WHAT'S THE GOOD WORD

Sermons for the Pentecost Season (First Half) Series C

**Dick Frazier
Dan Hamlin
Dick Hunt**

WHAT'S THE GOOD WORD

ISBN 0-89536-384-4   PRINTED IN U.S.A.

Dedicated

to our children —
 Janis, Laura, Eric, Anne,
  Katherine, Krista, Jeremy,
   Cynthia, Aaron, Jane, and Daniel —
    that they may ever know and
    live in Christ our Lord;

and to our wives —
 Marj, Nancy, and Sally —
  God's interface for
  that new life.

TABLE OF CONTENTS

FOREWORD

These sermons are based on the second lesson for the Pentecost Season (first half) of Series C in the three-year Lectionary.

There is a further dimension as well: To get the "church's sermon" preached demands certain responsibilities on the part of both pastor and congregation. Preaching needs to emerge out of a shared life, and out of inquiry between pastor and congregation into the meaning of God's Word and its application where people are or can be. To that end, the dialogical approach is a technique of good speech. Additionally, this approach occurs as the spoken word is supported by the use of drama, art, music, liturgical dance (I am never sure how that adjective really defines the noun); dialogues between and among pastors of the same and different persuasions. It includes sermon feedback sessions and what I believe to be more valuable — sermon seminars to prepare preacher and people before the sermon is preached. All of these and more are shared in the sermonic life of Trinity Church. Yet, there is still another dimension to these sermons.

One of the traditional definitions of preaching is "Truth through personality." A team ministry with several pastors affords the congregation opportunity to hear the truth through a variety of personalities. Each has a distinctive background, reveals the uniqueness of one's own religious experience, shares personal convictions, and demonstrates the qualities of one's own spirit, personality, and study. However imperfectly, our story is woven into God's story that the hearer-sharer may focus on his or her story. Of course, from time to time members of a team move on to other fields of ministry. Dick Hunt is now pastor of St. Andrew Church, Speedway, Indiana. Others have joined the Trinity team and have added new dimensions to our common life as a Christian fellowship.

It is not our approach to give the senior pastor a Sunday respite now and then by trotting out a pastor of youth on Youth Sunday, a pastor of education on Rally Day, a minister of music on some latter day Cantata Sunday, or one of our women staff members on Mother's Day. Each is, first of all, a pastor, sharing in pastoral ministry, and then providing leadership in specific areas of competency and interest. We are not set apart to preach. We are set apart to be pastors, shepherds, enablers. The pastor-shepherd is undergirded by God's Word, strengthened through prayer, refined by pastoral situations — wrestling with the relationship between faith and life where our people are — and enlightened by constant reading of a variety of materials.

The varying personalities enhance the witness to the truth of the Gospel. The church's sermon exists to bear witness to the Gospel truth: God has "committed unto us the ministry of reconciliation." It is a unique message; it is a magnificent message; it is an eternally essential message.

Dan, Dick, and I are grateful to secretaries Dorothy Mortorff and Christine Sieminski for their able typing and patience with us, and to the members of Trinity, Fort Wayne, for their response which enable the "church's sermon" to be preached.

Richard G. Frazier
Lent, 1979

HEARING AND SEEING

The Day of Pentecost
Acts 2:1-21

The Reverend Richard G. Frazier

Some time ago one of my partners in ministry used a story form to preach a sermon while one of our members drew illustrations which were projected on a screen. The visual and aural reinforced and complemented each other.

One can argue for either one of these dictums — "seeing is believing" or "hearing is believing." It occurs to me that both are vital for a Christian community to experience the reality of God. In the learning process the visual memory and auditory memory work together for good education. Telephone companies have experimented with the video-phone in which people are both heard and seen. Combining the visual and aural fosters communication in business conference calls, but I am told that marketing the video-phone for individual homes is still a question mark. And there are those times when we do not mind being heard, but to be seen? Like two-thirty in the morning or while in the shower . . .

Yes, our visual culture is a mixed blessing. We are enhanced, of course, by the beauty of nature, art, and architecture; however, the visual can so engulf us that we fail to read much any more or even talk to one another. A recent magazine article suggested the need in our homes for a common hearth room where the family can be together for cooking, eating, talking. But if each family member spends most of the time in looking at television, for instance, where is any real togetherness?

This applies equally with our aural culture. I have shared with you the writings of that anthropologist who writes like a poet, the late Loren Eiseley. Discussing man's imagination creating a region beyond the visible spectrum, Eisley suggests that moment in mankind's long history when a way was invented,

" . . . *to pass knowledge through the door-*

way of the tomb — namely, the achievement of the written word. Only so can knowledge be made sufficiently cumulative to challenge the stars. Our brothers of the forest . . . do not possess the tiny figures by which the dead can be made to speak from those great cemeteries of thought known as libraries."

So, too, with the spoken word. Yet I know couples who "talk" together incessantly but there is no communication. Each abuses the other verbally.

The story of Pentecost is dramatized as both a visual event and a speech event. It combines the aural and visual, the eye and the ear. These are re-created whenever two or three gather in Christ's name, their hearts open to God's spirit. And thus one day in Jerusalem, as people gathered together, they were engulfed with both sound and sight — the sound of rushing wind, the appearance of tongues as of fire, people seeing and hearing one another. It was then that they "were filled with the Holy Spirit." Whatever else it means, the Holy Spirit, the present tense of God, was known through both the visual and aural.

In the fantasy movie "Star Wars," which celebrated the victory of good over evil and the possibility of a different and better world, Luke Skywalker, Obi Wan Kenobi, and others are able to overcome evil as they are open to the Force. The line occurs repeatedly, "The Force will be with you always." The Christians' force is rather more specific and substantive. Indeed, it must be seen in the context of Christmas, Easter, and Pentecost — the great festivals which belong together. At the Christmas incarnation, it was God invading planet earth, "God with us." At Good Friday and Easter it was "God saves us" — saves us from

---

*Loren Eiseley, **The Invisible Pyramid** (New York: Charles Scribner's Sons, 1970) pp. 62-63.

death and sin, the separations of our lives. At Pentecost it was "God in us" — empowering and giving us the urgency to share, to witness.

Jesus had affirmed to his disciples that even though his physical presence would be gone, there would be an invisible presence of power working with them forever. That spirit is not always manifested in the same form or style. Meister Eckhart, the German mystic of the thirteenth century writes: *"God does not work in all hearts alike, but according to the preparation and sensitivity he finds in each."* God does not place us in a mold wherein we all look alike, act alike, dress alike. He works in each of us in different ways, and each responds differently. The fact is that God is at work in your life and mine.

Yet we can easily clog the channels. An over-concern with Pentecostalism can scare us away from Pentecost. An emphasis only on emotional experiences can make us into a religious "Johnny-one-note." A religion devoid of emotion and spontaneity soon becomes dull and drab. Or, in the business of living, some may spend only on themselves. We can shut out the spirit by being too protective of what we have. Our goods and possessions then become liabilities, rather than blessings. Have you found it to be true that when we are unable to hear one another within families, marriages, friendships, we avoid seeing one another?

God's spirit comes to strengthen, guide, and chasten us where we are in the daily tasks of work and worship. He is at one time our comforter, advocate, admonisher. We are freed to respond or to turn away from his guidance, but the power is available. And one of the reasons is that he enlarges our capacities to receive his gifts. When St. Paul lists the gifts of the spirit — and there are several — the *"greatest of these"* he states, *"is love."* It is love which seeks the good of the other, sacrifices for the other, breaks down the barriers between, such as neighbors' fences, the generations, the conflicts between races.

The spirit can lead couples to examine their style of communication so that they may begin to see each other as persons and to hear each other. Methods of behavioral psychology such as Transactional Analysis provide resources to that end, but no form can help unless we are led to see, to hear, to listen, to watch, to act.

One day on the Damascus Road, St. Paul saw the dazzling light of the Son of Righteousness. The vision freed him to hear that awesome voice . . . *"Saul, Saul, why do you persecute me?"* He was then freed to hear the good words of the gospel from Ananias. The spirit unites us, brings out our best self, makes us whole, gives us peace. The story is told of a boy in a family who never washed behind his ears, came to the table dirty, his hair uncombed, clothes ragged-looking. His parents bribed, coaxed, pleaded, scolded, did everything they could to make him be clean and polite but to no avail. Whenever he went out the door, he SLAMMED it. Then one day he came to the breakfast table — his hair was combed, his clothes and finger-nails clean. It seemed he had even washed behind his ears; and when he went out the door, he closed it gently. What had happened? He had met Susie; a new love principle had come into his life. That can happen to us when God's spirit gets within us. A new love principle enters, and we are whole as nothing else in all the world can make us whole. But the non-verbal (sight and touch) and the verbal (I love you) reinforce each other.

Yet the essential meaning of Pentecost was directed to the community of faith. The Spirit called the church into being. We are God's people in community. It is through the church that we can find

God's power on the personal level.

The church is "one body," as well as "one spirit." In belonging to the "body" we belong to the "spirit" and do so whether we are able to "feel" the spirit or not. One helpful way to see the relationship of church and spirit is through fellowship of what we call the Koinonia of the spirit. When we share intimately with each other in supportive ways, because we share together God's Spirit and Power, there is koinonia.

In his book **Wind, Sand, and Stars** Antoine de Saint Exupery tells of pioneering pilots exploring for safe air routes over the Andes in South America. A deep bond of togetherness grew between those men as they flew amid the dangerous crags and caught the treacherous down currents. Realizing what was happening, Exupery observed that great friendship does not come as two people stand looking at each other, but rather as they look upward and outward toward a common goal and a common task.

God did not think up the idea of Holy Spirit on the day of Pentecost, nor shall I recite the historical record for you. Yet the church was endowed with God's spirit in a spectacular way on a specific day — fifty days after the first Easter — when they were "all together in one place." God could do something through their togetherness which he could not do otherwise.

If we can clog the channels of God's Spirit as individuals, we can also clog the channels within the community of faith. Ralph Waldo Emerson once remarked that *"First, the spirit builds its house, and then the house confines it."* True, the house can confine the spirit and the church is good at that, but it is the spirit which builds the house. There is in the mind of the creator a creative intent. One question we as a church staff ask ourselves repeatedly is this: "Are we using people to keep a big building afloat, or are we using the inherent power of our faith and facilities to help people?" It is an important question to guide our ministry.

I believe the spirit is working within us in new and exciting ways: In our worship together, as we wrestle with God's truth, and in the many ways we seek to translate that truth into life, confronting issues and people within and beyond the church walls. Many church members are discovering or re-discovering the reality of loving and being loved, of sharing and being shared. I am thinking now of such recent events in our parish as the retreat for the Koinonia groups, a handful of people who have been meeting to discuss the complicated issues of bio-ethics, those tutoring children in the West Central area, the youth helping shut-ins with spring housecleaning, of so many hands reaching out to our newest refugee family, of people willing to be trained to care for others and to share the good news of our faith.

If we would paint THE SPIRIT OF GOD on the side of the Goodyear blimp and moor it to the spire of Trinity Church, it might cause a flurry among the pigeons and make a passer-by gape; but just as nothing is able to drive pigeons away, nothing will really speak to the gapers or bring them in unless our life together is led and filled with God's spirit. This includes the worship service which provides variety within a familiar form, aids for preparation with the element of spontaneity clearly allowed; teaching that is personal rather than coldly rational; a sharing which doesn't call attention to itself; a discovery that each of us is part of the body of Christ, chosen as God's own people.

As we share together in worship, the oral (spoken and sung word) and the visual (the cross, colors of the church year) become a vital channel of God's spirit. See some of the ways that combination works:

Forgiveness is dramatized in the classic

architectural form of this church — the cruciform — a man stretched on a cross. And Sunday by Sunday as we enter this nave, the visual reinforces the words of absolution.

The inscription across the face of Trinity's pulpit is a mixture of Latin and Greek "Predicare Christum Crucifixu" which means, "We preach Christ crucified." Its visual reminder infuses the oral sermon.

The visual elements of wine and bread in the holy communion are signs and tokens of the words of absolution and celebration.

And sometimes we sit in church and are glad that no words are spoken. It is enough just to watch the flickering of candles and sanctuary lamp, the symbols in stained glass, just to see the gothic arches receding into the distance. We worship God here through the spoken and sung and written word. But his presence is also known when no words are spoken. This "Hallelujah in Stone" speaks to every worshiper and passer-by of that glow of glory which, save the church, no agency on earth can provide.

As our eyes march around the church nave, they eventually focus on the largest of the stained glass windows. The north window captures the biblical story of the Transfiguration. That window looks down, not only on a congregation at worship, but on a busy downtown street, a funeral home, the Chamber of Commerce building. These are stark reminders that our worship issues in witness through the busyness of life . . . and death . . . through the politics of the city and hundreds of committees and clubs doing hundreds of needed civic enterprises amid the dusty streets wherein we live and work.

Yes, the visual and aural combine to make us aware of God's spirit and to enable us to receive him. This prayer of Evelyn Underhill from her "Veni Creator" was written for Pentecost eve. We can make

18

it our prayer:
> When the morning wind
> Blows down the world,
>   O spirit show Thy power;
> Awaken the dreams within the languid mind
> And bring Thy seed to flower.
>
> Amen

THE PEACE OF GOD

First Sunday After Pentecost
Romans 5:1-5

The Reverend Richard G. Frazier

One of the more exciting facets of my college life came through an invitation to play with the Springfield, Ohio, Symphony Orchestra. My chair was third trumpet. (There was in that orchestra a grand total of three trumpets.) And there I was at the first rehearsal — ready, tuned, excited, and a little fearful. Fear quickly turned to embarrassment as the conductor, Guy Taylor by name, stopped the rehearsal and asked, "What in heaven's name is the third trumpet chair playing?" — or words to that effect. It seems that some of the ancient manuscripts we used required not only reading and counting, but transposing, changing the key as we played, a factor that neither the director nor the other trumpet players shared with me, nor I, in my excitement, noted.

Playing an instrument "in the wrong key" fosters disharmony, discordance, chaos, and no little tension for the instrumentalist, director, and orchestra. Being "out of key" with life is rather common — call it stress, tension, anxiety, or whatever. A woman once said to her physician, "Doctor, I am all run down!" He examined her thoroughly and made this diagnosis, "Madam, the trouble is not that you are all run down. The trouble is that you are all wound up." How many are living, in the words of Thoreau, "Lives of quiet desperation."

Millions of sleeping tablets are consumed by the American public night after night. Indeed, so real is the sleeplessness of the public, so tense are they, that it is difficult to put people to sleep even with a sermon — not impossible, just difficult. It is easy to elaborate on, even pontificate about, the things which make us out of tune, which rob us of peace. But let us think together about the peace which God offers us. First of all, what peace is not.

For one thing, peace is not a resignation from the world, a denial of our feelings. Yet this is how some of the eastern meditational teachings so popular today speak of peace. Novacain the heart, kill the feelings, deaden the desires, isolate yourself, avoid controversy, talk about anything except religion and politics. Be unmoved by what you see around you, hold back, hold back. Then you will discover peace. But can anyone live or want to live with that kind of approach?

Second, God's peace does not keep us from difficulties or enable us to escape tension and trouble. Consider exhibit A in the New Testament, the writer of this passage. What St. Paul did not receive from Christianity was peace of mind in any shallow sense, nor need I catalogue every single item in the long list of his trials and burdens " . . . *beaten, in peril, in pain, in hunger, in thirst, in cold and nakedness.*" Then, too, there was the persistent, perpetual thorn in the flesh perplexity. "Paul, we have almost forgotten the record. Who has a better right to speak from experience than you have?" His testimony comes from a trial-tested life.

Third, the peace we are offered does not come packaged with three easy lessons. No mental gymnastics to tone up our spiritual muscles. Recently, I received a letter from a group, similar to many letters which have offered to give me peace and to answer all my prayers. All I had to do was send in my requests (and a contribution), and they would take care of all my needs. It was simply too easy. The Bible is not a package of gimmicks and devices by which we are guaranteed peace of mind, and yet how often people try to play God with us.

What, then, is the peace of God about which Paul speaks in this fifth chapter of Romans? The apostle places it in the context of our "being justified." It is God's intervening actions through Jesus Christ which justify us. He cancels our debt, dismisses our liabilities, and places us in the center of his love. When we accept this in faith, we have peace with God and peace with ourselves. This relationship puts life into balance and sets us free to get on with making something beautiful of the precious gift of life entrusted to us. In other words, at the center of God's peace is a vital relationship with God. Indeed, our ministry together as a congregation means to share, to grow with one another in that relationship because we have a common bond with our Lord in his church. We are justified. We are in the right key. Peace is the opposite of tension and chaos. It is a calmness, but it is more. Essentially, it is a relationship between one and God. The calmness, the peace is a consequence of the relationship.

"God's peace" involves bringing to his presence in all our hopes and fears and needs. *"In everything,"* wrote Paul, *"let your requests be made known unto God."* We do this, not just in speaking, but also in listening, word focusing, meditation, silence, as we have explored in various seminars the purposes and methods of meditation. But whatever our methods and whatever words or posture, prayer is the expression of a relationship. At the heart of that relationship is the phrase "in Christ's Name" or "through Jesus Christ our Lord." When I pray "in Christ's Name," I pray in the relationship of a child to a father, one which is not mine by right but by the action of God in Christ. Thus I bring everything to God as a trusting child brings everything to his father. G. A. Stoddard Kennedy expressed it:

Peace does not mean the end of all our striving,
Joy does not mean the drying of our tears;
Peace is the power that comes to souls arriving
Up to the light where God Himself appears.

If "being justified" brings us into relationship with God, it also speaks to us of being accepted by God. When we know God accepts us, we can begin to accept ourselves and to realize our best self.

For one thing, we are of vital importance. Everyone's part in the community of God's church, like everyone's part in an orchestra, is important. The point where the conductor of the Springfield Symphony halted the rehearsal to inquire about the third trumpet player's sanity was a two-bar continuum solo. Why the composer provided that is beyond me, for a third trumpet player should be a math major, given the fact that he spends more time counting rests than blowing sounds. Historically, composers did not write much for the third trumpet. The violins and other strings have most of the fun. Yet here was a composition (frankly, I forget the name of it . . . simply remember the experience) wherein there were two bars of music; and if the thing was going to work at all, the lowly third trumpet player had to make good. He was of vital importance.

In the life of the congregation, whether in Rome or in Fort Wayne, as the Bible is forever trying to teach us, each one as a baptized child of God is uniquely important. In our Ecclesia, one of Paul's image words of the church, and as the original word denoted, each one has an equal right and an equal responsibility.

What shall we do with our weaknesses and limitations and difficulties, the things that defeat peace? Part of accepting the self is to realize them, as well as our strengths, share them with our God, and in his power live creatively within them.

Major Whistler once served as the Commandant of Wayne's Fort (the new replica of that fort is a welcome addition to our community). Whistler's son became a famous artist. But he started out to become a general, to follow in the vocational footsteps of his father and grandfather. He was dropped from West Point because he could not pass chemistry. Milton accepted his blindness and wrote a classic that will stir the mind and soul as long as one is able to read.

This is not to indulge in vanity and conceit, but I think that much of our tension stems from self-degradation and a lack of confidence. Peace is not avoiding trouble or seeking to be rid of all difficulty, but it is enduring or seeing through the struggle, enhanced with God's strength. A wildflower sometimes grows through a crack in the fence as beautifully as it does in an open field. Dietrich Bonhoeffer wrote inspired letters from his prison camp where he awaited his execution. Was it Neibuhr who actually wrote this oft-quoted prayer, "God show *me how to change the things that can be changed, to accept the things that cannot be changed, and to have the wisdom to know the difference"?* When we have accepted the fact God has accepted us and begin to accept ourselves, we can accept others, even share that self; and that, too, is part of the peace of relationship.

This leads us to the point of sharing God's peace. We keep it by giving it away. There is something even a third trumpet player must learn, as well as, I assume, a rock guitarist or troubled trombonist or busy bassoonist, that all should work together, fitting their parts, subject to the director's leading, into a stirring music.

For this very group of people with varied backgrounds, emotions, needs, ways of expressing faith — this very group called a Christian congregation — is called together by God, nurtured for sharing with one another and others. Our touchstone is not a political philosophy or a social philosophy. Our touchstone is the Christ, his person, teachings, and ministry. In him is our peace.

We ever need to grow in our relationship with God. Part of that is finding refreshment in life. Before he faced the end of his ministry, our Lord went off to the coast of Tyre and Sidon, the Miami Beach of that day. How often Scripture punctuates the story with these words, " . . . *and Jesus departed to pray.*" We, too, need such times. With our heartaches, tensions, temptations, the times when we are out of tune or playing the wrong key, we need to grow in that relationship. Are we any less in need of the power of prayer than was Jesus?

Can we take a few minutes during the day, a few days during the year? There is always the danger, of course, that we just run away — to bingo, to Miami Beach, to the movies, and back to bingo again. Do we not need to bring the resources of Scripture, prayer, a good book, music, or art, even someone of maturity with whom we can reflect? Can we place ourselves in the context of growth experiences, whether serving, prayer groups, Bible study, retreats, circles, sharing groups, reading and reflection, and, not least of all, our worship together? We can share in the companionship of those who have struggled with the relationship. Our library contains many of the classics of devotional literature. To read the spiritual classics is to explore what St. Teresa called "*the mansions within.*" Such exposure can bring refreshment to our souls, comfort in knowing that even God's great ones wrestled with faith and peace and relationship as do we, and insight into working through those things which drag us down.

The peace of God does not rest on any human device. "*Rather,*" says St. Paul, "*since we are justified by faith, we have peace with God through our Lord Jesus Christ.*" That relationship enables us to live in the right key.

GOD'S INTERFACE

Second Sunday After Pentecost
Galatians 1:1-10

The Reverend J. Richard Hunt

28

His beard was flecked with brown. His blond hair a little messed up from working outside, which is where he had just been. He said he's quit early to come and talk.

"I don't exactly know what's happened. But I do know I want to be part of the church, this church. It's like a light has just been turned on for me. I feel a freedom in this place to love and find answers." He said he'd become a baptized non-believer. Now he felt an urgency in his life.

"I know God's calling me, but I don't know how to work it out. And besides this sense of urgency, I keep hearing the word 'patience.' " He was in his early thirties and he was feeling a movement he's never felt before. "I know I can find answers in this place. There's no condemnation here. All the people are children of God. They're friendly and open. It's easy to get lost today. There's so much bad happening." That's some of what he said to me. I just listened and resonated with his urgency, with his joy at the door he saw before him, and with his struggle for patience.

I didn't quote Paul to him; but I thought of his words in Galatians:

Grace and peace to you from God the
Father and Lord Jesus,
who gave himself for our sins
to deliver us from the present evil age
which is the will of our Father.

My friend was experiencing the grace and peace of moving back and forth through his door. Grace saying, "You are loved by God." Peace assuring, "You have a place with him who loves you." Both embracing him with the message: "Jesus gave himself for you. You need not be lost or alien. He delivers you from the present evil age."

What kinds of doors are you confronting? What lights are "on" or "off" for you? Where in you does urgency and patience wrestle? Paul says that there is no experience that we may encounter that is not common to all people. God provides a way through.

Paul meets us, as he did the Galatians, at the point of our temptation. We are tempted to yield to despair and, in alienation, to get further lost. But it is the will of the Father to give us the Kingdom. He seeks us out. He bids us rest in the assurance of his love and trustworthiness. He invites us in to be his servant and friend. He invites us into a large place where we might find our answers, where we might grow in awareness of God's presence, where we might blossom and bear fruit with patience.

My bearded friend rightly sensed that the parish is the place provided in God's scheme of intimacy. The parish is a place to love and to be loved. The parish is a place to value life and to have our life valued. The parish is a place where we can talk and listen and sort out ourselves and, with patience, find out what it's all about.

In the face of the evil times that seek alienation and self-absorption, rather than intimacy and the care of others, the parish is God's interface between his Kingdom and the world. As with any interface, the parish is the common boundary where information moves back and forth. An interface is also a body of problems, considerations, and practices common to two or more different fields of enterprise. It is the common ground between God and his world of people.

God does not allow himself to get self-absorbed. He listens to us. He comes to us. He embraces us, individually and corporately. We must not allow ourselves to be self-absorbed, either. We can listen to God and come to him and embrace him.

Thus, in dialogue with God at this point of interface, we can listen to and embrace each other as we work together on the problems, considerations, and practices inherent in the whole community's health.

That interface model is useful in seeing that we are each the temple of the Lord. We are the interface between God and another person. Paul put it:

We are ambassadors . . . God making his appeal through us. Our message is that God was making all mankind his friends through Christ. (2 Corinthians 5)

The parish, you, individually, are part of the body of Christ: God's interface.

My friend intuitively is aware of God's presence in the mix of people called to this place to study his word and worship. Where God is, a person may live and grow to be a more wise and caring person.

My friend told me he's just had the light turned on. He is now exploring the large room God has prepared for him and all his other children. The Lord is restoring to him the joy of his salvation.

The Light is on and the door open for him, for you, and all people. Be his invitation for all you meet.

32

THE ARABIAN PASSAGE

Third Sunday After Pentecost
Galatians 1:11-24

The Reverend J. Richard Hunt

What do these people have in common?

Wade is a thirty-year government employee. He's going to retire next year. He'll be fifty-five-years-old and very successful in his work.

Sue is a thirty-six-year-old and just had her fourth healthy child. She's decided, after long reflection with herself and her husband, to undergo a tubal ligation to prevent further pregnancies.

Mary and Bill have just gotten married at twenty-seven-years of age. It's the first time for them both. They have been highly successful in their professions and living very independent lives.

John and Joan embrace in tears of grief. Their fifth son has just died of leukemia. Just seven years old. Four weeks ago he was struck down by the disease and wiped out in those four weeks. They stand painfully at the end of that exhausting ordeal.

What is there common in these diverse human situations?

Notice that in each situation the people have come to the end of one period in their life and are faced with something new.

Notice, also, that all the people have been successful.

Wade — successful in his job

Sue — successful in bearing children

Mary and Bill — successful in being singles

John and Joan — successful in parenting a family of five boys, also in helping one of them through a very painful death.

A door has closed for each of them. They stand on their success looking into a new country.

St. Paul had a similar experience. Let's see how he handled it. Fresh from his success as one who was precocious and more zealously devoted than any of his peers to the traditions of his ancestors, Paul steps through an unexpected doorway on his way to Damascus. He steps from his successes on to a new road leading into a new experience of his life's meaning. Paul tells us he did not go to get pre-packaged answers; instead he went away into Arabia to meditate and to confront the Lord.

"I will drive him into the wilderness
where I will speak with my servant,"
says the Lord.

After that conversation with the One to whom he spoke intimately, Paul could say some remarkable and instructive things.

Jesus revealed to me what I know.
God called me to serve.
Then he revealed what I might do —
Speak his good news.

What was the good news he learned from the mind of Christ?

Paul says, *"I count all as dung, as trash, to be thrown out in order to know Christ Jesus my Lord."*

What was the "all" he was ready to dispose of?

On his success, his former life style, he was closing the door. He stepped into a new life united with Jesus Christ to experience the power of his resurrection, to share in his suffering,

and

to become like him in his death in order that he, too, might be raised from death to life.

That is the language of intimacy and growth.

We may benefit from Paul's learning experience. Every stage of growth in our lives is a passage into a new place. It is a passage into growth in which I must give up what has worked and accept the insecurity and suffering inherent in untried skills.

As a crawling child must give up his success as a

crawler when he stands up to step into the country of those who toddle and finally walk, the crawling child dies and is resurrected as a walking life.

The mind of Christ informed Paul and us that as Christ did not hang on to past success and position but gave it up to be with us even through death, we can go on to such caring and intimacy with each other from threshold to threshold throughout our life together.

To grow up into Christ we move from death to life as we share in our suffering. Paul's Arabian passage is a model for our many passages. Let go what lies behind. Take hold of hope, Jesus Christ, who has gone before us and waits on the other side of any door we'll ever go through.

He waits to shepherd us. What doors are closing in your life? If you feel as if you are in the wilderness, be assured that is where the Lord speaks to us that we might shepherd each other.

38

A NEW WAY
(A Children's Message)

Third Sunday After Pentecost
Galatians 1:11-24

The Reverend J. Richard Hunt

Centering

Do you have a gold fish?
Have you seen this little plate on my door?
Do you see the fish shape on it?
That fish stands for or symbolizes the Church gathered together around Jesus.
Make a fish with your finger in the air.
I have a story about a fish. I'd like you to hear.
Listen.

Read **Swimmy** (Leo Lionni, Pantheon Book, 1963)

Message

When Swimmy came to the fish who were afraid, what did he do?
He helped them form a whole new way to live and help each other.
When Jesus came to Paul, he helped him stop being afraid and find a whole new way to live.
When Paul came to a town, he gathered people in a group called a Church, which was symbolized by the sign of the fish.
Make a fish again.
When you see the symbol of the fish or a real fish, remember Swimmy and Jesus. Jesus, like Swimmy, is the eye of this "fish," this parish. He helps us see new ways to shape our life together so we can take care of each other even when we're afraid.

Prayer

Thank you, Jesus,
for helping us get together
and learn new ways
to care for each other.
Help all your children. Amen.

42

REALIZING LIFE

Fourth Sunday After Pentecost
Galatians 2:11-21

The Reverend Richard G. Frazier

44

Are you realizing life? Perhaps you think that is a facetious question or a bit of preacher rhetoric, and maybe so. But I hold it before you as a key question flowing out of God's Word and a key question for the living of these days.

Recently, we shared in our church theater Thornton Wilder's engaging play, "Our Town." There is a scene in the last act of that play which vividly calls us to life. Emily has died and has been granted permission to come back for a time. She has arrived at the graveyard at Grover's Corners to experience the same things that happened before but with the difference of a new perspective. The day she chooses to live is her twelfth birthday. Her mother is preoccupied with preparation for the celebration, her father returns home from work exhausted, and only Emily is aware of the few precious moments of time. She pleads, "Mama, just look at me once as though you really saw me. Let's look at one another." But no one hears her, for Emily is just re-living the day, not changing it. She can stand it no longer and cries out, "I can't go on. It goes so fast. We don't have time enough to look at one another. I didn't realize what was going on; I never noticed it. Oh, earth, you are too wonderful for anyone to realize you." And then she turns to the Stage Manager and asks through her tears, "Do any human beings ever realize life while they live it, every, every minute?"

From the prose of Thornton Wilder we turn to the poetry of T. S. Eliot. He pictures the fear of life, the fear of embracing life, thus getting lost in the humdrum patterns and ruts of every day. He has his chorus of **Murder in the Cathedral** say, "We do not wish anything to happen. We have lived quietly, succeeded in avoiding notice, living and partly living, living and partly living." Are we realizing life?

This speaks to the question of identity. From the

baby's non-verbal question, "Who am I?" to the child who responds, "I'm Johnny Jones. My dad is better than your dad. My mom can bake a better apple pie than your mom." The child has an amazing affinity with parents, and there is no greater joy for me than to walk in the door in the evening and be greeted by wild-eyed, ready-for-action children. But when the child becomes an adolescent, he no longer wants to be called "Mr. and Mrs. Jones' little boy Johnny." The links with the parents lessen as he plays at being a person in his own right; and if you really want to have a mess on your hands, try to kiss him when you greet him at Back-to-School Night.

The young adult struggles with the question of "Who am I and who do you say I am?" When no identification is offered as needed, the young adult turns either to mass personification of adulthood, something like the **Playboy** look, or produces an exaggeration of some identity.

It is my experience that people of all ages are wandering around asking, "Who am I?" Some time ago a man in his early forties said to me (and many others have shared varieties on the same theme), "I am trained for a good profession, but I am bored stiff with my job. I don't want to die before I live." This particular young executive has, in the eyes of many, every material thing to make him happy . . . and yet . . .

Many people reach the middle years with feelings of triviality, emptiness, and futility. They may have a sense of vital things going on in the lives of others, not in their own. We know how to add years to our life but not always life to our years. Edna St. Vincent Millay expressed it in her poem, "Ashes of Life":

Life goes on forever,
  like the gnawing of a mouse,
And tomorrow and tomorrow and tomorrow,

There's this little street and this little house.

Another, in the later years of work when it is too late to change jobs, reaches the point of no return and must settle for what he has. Boredom easily sets in, and he sees the years stretching out before him in endless succession. He wonders if he can make it to retirement or if there is anything after retirement.

Identity refers to an organizing center to one's experiences — a place, a direction. St. Paul experienced identity in the relationship he described in these words, "I live, yet not I, it is Christ who lives within me." Paul had been bred in the way of the law. He who once passionately hated the gospel of Christ now passionately realized life through the same gospel of Christ.

The Apostle begins, *"It is no longer I who live."* That is a strange phrase for these days. An obscure *ism* has infected much of our citizenry — it is the *ism* of solipsism. We usually refer to it in less technical names, such as "self-fulfillment," the "me culture," the new "Narcissism," "Hedonism," and plain selfishness. In practice, solipsism inspires individuals, in the words of a magazine writer, to subordinate or abandon jobs, politics, civil service, church life, family responsibility, in favor of self-realization classes, exotic exercises, getting stroked with rabbit fur, communal hot-tubbing, extra-marital sensations, and other pursuits imagined to produce pure happiness. Seeking to realize life in self-fulfillment to the exclusion of all else is self-delusion.

The Greeks had a mythological character, Narcissus. He was the darling of the swimming pool set, except in this case he did not dominate the swimming lanes or the diving board. For that matter, he did not sit beside the pool dispensing drinks, seeking a tan, or ogling the girls. Rather, he gazed into the pool — at himself. He was fascinated with his own image. The Greeks, at least, had the good sense not to worship him. How is it with us? Do we make him a god?

Again, Paul speaks to us, *"I live, but it is no longer I who live, but Christ who lives within me."*

When Christ lives within us, we are his children, related through him with our Father God. The AP release described her as the woman with no name — a mystery for thirty-eight years in the custody of the state of Illinois. During the Depression she was found dazed beside a rural road. No one knew her. She was not insane. She just could not remember who she was. There already were three Mary Does in state mental institutions. Mary Doe-four lived in institutions for thirty-eight years not knowing who she was.

The Sacrament of Baptism speaks to the problem of identity, answering the baby's non-verbal question, "Who am I?" In effect, the sacrament says that in addition to being a child of your parents, you are a child of God, participating in the benefits of Christ's death and forgiveness and resurrection, made an heir of his kingdom. There is always a surge of emotion for me as I announce . . . "Daniel Llewellyn, I baptize you in the Name of the Father and of the Son and of the Holy Spirit." Occasionally the pastor meets some strange names at the baptismal font. However, usually he meets family or biblical names popular at the moment. Whatever, names are not mere labels. Our baptismal names represent us as persons. We have identity, relationship.

When Christ lives within us, our own individuality is not extinguished or absorbed into some kind of nirvana. We have the freedom and responsibility to develop the self, to act. But now the mind of Christ gives content to the self.

God brought out the best self in Zacchaeus. God got hold of a rough and uncouth Simon and transformed him into the Peter that was within him all the time. God took the bitter cruelty of Saul and called forth a power and love that made him the Apostle Paul.

Christ living within us means participating in his gifts — forgiveness, kindness, personhood, patience, reconciliation. We share his purposes and life style, knowing that the risks, priorities, costs involved are part of what Paul described as *"being crucified with Christ."*

When Christ lives within us, we gain a new attitude toward death. St. Paul wrote, *"to live is Christ, to die is gain."* "Gain," in English grammar, is a modifying word. It means, "more, a greater amount." To live in Christ is a relationship: To die is to find a greater relationship. And thus eternal life, as I understand it from Holy Scripture, is not concentrated on the landscape or the geography of heaven — or even hell, for that matter. We do not know precisely where they are. The image is one of relationship. Our Lord said, *"I go to prepare a place for you that where I am, there you may be also."* Thus, eternal life begins now, today, in the relationship of trust with our Lord, one which goes on through the door of death into a greater relationship.

When Christ lives within us, a person is going to have problems, even despair; but one need not be overcome by it for the very fact is that we are in harmony with the power and love of God. And this has come about, not through good deeds, but because God accepts us as we are and invites us to accept his acceptance of ourselves.

When Christ lives within us, there is growth amidst our ups and downs. One of my concerns with the movie, "No Longer Alone," speaks to this. The real-life story of Joan Windmill is one of loneliness, fear, despair; and we can identify with Joan. We, like

Joan, need someone to turn to. For about two hours of the movie we relive Joan's tragic life. For about ten minutes we see her give her life to Christ at a Billy Graham Crusade. Of course, I believe that doing so was the beginning of much joy for Joan. She has become a new creature, no doubt about it; but the movie didn't share any of her wrestlings of faith. Christ living within us implies continual battles to remain faithful and continual decisions in the midst of life. We are all not merely beings, but becomings, growing in that relationship with our Lord.

When Christ lives within us, we are not some kind of religious lone ranger, forever doing our own religious thing. In the relationships with family and job and church and society, do we consider only me, my, and mine, and then ride off into the sunset? The image of Christ living within us is not a lone ranger image. It is more like the image of an astronaut. The astronaut has to study, be knowledgeable, as does the Christian need to be knowledgeable about Scripture and faith, relating it to his or her own life experience, ever willing to take risks. The astronaut knows the interdependence among everyone on the spaceship: that they must work together, and all the people on the ground, the backup crews, all of them must work together if the mission is to be successful. So, too, in the church. We are surrounded by a cloud of witnesses; we are interdependent. That's an image for our day. When Christ lives within us, we are not lone rangers going off on our own, but like astronauts working within a community toward a common goal.

When Christ lives within us, our eyes are opened to see the lines of suffering love on God's face. There is prompted a dedication to a larger purpose, to extend a hand, to live a life, to nurture others, to share our selves.

A Civil War story is told about the close

relationship of Captain Russell Conwell and his orderly, Johnnie Ring. One day in a brisk battle the troops retreated across a river, burning the wooden bridge behind them. In so doing, they cut off the escape of the orderly, who had gone back to bring the captain's sword. He tried to cross the blazing bridge, only to fall into the river, his clothing in flames. The men dragged him out, and he returned to consciousness. He smiled when he found the sword still safe at his side. He took the sword into his arms and died. It is said that Russell Conwell made a vow that thereafter he would live not only his life, but the life of Johnnie Ring. When his famous lecture "Acres of Diamonds" earned him millions of dollars, he gave most of it to a hospital and to Temple University. Wouldn't it be fair to say that Johnnie Ring gave at least half of the money? And isn't it accurate to say that for Russell Conwell to live was Johnnie Ring?

In some such way the opportunity of the Christian is to let Christ live in him. Of course, if Jesus were here in the flesh, he would be very different from any of his disciples. And yet Jesus lives in his disciples — in the men and women whose only glory is that Christ lives in them.

Are you realizing life? William Cowper prayed to be defended from the task of *"dropping buckets into empty wells and growing old in drawing nothing up."* St. Paul shares the perspective, the infusion, the power by which he realized his life, *"I live, yet not I, but Christ lives within me."*

WISDOM IS CHECKING OUT THE WIRING AND FOUNDATION

St. Peter and St. Paul, Apostles
1 Corinthians 3:16-23

The Reverend Daniel L. Hamlin

Shalom!

In the Second Lesson for this day, Paul is speaking to the congregation at Corinth where we get in earshot of some of the difficulties inherent in the melting together of two different approaches to human existence into a third approach that was, given their similarities, certainly unique from either of them. One group within the Corinthian congregation is claiming superior knowledge of Judaism or Christianity. Paul rebuts with the categories of that which is wise and foolish in God's eyes. I would like us to tap into this message of Paul's by looking at what no one of you could possibly see as foolish, and that is that wisdom is the investment of our financial capital. I want to suggest two important areas to check out in purchasing a home, that is, the structure's wiring and its foundation. I do so only because they have a correlation to our human structure, i.e., the body.

Each day, calls come in to the office reporting the happenings among a people who have been very "successful" in acquiring that to which their wiring turned them. "Wiring" is a reference to that segment of life wherein we were probed, pushed, and pulled through with the wise wisdom of the generation. That wiring said: work hard, stay in school, take care of yourself, keep your eyes open to seize opportunity, your hands clenched for those who would exploit you, your head clear to read the fine print; run with the right crowd, and your board will light up like a psychedelic rainbow of freedom, fame, fortune, and fraternity.

And each day the calls keep coming in to the office like telegrams: Thank you, Pastor, for talking with me . . . STOP . . . I'm not sure I know how to handle this . . . STOP . . . But they've suggested with no guarantee . . . STOP . . . Police protection . . . STOP . . . Separation . . . STOP . . . Divorce . . . STOP . . . Relocation . . .

STOP . . . Psychotherapy . . . STOP . . . Chemotherapy . . . STOP . . . Surgery . . . STOP . . . Karate . . . STOP.

Being that we all live within body structures where the works are on the inside, I am often tempted to respond to these traumatic telegrams: Yes, I know you are relatively new, certainly not old in terms of years . . . STOP . . . I think you might want to consider rewiring the structure and reworking the foundation . . . . STOP.

Let no one deceive himself. If anyone among you thinks that he is wise in this age, let him become a fool that he might become wise. For the wisdom of this world is folly with God. For it is written, "He catches the wise in their craftiness," and again, "the Lord knows that the thoughts of the wise are futile." (1 Corinthians 3:18-20.)

Every one then who hears these words of mine and does them will be like a wise man who built his house upon the rock; and the rain fell, and the floods came, and the winds blew and beat upon that house, but it did not fall, because it had been founded on the rock. And everyone who hears these words of mine and does not do them will be like a foolish man who built his house upon the sand; and the rain fell, and the floods came, and the winds blew and beat against the house, and it fell; and great was the fall of it.

And when Jesus finished these sayings, the crowds were astonished at his teaching, for he taught them as one who had authority, and not as their scribes. (St. Matthew 7:24-29)

It needs to be stated that the original wiring referred to above is not "bad" in the sense of somehow being "evil" or even "faulty." By no means is that intended. The wisdom and wiring received from home, parents, grandparents, school, and even from church in our formative years has everything to do with our survival as a people, individually and collectively. So the intention is never to make small our natural, self-evident endowments by birth, nurturing, and heritage. Having said that, however, something else must be said in the light of biblical teaching and experience: The wiring received in being an offspring of this great country, and its tendency to general religious heritage, was never intended to withstand the rigors and the demands of living in the skirmishes and clashes of people and groups, each clutching and clawing at their inalienable rights to life, liberty, and the pursuit of happiness. That temporary patchwork, wiring, and wisdom run out and burn out the face of such as to conclude that even gifts are of little value unless they are appropriated and assimilated into the bloodstream to make us "live."

All Scripture is inspired by God and profitable for teaching, for reproof, for correction, and for training in righteousness, that the man of God may be complete, equipped for every good work. (2 Timothy 3:16-17)

Let no one deceive himself. If any one among you thinks that he is wise in this age, let him become a fool that he may become wise. (1 Corinthians 3:18)

Jesus shows, in the story from Matthew which he placed at the end of his Sermon on the Mount, that he wasn't interested merely in training or teaching us. Jesus was showing us in this story how much he cared for us by insisting that we build our life's house on a rock foundation. He literally takes us by the hand and invites us outside to show us the threatening sky so that we can draw our own grave conclusions about the sand pile in which we are planning to lay footings and foundation. Jesus forces us to think about tomorrow, not so that we will forget about today, but so that we won't forget today's needs and necessities!

When a bomb drops in your backyard, somehow checking its serial number, who manufactured it, its color and weight does not cross the mind! Jesus was so convinced of the truth of what he was saying, that those who heard him and did nothing about it he called fools. *And every one who hears these words of mine and does not do them will be like a foolish man who built his house upon the sand. (Matthew 7:26)*

What Jesus saw people spending their time doing was not categorized as "sin" as much as mere nonsense. The portrait of the person Jesus is painting in this story is not a "bad" person so much as a crazy fool taking up precious time on the nonessentials instead of laying up foundation. Autobiographical reading confirms what Jesus taught, for it often reveals the lives of the famous and the wealthy, people who, by their own admission, have spent a good portion of their lives on less than fulfilling pursuits. Katherine Mansfield, the famous writer of short stories and plays, said when she came down to the end of her life, "I am ashamed of all of them. Not one of them would I dare to show to God." The end of life — that is important. Ty Cobb, a legend in American baseball, indicted himself before he died. He confessed, "You cannot eat baseball, and sleep baseball, and study baseball year after year and just stop like that." That's what Jesus is trying to say in this story. You can't put everything into anything and expect to weather the time when your baseball days or professional days are over. If the only thing we have read religiously all our lives is the newspaper, if we know the statistics on each all-American better than we know what Jesus said and did, God, help our folly.

Certainly the church is not outside this probing of that which is wise and that which is foolish. I remember that I had avoided biblical study in my ministry essentially because my life experience in the church before entering it professionally only registered "failure" when Bible study was mentioned. The fact that I spent ten years in my profession without any member asking for Bible study was a pretty clear indication that many others had similar experiences with that which I now consider the wiring and foundation of a Christian's life perspective. I want you to know that the church is not exempt. I believe that motivation and mission can become mixed and muddled in the minds of parson and people without the attitude of being a student of his manual on what turns you on and keeps you on! Wisdom is checking the wiring and foundation.

With a little bit of checking you would find that Jesus was not a person that you would want to avoid. Rather, he is one who supports your life, would come to the ball park and would keep in style. What he saw as foolish was to departmentalize — to pigeon-hole God out of the ball park and the office to that dress-up Sunday morning hour called "church." That was the scandal Christ came to expose.

Spending an hour a week glancing at the blue-prints, thinking that, through some magic process or mystery of God and religion, one would "experience" the security and contentment of having a well-built house in which to live out our days without ever rolling up the sleeves and breaking ground, is the foolishness that has been encouraged to keep attendance up and our Sabbath gatherings largely ineffective.

Every one then who hears these words of mine and does them will be like a wise man who built his house upon the rock . . .

Jesus allowed the wormwood, permitted the gall, accepted the rugged cross, gave up his life . . . so that we might have rock. There is only one kind of foundation for a person to build his life upon — rock — the kind of solidness that Peter said he found in Jesus when, in answer to the Master's query about fading disciples, *"Will you also go away?"* Peter blurted out, *"Lord, to whom shall we go? You have the words of eternal life!" (John 6:66-69)*

Everything going on around us may be connected to building: scaffolding, decoration, looking good, feeling good. But it is not life itself. It is not foundation. The wise person has to have that first. Everything he does will be funneled into foundation; for he finds that what was once an attraction has now become a need to continue strengthening and completing the house that God designed. Such a Christian orientation to living was once described to me as a comfortable coat. Do you know how you feel when a coat fits right in all the right places? You look good in it and you feel good in it; you wear it with confidence wherever you happen to be. A Christian life style is like a comfortable coat. It's not to say that the coat doesn't ever get soiled, or wrinkled, or need cleaning, or patching here and there. No, but it fits and you are comfortable wearing it! Another translation has it: *"Now, everyone who listens to these words of mine and acts upon them will be like a sensible man."* The Gospel is not seeking to entertain us or sweet talk us into something to keep the institution going and jobs available. It is the only thing that makes any sense for our lives — to "remember him," "come to him," "pray," "comfort," "help," "love," "forgive." Christianity begins with a noun, but it comes to the verb "do" (and it never comes to anything until it does). We may not be able to understand all of the Bible, but that isn't my problem. What bothers me most about the Bible is what I understand all too clearly.

" . . . *and the floods came, and the winds blew.*"
Faith will not stop the storm from coming, but it can take it. If, through the years, we have eaten, studied, digested, and slept with his blueprints, drawn on the wealth of example, gained strength and joined hands with those who are looking at the same blueprints, built broad, and deep, and solid, we shall not be continually anxious. We shall be able to handle disappointments as not being ultimate happenings; not so intent with the immediate — to be able to laugh at ourselves and life when people and events would have us wrinkle our brows with its seriousness.

What if the company or the spouse said, "I'm through with you;" if the reputation were ruined; the savings gone up in smoke; our health broken or our dearest kidnaped, and we were left deserted, dying? According to Christ, everything depends on what we build our life on: rock or sand. If rock, well . . . the storm will test us and in the darkness we may lose our temper, our patience, maybe our faith; but not for long, for we shall know that all shall be secure in the eye of the storm.

When we are responsibly taking heed of the message of this parable and are building our life accordingly, we will know, as did our hymn writer, "who trusts in God's unchanging love builds on the rock that nought can move." "On Christ, the solid rock, I stand; all other ground is sinking sand." Wisdom is checking out the wiring and the foundation.

Be a blessing.

FREEDOM IS RELATIONSHIP

Sixth Sunday After Pentecost
Galatians 5:1, 13-24

The Reverend Richard G. Frazier

People long for freedom. People fear freedom.

Perhaps you have seen the small, rectangular, brown box with a metal arm extending from its top. As one pulls the arm, the door slowly opens and a little green man from within begins to find freedom from his box. Then as soon as he is released from bondage, he slowly returns to the original position as the box lid closes over him. It is a visual parable.

People long for freedom. People fear freedom.

That is what Galatians is about. Certain folk had come to persuade the Galatians that Paul was not a real apostle and that his gospel was a watered-down article that could never assure them salvation. Salvation was impossible, they said, unless you lived according to the law. They indicated Paul received people in the church without the law because it was easier, and he was more interested in numbers than in truth.

Paul's responses are free of excuses or bitterness. He takes the positive. His reply ignited the truth of spiritual freedom. All that mattered to him was faith which works through love, not a code which works through fear. The emphasis was on a personal relationship to God as we know him in Jesus Christ. In Ibsen's **Brand** the preacher senses the grim demands of following the law in piling up good works. In his stern persuit, he succeeds in only making a hell for his family, his parish, and himself. In the end, when the avalanche is about to engulf him, he hears the message of God — God's grace — a self-offering, self-giving love.

Through that which Paul saw and heard in Christ, he felt for the first time that the God of his fathers was not only the Creator, not only the Law-giver, but also the lover of every human being he had created. Because of God's revelation of love through Jesus Christ, he knew he was accepted even with all his imperfections; and if God accepted him, he could live a full life — free to be. Thus his perspective for those who were being tempted to follow a code. Thus his confidence even as some condemned him.

Freedom Is Bondage

People long to be free — economically, relationally, politically, individually, sexually. On every corner there are hucksters packaging and pushing their freedom-wares.

The freedom about which Paul spoke is an inward, personal experience. It is to be found by way of commitment to something beyond ourselves, specifically to God as we know him through Jesus Christ. If we are to be free, we have to be bound. Freedom, then, is a by-product of God's acceptance of us, as he names us his children, heirs to his Kingdom, a relationship given to us in holy baptism and constantly renewed in the sacrament of holy communion. P. T. Forsythe makes the point that one's first responsibility is to find, not one's freedom, but one's master.

Freedom is being mastered. More to the point, freedom is being mastered by something or someone worth being mastered by. Two men, like Nero and Paul, lived in the same city at approximately the same time. They both are mastered men. Nero is the slave of his passions; Paul calls himself the slave of Christ. But we judge Nero yet as under a shameful tyranny, and we remember Paul saying, "For freedom did Christ set us free."

The dancer leaps with grace because she is released from the woodenness that imprisons most of us. Yet she is bound to rules of dance and the discipline of practice, practice, practice. The trumpet player in a dance band is released to "take a ride";

that is, play with freedom, not bound to notes on a page. Yet, he must be faithful to the key in which the particular song is written. For St. Paul it was more than his will that provided freedom: It was being bound, mastered by the gospel and the person of the gospel — Jesus Christ our Lord and Master.

Bound to Christ, then, we are free to be, to pray, to grow, to risk, to do. We may break the relationship, get lost and separated from God, from each other, from our best selves. Sometimes we locate the cause of our frustration within ourselves. That humorous Andy Capp of the comics who, at the same time, represents a despair more agonizing than our own and punctures the pomposities of society, including church folk, is free from labor, discipline, responsibility, duty, but is a slave to his own self-regard.

At other times we locate our frustrations in the rules and principles that seem arrayed against our pleasures. We give a ready endorsement to Rudyard Kipling when he flings his pen at unwarranted restraint and writes:

Ship me somewheres east of Suez,
where the best is like the worst,
Where there aren't no Ten Commandments,
and a man can raise a thirst.

But is this freedom? Really? Look at the Prodigal Son; feel into his experience — his throat parched, his skin dry, his body athirst for the muddy, grimy, filthy waters in which the pigs were wallowing. What was the prodigal's sin — engaging in wine, women, and song in a far country? Not essentially. Some fifty children of our music and drama ministries recently portrayed the story of the Prodigal Son in the delightful "Barbecue for Ben." Etched on their minds and ours is the fact that the prodigal's sin was being separated from his father; and only as that separation was healed did he find freedom and, hence, life. Christ saves us not from pain or errors or even physical death. He saves us from the broken relationships, the separations of our lives. He won us; we did not win him. He saved us; we did not save ourselves.

In his book entitled **Night Flight,** Antoine de Saint-Exupery, the late French aviator and philosopher, describes the lost feeling of the aviator in the midst of the darkness. Finally, hearing the whisper of the radio control operator, he frantically asks him to flash the signal at the airfield to learn whether or not the light he sees on the horizon is safety or a star. When the man replies that he has flashed the light, the flier sees nothing; he knows that he has not yet found the light which will guide him home. The Christian, with his eyes on Christ and his church, has no doubt that if he walks through the woods or flies through the darkness of the night, he can never get lost. He is free. Bound to Christ, we are free, not from grief, but from a grief which causes us to become morbid and grinds our lives down to a halt. Bound to Christ, we are free from meaninglessness.

Bound to Christ, we are free to be. What binds you? Do you sometimes find yourself "boxed in," like the little green man? Is your box a career which tempts you to compromise your values in order to get ahead? Or your box may be your appearance, a preoccupation with the way you look or hope to look. Do we remember that what we ARE is more important than how we appear? I do not mean in any way that we should be careless about our appearance or cleanliness, but isn't the product more important than the package? Are we bound by our peer group, tempted to follow their lead, even though we may know that what they are doing, advocating, becoming is not what we want to do, advocate, or become? Who is our Master? To what are we bound? Our answer will determine whether or not we fear freedom and what kind of freedom we will find.

Free To Do

If the law is moral insight, the gospel is moral motivation. People freed from the old law by Christ but controlled by his spirit reap the fruits of his spirit — love, joy, peace, patience, kindness, goodness, faithfulness, gentleness, self-control. If his spirit is in us, then we live by it, walk by it, do the deeds of it. As the spirit of Christ shows in our decisions, our words, our deeds, we have meaningful morality; and only as we use Christian freedom to nurture Christ's spirit as our guide, do we seek to cooperate with what God is doing in our age. External restraints are exchanged for internal constraints of our joy in Christ. Free from the bondage of the law, we are free to serve in love.

We are free to share relationship with others. We *over* not only talk about brotherhood but refuse to stay out of neighborhoods with open occupancy covenants. We not only agree that lust is polluting and destructive, but are willing to examine our sexuality in the light of the personhood and purpose in which God created us. We not only affirm the importance of building up the neighborhoods of a community but will appropriate revenue sharing funds or seek in other positive ways to make this a priority.

The Soviet Union is able to allow some measure of freedom in the church because the church is kept in its own house. There is no mission. There is no group ministry. There is no judgment allowed regarding the state or society. Isn't it interesting that in the west, many voices lifted up against communism also speak against a church in mission — to its neighborhood, its community, its social issues, its relating faith to life. They seem to desire a domesticated church occupied in serving only its own house.

People long for freedom. People fear freedom.

The man in the box finally found the freedom from within and immediately withdrew into the comfort and security of that box. He avoided all relationships. Yet, isn't it so, it is through relationships within the communities of faith, family, neighborhoods, committees, sharing that God reveals himself to us and we find life.

An example of this can be found through the Christian virtue of meekness which, like the rest of the Christian virtues, is a by-product of a life whose freedom is in Christ. I remember the illustration somewhere in Zane Grey's westerns: When the wild horses of the West were brought under control by the cowboy, it was said that the horse was "meeked." All the fire and power and life of the horse remained, but these were subject to the cowboy's touch of the reins. Thus, meekness is all the power, the courage, the freedom of the Christian but always subject to the touch of the master's reins. In the biblical sense the meek are those who have been liberated from the bondage of fear. The opposite of meekness is not self-assertiveness but arrogance. The meek can accept themselves because they know they are accepted, affirmed, freed. They have worth; they have value; they do not have to become defensive. The meek are free to be. In the words of Robert Frost, "One way of putting it would be that you have freedom when you are easy in the harness."

We are bound, not by fear, but by a way of life personified in the person of Jesus Christ. There will be growing pains. We will not be free to do everything we like to do, but we will be free to be the person we are capable of being and becoming.

The call to freedom is a call to the law of love, to relationship with one who can be our true Master. How is it with us?

REACH OUT AND TOUCH SOMEONE

Seventh Sunday After Pentecost
Galatians 6:1-10, 14-16

The Reverend Richard G. Frazier

One of the folk anthems our youth choir likes to sing includes these words:

Lonely voices crying in the city,
Lonely voices sounding like a child,
Lonely faces looking for the sunrise.
Just to find another busy day.

Lonely voices come from busy people,
Men afraid but too ashamed to pray.
Lonely faces do I see,
Lonely faces on my memory.

Lonely eyes I see them in the subway
Burdened by the worries of the day,
Men at leisure, but they're so unhappy
Tired of foolish roles they try to play.

Lonely people do I see
Lonely people on my memory. *

My predecessor at Trinity, Dr. Paul Krauss, counseled: "The preacher must be sensitive to the burden that is in every pew." Another Paul wrote, "Bear one another's burdens, and so fulfill the law of Christ." A recent advertisement by one of the telephone companies invites us to "Reach out and touch someone."

A report came to the Apostle that the congregations in Galatia were on the point of casting aside the Gospel and denying his leadership. That added to his already heavy burdens. He invites the readers to a relationship with God in Christ, to freedom, to obedience. As is his usual pattern, the theological teaching, in this case discerning the difference between law and Gospel, between slavery and freedom, is followed by practical application. One thrust is to discuss what it is to live out the law of Christ, the law of love.

Of several reponses we focus on two — sharing the burdens of others and bearing our own burdens. Strange contradiction, you say? Maybe so. Yet, with the light of the Gospel, we see that the primary question for Paul was not, "How can I get rid of my burdens or avoid sharing the burdens of others?", but "how can I fulfill the law of Christ?" Will you then consider with me something of what this can mean for us.

Bearing One Another's Burdens

The need to "bear one another's burdens" can be fulfilled on the personal level. Do I hear someone protest, " . . . how can anyone bear the burdens of the world or even begin to meet needs which surround us . . . it is another example of the generalizations and irrelevancies of religion."

It is a pertinent question even though often asked with impertinence. Where DO we begin? How can we help when obviously there are so many in need? How easy it is to develop what Norman Cousins called "compassion fatigue." He was speaking on the occasion marking the one-hundredth anniversary of Dr. Ida Scudder, founder of the Vellore Christian Medical Center in South India. He recalled the relief efforts he had seen in India when millions upon millions were homeless and many were sick. There were Western doctors who were highly motivated and went out to India to do their stint in ministering to the needs of the masses. In no time at all, they developed "compassion fatigue." "They help one person and ten march up behind; they help the ten and one-hundred step forward."

Here is the response of Mr. Cousins: "They missed the point that Dr. Ida knew and people like Dr. Schweitzer knew, which is, you do not look beyond the one in front of you. You never know how many people are helped because of the *one* you helped."

In our own lives do we not need to focus carefully on meeting the need of the one nearest at hand. Should we fail him or her, the wider circle may never be reached. The service that we share with others is the plus element beyond what is comfortable and what we know inside that we ought to do. It is the margin that the law of Christ, the law of love keeps before us.

Several years ago a professional basketball player, Maurice Stokes, fell and struck his head on the floor in the Coliseum in Cincinnati. He was taken unconscious to the hospital and for the remaining fourteen years of his life was a helpless cripple. For more than six months he was in a coma. He was never again able to speak.

Shortly after he was taken to the hospital, Jack Twyman, one of his professional teammates, went to see him. He found Maurice's mother at his bedside, weeping. She was anxious about how they would pay the mounting hospital costs. Jack Twyman took it upon himself to do something about it. He went to the officials of the National Basketball Association and made a plea that they have a special game for the benefit of Stokes. The game was held and $10,000 was raised.

As a result of that game, people all over the country sent their contributions. Because one person shared the burden of another, wider circles of people became involved. There were many problems along the way, and Jack Twyman kept probing to find the truth. It was six years before Stokes could move a muscle. He finally was able, through rehabilitation, to move a little bit; and when, after agonizing years, he was able to move his fingers a little, Jack Twyman bought him an electric typewriter. He wrote his first words on the typewriter: "Dear Jack, How can I ever thank you for all you have done for me."

After the death of Maurice Stokes, Arthur Daley wrote these words about him: "Perhaps there is something symbolic about the fact that Maurice Stokes died in Cincinnati's Good Samaritan Hospital; after all, it was a good samaritan who sustained him there."

"Bear one another's burdens and so fulfill the law of Christ." And that occurs not just in the dramatic newspaper-worthy examples. Any pastor knows of the hundreds of people who fulfill Christ's law, never calling attention to themselves. Often we share the burdens of others simply with our presence, when no words are spoken because there are no adequate words to speak.

The Joseph Baylys, in the course of several years, lost three of their children. In the book, **The View From a Hearse,** Mr. Bayly shares his honest feelings when one of the children died: "I was sitting, torn by grief. Someone came and talked to me of God's dealings, of why it happened, of hope beyond the grave. He talked constantly. He said things I knew were true. I was unmoved except to wish he would go away. He finally did. Another came and sat beside me. He didn't talk. He didn't ask me leading questions. He just sat beside me for an hour and more, listened when I said something, answered briefly, prayed simply, left. I was moved. I was comforted. I hated to see him go."

We "reach out and touch" and "bear another's burdens" in the common everyday caring, listening, and presence with our neighbors, even as Salinger describes Bessie's caring for someone ill in **Franny and Zooey** with "the consecrated cups of chicken soup."

Burden-Bearing Within the Community of Faith

"Bearing one another's burdens" happens beyond our personal sharings. Indeed, Paul is thinking here of our life together in the community of faith, the church. There are a myriad of ways this kind of sharing takes place in the life of this parish — groups of people, organized and unorganized, reaching out to others. A significant forward step for us is found in the training sessions as we seek to enable people to listen, to care — sharing with them the biblical concepts. Our curriculum which combines the Stephen Care Series, Bethel Bible Study, LCA Word and Witness program, plus our own approaches, is bearing fruit.

I am thinking just now of what may sound like a strange illustration to you — the relationship between our budget and bearing burdens. Yet, march through the fiscal budget of our parish, some $625,000 worth, and on every budgetary line you can see monies being translated into the bearing of burdens. Let me suggest a few:

Worship — The work of God's people gathered together to be strengthened for our work/ministry/life in the world;

Pastoral — Shepherds, enablers providing a ministry of word and sacrament;

Education — Nurture for all ages through classes, seminars, learning trees, camping, small groups, retreats, koinonia and sharing groups;

Fine Arts — Enriching our educational ministry for all ages through music, drama, art, and dance;

Fine Arts	The first step in "evangelism" is to train people to care for people through our Growth Institute, neighbors, deacons, deaconnesses, Good News ambassadors — some three-hundred fellow members already trained and ministering through these specific areas;
Property	To maintain and enhance our exquisite, functional "home base," where members of the community of faith gather to be equipped for their several ministries in the world;
Benevolences	A minimum of one-third of our income flowing out for others — from the neighborhood ministry to LCA world missions with specific aid in Alaska, Liberia, and Japan; from community needs to the synodical and LCA ministries; from local ecumenism to the Lutheran School of Theology at Chicago; from the alms fund to sharing in the needs of the hungry through the LCA; from support of institutions and agencies for the aged, family counseling, released time education, to contingency funds which enable us to respond to emergency needs.

This is merely suggestive and not, God forbid, to pat ourselves on the back. Yet, read the budget sometimes in the light of bearing burdens. It is a good perspective.

Bearing Our Own Burdens

Paul was conscious of others aiding him to work through his burdens. He rejoiced because of the "brotherhoods of faith" in Philippi, in Corinth, in Ephesus, in Colossae, in Rome, in Galatia. To the Ephesians he wrote, "you shine like stars in a dark world."

Then we meet what at first glance may seem like a contradiction. "Bear one another's burdens" . . . "Each one will have to bear his own load." Or as the New English translation has it, "for every one has his own proper burden to bear."

"Bear" means not only support, equip, bring forth, give. It also means "to endure." As I understand it, we bear our own burdens not only in accepting our responsibilities, but in sharing our needs with God through the relationship he offers us in prayer and worship. No burden is a secret from him. No burden is too great for him. Thus our prayers can rightly begin with our needs as we see them, expressed in whatever words we know in whatever way is natural for us. Central in the relationship is the phrase which gives our prayers perspective, "Thy will be done."

Yes, even pastors need to hear, believe, and accept God's acceptance of us, to take hold of the strength he gives us to see things through, to take to heart the words we pronounce for others: "In the mercy of Almighty God, Jesus Christ was given to die FOR YOU, and for his sake God forgives you all your sins. To those who believe in Jesus Christ he gives the power to become the children of God and bestows on them the Holy Spirit."

Then, too, one way we learn to cope with our own burdens is by sharing them with others. Do you feel with me the difficulty not to be ashamed when we need comfort . . . in some grief, some separation, some wrestling with faith? Are we too ashamed, too proud to seek help, to open ourselves? Have we learned that it is as blessed to receive comfort as it is to give comfort, that it is as human to need to be consoled as to console?

I vividly remember one Wednesday morning as I sat in on a breakfast group in our parish. There had been some ten deaths within two weeks and a great amount of grief was at work within some unusual situations. There were a large number of emotionally exhausting problems in counseling, and the on-going listening to concerns. I was emotionally and physically drained and began to share with those at the table my own exhaustion. My burdens were being shared. I soon sensed sympathy and understanding emanating from faces, voices, gestures of those around me. Only a few words were spoken, "Are you taking yourself too seriously?" . . . and I needed that . . . "I have found, as you have, the strength of God's everlasting arms to see things through." . . . I needed that . . . "Why not take a good book and hole up for a day or so somewhere beyond any telephones and people?" . . . and I needed that. No moralisms. Just sharing. But most of all it was through the non-verbal presence of these friends that God comforted me, and I was better able to bear my own burdens. There was the reminder that those who spend a great deal of time comforting others also need to be comforted. Indeed, it is in opening ourselves to the comfort of others that we are aided in bearing our own burdens.

The heaviest burden ever borne by man was borne by Jesus on the Cross. He struggled with his own burdens . . . "I thirst . . . my God, why . . . it is finished . . . into thy hands I commend my spirit." He reached out and touched those at the Cross . . . "Father, forgive them . . . today, thou shalt be with me . . . woman, behold thy son; son, behold thy mother." His facing and living through suffering, pain, death, and then his resurrection triumph over sin and death enable us not to escape burdens but to see them through.

"Lonely Voices."

"A burden in every pew."

"Reach out and touch someone."

Or as another folk anthem expresses it:

Reach out and touch a soul that is hungry;
Reach out and touch a spirit in despair;
Reach out and touch a life torn and dirty,
A man who is lonely, if you care!
Reach out and touch that neighbor
    who hates you;
Reach out and touch that stranger
    who meets you;
Reach out and touch the brother
    who needs you;
Reach out and let the smile of God
    touch through you.

Reach out and touch a friend who is weary;
Reach out and touch a seeker unaware;
Reach out and touch,
    though touching means losing
A part of your own self, if you dare!
Reach out and give your love to the loveless;
Reach out and make a home for the homeless;
Reach out and shed God's light in the darkness;
Reach out and let the smile of God
    touch through you. *

That is "walking in the law of Christ, the law of love!"

WHAT'S THE GOOD WORD?

Eighth Sunday After Pentecost
Colossians 1:1-14

The Reverend Richard G. Frazier

It's amazing when you think about it. Here is St. Paul writing a letter to the Christians at Colossae, concerned about their "heresy." We are not told precisely what it is — some errant philosophy, vain deceit, worship of the spirit which seemed to issue in an asceticism and legalism foreign to the gospel which the apostle lived and taught. The people were being led astray by teachers who doubted the sufficiency of Christ. Codes took preference over persons, and the situation called for prompt attention.

In view of this fact, how do we account for Paul's approach? He begins the letter, not with a two-gun blast at their heresy; nor does he send his Colossian contact, Epaphras, to begin a witch hunt or take a survey. Rather, he offers a prayer of thanksgiving. Listen: "We always thank God the Father of our Lord Jesus Christ when we pray for you because we have heard of your faith in Christ Jesus and of the love which you have for all the saints, and of the hope which is reserved for you in heaven."

No badmouthing here. No tearing down. It's not natural. In our own personal or congregational life, how often we respond to something we find difficult, new, or threatening with negative words!

Or perhaps we don't "word" at all. Two people who make me listen more than anyone else are my dentist and one of the barbers I visit. What else can I do when the dentist fills my mouth with wads of cotton and an incredible variety of hardware? I am ready to respond to some statement at the same moment my tongue is stiff with novacain. Speech is impossible.

The experience with the barber is somewhat different. As soon as I hit the chair, he is off and running with talk, talk, talk. The torrent of words is so swift, I rarely get into the swim. He talks at me, not to me. And there I am in the chair listening, listening, listening. When he pauses to take a breath, I hurriedly get a word in: Simply, "Do you share all of these words with your wife when you get home?" "Oh . . . well . . . we don't 'word' at all. Not more than a dozen words pass between us. The food is on the table when I get home, and a television, too. We have another television in the living room and even one in the bedroom. We simply don't talk. But think of the arguments we avoid." Frankly, I didn't dare. Do we talk with each other in our families and congregations?

But there is also good wording. When two of my daughters were somewhat younger and Katie would do something to her older sister, Anne wouldn't hit back or yell. She had learned how to care for the situation. She would simply look Katie straight in the eye and say firmly, "Katie, you are a BAD girl." And Katie would melt, running off to her Dad, pleading, "Dad, am I a bad girl?" A good word was needed even before exploring how she really felt. How much we need good wording within our families and congregations! Not a phony hail fellow or a sentimental "nothing is wrong," but a good wording that has substance. The Gospel "good words" us and St. Paul, fully aware of the problem, "good words" the Christians in Colossae.

And every enterprise I know that frees people, including Alcoholics Anonymous, Overeaters Anonymous, and every expression of Christian faith is, at bottom, an attempt to good-word a person, enabling him to accept himself because he is accepted, empowering him to be free of his self-damaging dependence upon alcohol, overeating, self-pity, fear, guilt, or whatever else is sabotaging his humanity.

A little girl was trying to get a turtle out of its shell, and her uncle told her to take the turtle to a fire and warm him up, and he would come out by himself. The uncle was reported to have said, "People are like turtles. Never try to force a fellow into anything. Just warm him up with a little human kindness and more than likely he'll come your way." Is that the way it is with you? It is with me. Indeed, are we not all more likely to be persuaded by the loving spirit, rather than the belligerent attitude?

St. Paul's gratitude contains both an appreciation for their faith and brings to focus other needs. The writer of Proverbs has it, "A wise man is esteemed for being pleasant; his friendly words add to his influence." And again, "A soft word turns away hatred, and a harsh word stirs up anger." Now, what is the reason for Paul's thanksgiving? What is the clue by which he speaks of gratitude and thanksgiving? What's the good word? It is wrapped up in that phrase, "The hope laid up for you" or, as the New English Version has it, "You have grasped the hope reserved for you in heaven."

How do we consider hope? Is it, in the words of a popular song . . . "You mustn't sit around and mope, you've gotta have hope — miles and miles of hope." Is it a matter of bucking up our spirits and climbing up a ladder of good deeds? Paul underscores this hope as God-given. God's amazing grace singles us out before we can know it or be aware of it. God says "Yes" through the sacrament of baptism . . . You are mine, a child of God, an heir of my Kingdom. We are both good-worded and gifted in baptism.

Is hope mere wishful thinking? A young person might say, "I hope I pass that history examination." If he has done his homework, his hope has some substance. If not, it is mere wishful thinking.

Is hope only an escape from the difficult realities of our lives? Is this the good word to us? If we think in those terms, even hope for the same, we will soon dispense with such words, for they provide no lasting effect of goodness, are subject only to our feelings. And if hope is dependent on our feelings, we will be high one moment and downcast the next.

Living in hope always has Christ at the center. This is the essential message Paul wanted to get through to the Colossians. They and we are called upon to focus on Jesus as the source and goal of our faith and hope. Faith and hope are centered, not in creeds and codes, but in a person, the emergence of Jesus of Nazareth. Christianity focuses on God's revelation of the Christ.

Living in hope can then encounter the worst, as Jesus experienced the worst that people would throw at him. By facing and living through such, he is our Redeemer and Savior, saving us from the separations in our lives, our lostness, our sin. Hope springs out of a crucifixion, the cross being a symbol of victory.

In the narthex are three of the loveliest windows in Trinity Church, gems of color, exquisite in their simplicity. Love is portrayed by Francis of Assissi, Courage by Barnabas, Hope by Stephen. Is it not strange to link Stephen with hope? Certainly his witness to the Lord and the truth of his beliefs and convictions did not get him out of trouble. He did not escape anything. Yet the symbols above the head of this first Christian martyr, the crown and laurel, are the signs of victory. In the midst of his difficulty, as recorded in Acts, "His earthly judges saw his face as if it had been the face of an angel." And who knew better that hope does not get us out of trouble than Paul himself? It was not a way out but a way through.

Living in hope gives us perspective when we are tempted by the cultists. Never in all the years of my ministry have I witnessed the emergence of so many so-called religious sects and pseudo-religious cults. Is this not strong evidence that we are living in a time of enormous insecurity with the need of protection from society's rough edges? Most of us receive these supports from our family, our community, our community of faith. Yet many look elsewhere — some, frankly, because they are turned off by the churches who turn them away. Yet our Lord cautioned us to beware of "false prophets" — those who seek to propagate their own version of truth, rather than the truth of Christ, or those who seek to attach others to themselves, rather than to the Christ; and the result is often division and tragedy, instead of building up faith and unity. Keep God, as we know him in Jesus Christ, at the center. Again, this is the essential message Paul wanted to relate through this letter.

Living in hope deals with the despair that so often confronts us. In the Peanuts cartoon, Charlie Brown is talking with Peppermint Patty who says, "Years are like swimming pools, Chuck. We jump in one end and we splash around until we reach the other end. How was your year, Chuck?" And the pensive Charlie Brown replies, "Somebody let all the water out." Do you sometimes find a gap between what you are and what you want to be? There are those times when all seems to go against us and the water is let out of the pool of life. There is a difficulty in making sense of things. Christian hope includes the facing of despair because it always begins with the worst life can throw at us. Ours is not a bombshelter religion. Biblical hope unfolds in the midst of the mystery of life. Finding there the presence of the living God, as the hymn writer expressed it out of his own experience, "The love that will not let me go." It is this assurance which gives purpose to the cup of life with its strange mixture of joys and sorrows, pleasures and adversities.

In that poignant tale of African life, **Cry the Beloved Country,** Kumalo, the village priest who has suffered much, is speaking to Father Vincent. "It seems that God has turned from me," he says. To which Father Vincent replies, "That may seem to happen, but it does not happen. Never, never does it happen." Dare we so trust?

Living in hope, as Christ gives us the hope specifically through the resurrection, is not some carrot dangling at the end of a string at the "end of time." The hope, secured in the resurrection event, infuses the present. Our hope gives courage and strength to face and act and share right now. It is not a guarantee for a successful outcome of the difficulties of our world — injustice, suffering, massive imbalance of the world's limited resources, conditions of poverty, hunger, racism. It is enough to serve, to risk, to involve ourselves actively, knowing that even though not all the problems of the earth can be solved, we can still lift the levels of our community life — home, school, hospitals, neighborhoods, recreational facilities. This is because of our hope secured in one who faced and lived through and triumphed over suffering, injustice, sin, and death.

It is not to say "I hope this person will overcome his illness." It is turning our love and good wishes into prayer, as we often do publicly and privately, and into positive actions of help, as we comfort one another with the hope of our faith. It is not just saying, "I hope justice will be done for all people"; it is sharing in human suffering and misery in whatever way we can, beginning with the family circle and continuing with our neighbor and the world, the hungry and the poor, the unlovely. God counts on us. Indeed, we are the only ones he has, amazing as that may sound, to share in that ministry.

How is it with us? Paul hopes that by emphasizing the positive, the weeds of false doctrine will be crowded out. The people of Colossae are good-worded, thanked for the hope which is ready to be theirs and for what they have already done in the gospel; aware of the dangers confronting them, reminded of the hope that can be theirs as they center their lives in Christ.

What are your hopes? Do they have substance? God good-words us with the Word, what God has done in history, the Word by which the world was created, the Word which appeared in Moses and gave him the law, the Word which appeared to Abraham, the Word which infused the prophets, "The Word which became flesh and dwelt among us," the Word which is Christ who was crucified on Calvary, risen in glory. What are your hopes? Do they have substance? Are they centered in the One who is the resurrection and the life? So Paul's words are given to those times when we are tempted to follow some way other than Christ's.

We always thank God the Father of our Lord Jesus Christ when we pray for you because we have heard of your faith in Christ Jesus and the love which you have for all saints because of the hope which is reserved for you in heaven.

GOD'S SECRET

Ninth Sunday After Pentecost
Colossians 1:21-28

The Reverend J. Richard Hunt

Remember last winter?

I can. I remember the morning (it was five degrees outside) when our furnace wouldn't work. The temperature was fifty-five degrees and sliding. In its hypothermia, the thermostat made no click and caused no ignition. I checked the blower switch, all the switches on the furnace, and all their fuses. Nothing appeared faulty. I finally decided to call the service man. He came and fixed it. Want to know how? He flipped the circuit breaker on the main circuit panel. It just never occured to me to look there. That was a $24 lesson in trouble shooting my heating system. Want to know how I felt? Anguished and angry at myself.

You see, I have a very perfectionistic parent in my head. It thinks I should be perfect and lands on me with both feet when I make a mistake. That parent in my head never read Paul's parental advice on how to treat those who make a mistake:

> You should forgive him and encourage him
> to keep him from becoming so sad as to give up
> hope. Let him know, then, I beg you, that you
> really do love him. (2 Corinthians 2:7-8)

My wife looked at me in my anguished, angry state and said simply, "You don't have to be perfect."

I remember her saying that to our daughter when she was three and fussing about something not being just so. The three-year-old's rebuttal was, "Yes, Mommy; but some of us are trying."

I have a little boy inside me who didn't disappear just because I got to be forty-three. He's still trying to be perfect. But on this occasion, with Marj's words and Paul's encouragement and what I've learned about dealing with my perfectionistic parent during the past six years, I got hold of my inner child and held him close on my lap. I hugged him so he'd know he was loved and I told the parent, in my head, to stop hounding me.

I think this is an incident where I glimpsed what Paul means by "the secret" God wants me to understand.

The secret?

Christ is within me
to bring me into
God's presence.
Christ is within me
to help me become
a mature person
in union with Christ.

We can live in union with Christ. We can put our roots deep in him and build our lives on him. (cf *Colossians 2:6-7*)

God wants me to learn his wisdom and knowledge: If you would be perfect as God is perfect, then be merciful.

Paul passed that message to Corinth. I have passed that message to my inner child.

How do you deal with your inner child and the perfectionistic parent in your head?

A man I counseled over many months was in his sixties when he learned this secret. He told me one day: "I've learned that I can be as nurturing toward my inner child, what I call my 'immature self,' as I was to my son when he was a boy. I can stop trying to wring its neck and throw it in the trash. Christ nurtures me, and I can care, in the same way, for my inner child."

Christ is in you, the source of hope.

Christ is in you, nurturing you,
that you might grow up into Christ.

You can be Christ to your neighbor by being a person of forgiveness. You can, as Paul says later in the letter to Colossians, "do everything in the Name of Jesus."

Begin with the child living in you. Reach in and hold that "little one" close. And also reach out to the other children of God whose lives you touch.

YOU MEAN CHURCH?
ARE YOU SERIOUS?

Tenth Sunday After Pentecost
Colossians 2:6-15

The Reverend Daniel L. Hamlin

Shalom!

If someone would say to me, "As therefore you received Christ Jesus the Lord, so live in him, rooted and built up on him and established in the faith, just as you were taught, abounding in thanksgiving," I think he would be inviting me to join in a discussion focused on the theological and biblical life style versus the life style of a humanist or that of a deist. If the same statement were made to the rank and file churchgoer that I have known in my ministry, it would draw, nine times out of ten, the reaction, "You mean church? Are you serious?" So I will pose the same to you this morning: So this is Sunday and what are you doing in church?

Just because we are here today doesn't necessarily tell me that we know why we are here. I wonder how we would answer such a question from a person who wants and feels that he should be in church and yet does not know the reason. To say it is a habit is unsatisfactory to most because people are not accustomed to acquiring habits for the sake of having them. How would you answer the person who would put it to you this way: "You see, I was made to go to church all my life and now that I am older I really feel I should go to church, and I do; but for the life of me it seems all so strange and unreal somehow. I'm embarrassed at the answers I give my children when they ask me why we go to church. I'm embarrassed when they say, 'Daddy, you say the prayer at the table today.' I must know the answer, for I cannot continue something for its own sake. It all seems so unreal and strange."

I have been in such a situation before and have been asked such a question. I believe now, I would have been better prepared had I thought up the situation first and rehearsed my answer since a serious question is being asked and a serious answer is expected. The following, then, is a serious and rehearsed answer to the reaction, "You mean church? Are you serious?"

Let me commend you, first of all, for asking the important question. You see, many people never get to that stage. Either they just quit church or they just continue on never knowing or believing in the reality of church or religion in their lives and in their living. Thank you for asking the important question.

I might say that I go to church to worship God. That sounds religious and would probably quiet you. But I would rather try to explain. I must tell you now, however, that no easy explanation goes all the way in such things. Some of the best reasons are of the heart and of the imagination. You must listen with your heart and your imagination or you will find it hard to understand why I go to church.

You see, I freely acknowledge the strangeness of going to church, but on the other hand anything seems strange if we look into it deeply enough. For instance, we work in the office from Monday to Friday and try to get some rest and pleasure over the weekend. Now that does not seem strange because we are used to it. We feel there are reasons why we carry out such a weekly routine, but we do not often stop to consider those reasons clearly, do we? We can say we have to eat, support our families, maintain a home with modern conveniences and a few luxuries, and we want to get ahead. That sounds reasonable enough, but does it really explain why we work or why we should continue such a pattern in our lives?

As for me, there are times when the work routine seems an almost meaningless grind. Then I ask hard questions. What does it all mean? Is it worthwhile? How did I get caught up in this complicated machinery of living? How did I get into my particular corner?

When I ask questions like this I do not get easy

answers. The whole thing begins to look strange. I have a name, a post office address, a family, a place in the world's work. But who am I really? Someone else might have been in my place in all these connections, but he would not be the person that I am. What does it mean to be me? You see, the deeper we probe with such questions the more difficult they become.

You may say these are idle or morbid questions. I do not think so. I think they are the really important questions, questions to uncover the true meaning of life, its strangeness, its mystery. I think that life seems familiar and commonplace only when we carefully avoid asking the above questions. I believe that to feel life's mystery and suppose it to be as ordinary as it looks most of the time is to be mistaken about life.

If you ask me, then, why I go to church, I say, first, I go because the church is a place where the basic and final questions about life have been raised and dealt with, not avoided or forgotten. And I believe the questions have answers, whether we know them or not. If there are no answers, I cannot imagine why it is natural to ask questions. And as long as I ignore the basic questions about my life, I am not living it very satisfactorily.

I have said that church is a place where the basic questions have been raised. I do not mean that they are always clearly put or convincingly answered there. But they are not avoided. They are in the background of nearly everything said and done in church, especially in worship.

I am convinced that the basic meaning of existence is not dealt with in our daily routine of work and play. The machinery of our living keeps on rumbling and rolling us along on its prescribed grooves and, weary in body, we sleep and forget why we are even moving this body through the mazes. Such hard questions as to why we live at all are dismissed. The thought that occurs to me when I meet such busy people is that maybe they are that busy because they want to be. We can even decide what thoughts we will allow to surface in our awareness. Perhaps we would just as soon forget that such hard questions exist. Playing busy and important sometimes is the way people escape even hearing what's really involved in being human in the full sense; a way to avoid thinking about ultimate questions altogether.

It is easy to do. We can just keep focusing on the more immediate and practical questions that are answerable in some fashion. We may ask only how we can do what we want to do. You know, we have become so proud of our knowledge, so very self-confident that we have found that it can do wonderful things for us. Knowledge gives us earthy comforts, pampers us with conveniences, flatters us with luxuries, improves our health, lengthens our lives. Sometimes knowledge also acts as a mirror to reveal more clearly the bad, the beautiful, and the ugly streaks in our human nature, supplying better tools for exploitation and deadlier weapons to destroy one another. Knowledge enables us to do so much that we fantasize we can do anything. It isn't that fantasies are bad — it is just that fantasies are fantasies, and the difficulty begins when we believe them. It is then that we no longer ask real questions. We pretend they do not exist.

It could be that you feel okay with that life style, but I find that hard to believe because you asked the question to begin with, remember?

You may think that I am purposely and laboriously making your simple question unnecessarily complicated. I could give you simple and logical reasons why I go to church, but they would not explain.

The fact is that about 800 families in the parish I serve get up on Sunday morning, hurry up, put on clean clothes, drive or walk to a structure with strange objects in it, and sit down in dignified silence. They listen while an organ plays. They sing songs by unknown authors who lived hundreds of years ago. They hear language read from books written originally in Hebrew and Greek. A minister talks about things that happened in the dim past as if they were news flashes from the six o'clock edition. They hear prayers and maybe say some of their own. Sometimes they eat something that tastes like paper and wash it down with wine. They put money, which they might have used for something else, in a plate. They sing some more. They are blessed in words meant, when they were first written, for ancient Jews. They go out, greeting people they seldom see anywhere else, and they go home.

Simple? No, fantastic! How can such a thing be done at all? How can it possibly continue to be done in a modern society? What could such a routine and ritual ever have to say to people whose continued lives and livelihoods depend on whether the job continues, the surgery holds, and the energy lasts? What sense can it make to go to church?

Well, as I told you earlier, I go there, first of all, to face the questions of why we are in the predicament we are in, how we got into it, and what it means. I go there because I believe there are answers to such questions, and our only hope is not to evade the questions.

Are you still with me? Okay. One more thing about the explanation that in no way can be simple: I go to church because of what I hear there. I hear words which are old but are not worn out at all. They speak to me more personally than the words I hear or read in the papers. They speak to me at a deeper level than the news, the advertising, or the entertainment programs. I have lived long enough to know that no matter how analytical I am of human nature, others' and my own, circumstances can still come down on me to make me feel guilty and ashamed, and fearful. I know I dare not reveal as much to others. What would they do if they knew? That's right: get it together; defend yourself; play opossum, everything is cool. For my own skin, I transfer the judgment of my critics somewhere else, anywhere else. Don't you do that?

Being that I play that "I am no fool!" routine on the outside, inside I am crying out, calling out, pleading for something on which to grasp hold. I cry to the dumb earth. I pound with bruised fists on a sky that is pillowy soft and without substance. The only sound I hear is the hollow, desperate, lonely sound of my own voice echoing back only the questions, but no solutions!

I have been in church at a time like that. There I have heard the voice of another person cry: *"How long, O Lord? Wilt thou forget me forever? How long will thou hide thy face from me?"* And again, *"Be not deaf to me, lest, if thou be silent to me, I become like those who go down to the pit."* I know how this person felt.

I have been in church when I felt that some people whose lives once literally oozed with the power of love were suddenly possessed by the love of power and were waiting for me in ambush. And I hear words being cried out: *"Those who seek my life lay their snares; those who seek my hurt speak of ruin. Let them not rejoice over me who boast against me when my foot slips."* Whoever spoke those words, spoke for me.

I go to church because of what I hear there, beginning with such words as these. Whoever fashioned these words, when and where they lived, what language they spoke, makes no difference whatsoever. These authors did not know me, were not thinking of me. Yet I know them better than I know most of the people with whom I work. They come closer to me than most of my acquaintances do. They speak not only for themselves, but for me and to me. Their words make me know that I am not alone in my most secret grief and joy, as I thought I was.

If the words that I hear in church did no more than this, they would still be great, wonderful news. For they tell me that grief, and joy, and compassion, and hope are the family marks of humanity, not my own private prison. Guilt and sorrow have some dignity if they are the price of being human. I can carry my share of them then, and a little more than my share, if need be, without breaking.

And then, one more thing: I go to church to make some decent reply to my God. Now, I know that there are many other reasons why people go to church, including sheer custom, and because your spouse wants you to go. They work in me, too. But I have not always gone to church and I could easily drop out. I would not continue to go without the reasons I am giving.

If, through my intellect or spirit, I ascertained that power to be God, and if that power to make alive and keep alive is addressing itself to me, then it is imperative that I answer at once!

Worship is the name some give to that experience. Some call it communion with God. I like to look upon it as one part of his Creation seeking to make some decent reply to our Creator.

If it is my God who speaks to my innermost heart in the words of human speech, in the agony of mortal existence, then there is no decent response but worship: to recognize and adore him, to look to him for all good, to confess him before others, to throw myself on his judgment and his mercy, to thank and praise him, to obey and serve him. "*As therefore you received Christ Jesus the Lord, so live in him, rooted and built up in him and established in the faith, just as you were taught, abounding in thanksgiving.*"

While this seems like a rather complicated explanation to a seemingly easy question, as I said in the beginning, no easy answer is worth much when it comes to the most vital activity in which we participate in life. You mean worship? Yes, I am serious!

Be a blessing!

WHAT A WAY TO GO

Eleventh Sunday After Pentecost
Colossians 3:1-11

The Reverend Daniel L. Hamlin

Shalom!

The first preaching assignment as a newly ordained pastor was an invitation to speak to a class of graduates in my high school alma mater. I was to speak to a group of 1,500 to 2,000 people. My wife thought that such a first assignment might give me illusions of grandeur. I assured her, however, that while I was honored by the invitation, I was, at the same time, darn scared!

Jesus' saying about a prophet having no honor in his home stuck in my mind. While my message would be addressed to the graduates who didn't know me, I knew that I was going to be speaking to all my old teachers and athletic coaches, to curious boyfriends and old girlfriends who would come to see if eight years of higher education could make the fun-loving, rattle-brained, basketball-playing fellow they knew in high school amount to anything. While the odds were against the message being a Pulitzer Prize winner, the challenge was welcomed and the reunion with my teachers and coaches afterwards was hilariously funny.

Looking over that message, after having delivered it, well, let's say *some* wouldn't think it was a Pulitzer Prize winner. Being an egotist at heart, I thought there was a message there that St. Paul is trying to get through to us in the Second Lesson today:

If, then, you have been raised with Christ, seek the things that are above, where Christ is, seated at the right hand of God. Set your minds on things that are above, not on things that are on the earth.

When astronauts go into space they are connected to gauges on the ground so that those on the ground might have a constant reading of the astronauts' blood pressure in every situation of stress. Interestingly enough, a group of safety experts made a test for comparison's sake with automobile drivers, driving on the freeways of our nation. While the driver was traveling at turnpike speeds, a passenger in the back seat of the test car exploded a paper sack. The blood pressure of the driver, thinking the explosion was a blow-out, went up way beyond any situation of panic faced by an astronaut in space. I sight this comparison only to give you some idea as to the strain endured by me the first time I drove my automobile through Chicago. The first time through Chicago was after having been ordained in Kenosha, Wisconsin. My wife and I decided to take my mother-in-law to my first parish in Indiana so that she could see where and what her son-in-law had gotten her daughter into. Of course, that meant traveling through or in the vicinity of Chicago.

I had been in Chicago before, in fact, in New York City before, but I had never driven through by automobile. Having a little idea of what it might be like to drive in Chicago, I took out my map and sort of planned a route which I thought would take me around Chicago. When I look back on this experience now, it seems rather humorous. But believe me, it wasn't at the time. As I came closer to Chicago there began to be more signs, and more forks, and more junctions, and they all seemed to be telling me the direction I wanted to go. Things began to be just too much guesswork. So I traveled at least forty-five minutes in the opposite direction to find a person who could tell me what turnoff I should take in order to arrive in Indiana. I was very fortunate to meet up with any person, let alone the person that I happened to meet, because the way I had plotted on the map was leading me into a real jungle of traffic. But at this point, I could not change course without losing at least two hours of driving time. So I was destined to travel through that jungle of traffic.

The man told me to look for a sign which read Clinton East. He said to be sure it was this particular sign because there was one just like it which read Clinton West. Well, I thought to myself, that seems to be rather simple, and I was on my way again. They say ignorance is bliss. Well, in this case I took the prize! Little did I know what I was in for. Let me describe it to you as I wrote it down shortly after the first time through.

There were at least ten lanes of traffic all traveling in my direction. There might have been more, but I was pretty well occupied at the time not to care how many lanes there were. The cars were bumper to bumper, along side of me, in front of me, cutting in, cutting out at the pace of sixty to seventy miles an hour. There were signs, signs, and more signs. It took one person to drive and another just to look at the signs. It was fortunate I was not alone. It was the easiest place in which to get lost, and when one is lost there, man, one is really lost! To say the least, I gave a large sigh of relief when I could look in the rearview mirror and see Chicago back in the distance.

When I thought of Paul's words to the Colossians for this Eleventh Sunday After Pentecost (to seek the things that are above) I thought of this driving experience and felt I should tell you about it. For is it not the way, or much the same way we make our way through life? We have never been through life before. I suppose if we could have two lives, the second time through would be much smoother. Driving through Chicago is not much of a trick for me anymore.

But you see, we have only one life and we have only one time to go through life. Every minute, every hour, every day in life is a section of time to which we will never be able to return again. And life is no place in which to get lost, either! Most of us travel through life at the same blinding speed as did those drivers on those ten lanes through Chicago. If you asked me what I saw of Chicago, I could tell you nothing about the city. I was going too fast to see anything, and I was afraid of turning off the highway for fear that I would never get back on. That is the way we go through life, is it not? We travel sixty miles an hour, going here, going there, doing this, doing that, always too heavy-footed so that some of the more meaningful experiences of life are not savored, nor are the lessons they teach absorbed, nor the joy inherent in those experiences felt. Many times the only thing that we can be sure of is that we have been through life.

Probably, this is one of the most descriptive characteristics of Americans — this hypermania for speed and activity. And it is a characteristic that molds and buttonholes most peoples' life styles in our nation. It is like a person trying to start in four directions all at the same time. There are far too many people who are trying to follow all of the alternative ways, alternative directions; too many people trying to follow *all* of the road signs in life. And the result is that we end up never having been anyplace, never having seen anything, never having learned anything, never having been the better off for it. I remember, it was twenty-five years ago now (it's hard to believe that time does pass so quickly), that I sat among a class of eighty students as a graduating high school senior. All of us were seeking something from life; none of us was out to ruin our life. We were ordinary young people — ambitious, energetic, seeking from life fulfillment and satisfaction. I have seen some of my classmates since then, and I know many of them are leading happy, fulfilled lives. Some of them have seen far too much of life. They have covered the boondocks and waterfronts of many a city! And today that is where you will find them! Many of them who had high hopes and great dreams for the future are sick in mind. Their memories are filled with a mass of confused and varied experiences and their lives are in a broken and chaotic state. And a number of them, in tears, have confessed that instead of finding fulfillment and satisfaction they have found *starvation!*

Now, not all of them tried to travel all of the roads. Many who sought fulfillment and satisfaction in life decided, instead of trying to go the way of all the signs, to take one of the forks in the road and follow that.

There are a great many in America who feel that the key to satisfaction in life, the end of all the worries and problems in life, is the way of matrimony, for example. There is a story told of a couple who were being married. They were still at the altar when it came time for the minister to give his blessings and best wishes to the bride and groom. The minister gave his best wishes to the bride, and then said to the groom, "Well, Jim, you sure are a lucky fellow getting such a fine girl. I am sure with her, your problems will come to an end." It was about a year later that Jim saw this minister on the street. He said, "Say, Pastor, I thought you said all of my problems would come to an end when I got married?" The minister replied, "Yes, I said that, but I didn't say what end!" There is more truth in this story, I am sorry to say, than there is humor. The altar is not the place where problems begin but where the responsibilities of being a husband or wife begin. This is problematic in everyone's book. And sad is the sight that one sees who curiously travels such a road in America.

Many illustrations could be added of people being ambitious in heart who have sold themselves on road signs, i.e., wealth, power, fame, knowledge, freedom from home, freedom to be what they wanted, freedom to do as they please, which all led to dead ends. All of this is sadly true. This is not something that we want to dwell on today, but which I think has something very important to say to us, something I hope will stick to your ribs, as well as your minds.

I'm really quite well-acquainted with you and your experiences in life. I know all of us, for a few years in our growing up, were on a pleasure trip enjoying the scenery, having a very carefree time. Some of us have already faced some junctures in which the signals and signs have confused us. Maybe some of you are traveling through one now. Whatever the case may be, while all of us need no help driving in happiness on the open road with a number of lanes in which to maneuver, I think that I should warn you that there are more, larger, truly confusing junctures coming your way: junctions and junctures in which you will have passed the point of no return so that you cannot turn around and go back; junctions and junctures that you will have to travel through and not only make it through, but have to be heading in the right direction once through them. Now if you are going to stop and ask me which way to go, I will tell you. There is a sign that is above the others. Don't miss it. Of course, you shouldn't miss it, it is plain enough. This sign, in effect, says this road has all that is of first importance for your life. It is rich and radiant, full of all those things in life that are of lasting value so that you will want no more. You will want an eternity of this kind of traveling. The sign reads: *"Seek the things that are above, where Christ is . . . for Christ is all, and in all."* Not only will I tell you that this is the road to take, but I will also tell you that this is the way which was meant for you.

It was said of a happily married couple recently that they were meant for each other, that this marriage was really made in heaven. Maybe so. But in an infinitely profounder sense this is true of the relationship between God and ourselves. God has made us for himself. He made us for his companionship, for the doing of his will. Life, therefore, works that way, and it will not work any other way.

A couple, at Christmas time, gave their small child a Jack-in-the-box. One day as their child had heard its songs over and over again until he, as well as his family, was weary of them, he decided to see how well it would work in reverse. Well, he never found out. He only broke the machine. It was not made to work that way. Just as the Jack-in-the-box was meant to work one way, so it is with our lives. We cannot function satisfactorily without being in relationship with our God.

St. Peter, the disciple, laid it before us short and to the point in St. John's Gospel. Christ never made the terms of discipleship easy. He never coaxed anyone to join his church. When he had spoken plain words to the multitude and plain words to those who had been known as his disciples, "From that time on," says St. John's Gospel, "many of his disciples went back and walked no more with him." Jesus watched in silence the departure of these "sunshine disciples" who had lost their faith and zeal. Then turning to the twelve, he said, there must have been the accent of sorrow in his voice, "Will ye also go away?" Quick as a flash came Peter's beautiful and loyal answer: "Lord, to whom shall we go? You have the words of eternal life."

The same question Jesus asked his twelve followers is the question I ask you today: To whom will you go? What road will you travel if you travel not the one plainly marked? If I were never to see you again after this Sunday, realizing that you will go from this place to meet God-only-knows what junctions and junctures in your life, I would strongly reiterate: "Seek the things that are above, where Christ is." Don't miss

116

it! It is not only the way to go, but man, what a way to go!

Be a blessing!

I DON'T HAVE TO

Twelfth Sunday After Pentecost
Hebrews 11:1-3, 8-16

The Reverend Daniel L. Hamlin

Shalom!

We have all heard children arguing, seeking authority over each other. The phrase that continues in the fracas is today's sermon title, "I Don't Have To," followed by "Yes, you do," followed by "No, I don't," followed by "Yes, you do," followed by "No, I don't." We call such a confrontation a stalemate or an impasse because no one in this situation shows signs of accepting the other's expressed authority.

While it is frightening to read article after article reporting the outbursts of crime caused by the conflict of authority, the defiance of law and order is really no great shock to any student of the Scriptures. We have been resisting authority ever since God made the first restriction to our autonomy in Eden: *"And the Lord God commanded the man, saying, 'You may freely eat of every tree of the garden; but of the tree of the knowledge of good and evil you shall not eat, for in the day that you eat it you shall die.' "* (Genesis 2:16-17)

Anarchy denotes a state or condition of society where there is no law or order, not even divine. One enters into every decision-making moment armed with all the wisdom of the culture, prepared in one's freedom to suspend or violate any rule except that a person must be as responsible as possible for the good of his neighbor. It would follow that "responsible as possible" must mean, in any given situation, relative to the value system and feelings of any other participant.

Living in a time that demands clear, insightful decisions, it seems that all the old lines between right and wrong have been blurred and almost obliterated. And, of course, to meet these changed conditions, new situations, new problems, and new freedoms, a deluge of new laws has been written and passed. The reaction to these laws is handled very much like the quick-thinking political candidate who stood at a rostrum seeking to bedazzle his audience and make them want to vote for him. He made great promises and veiled boasts about how much he could accomplish. Then a man in the audience yelled out: "Hey! I wouldn't vote for you even if you were St. Peter!" "If I were St. Peter," the candidate yelled back, "you wouldn't be in my district anyway!"

The desire for freedom from authority was the impetus for founding these United States, says anthropologist Geoffrey Gorer in his book, **The American People.** The attitude of the people who came to these shores was such that "people or institutions, who 'push other people around' are bad, repugnant to decent feelings, thoroughly reprehensible. Authority over people is looked on as a sin, and those who seek authority as sinners." The quote from Mr. Gorer's book seems, to me, to point out that the motivation for becoming involved in anything, including the acceptance of another's authority, is the key to the immense entanglement in which we find ourselves in society. Life has become so complicated in every respect that there is a new hunger and motivation afoot in society to create new life styles that are simple, easy to grasp, and impossible to doubt.

It reminds me of the optimist who tells you that ten years from now you will be able to laugh at today's troubles, but is careful not to mention the new troubles you'll have then. And that same optimist would tell you that you have to believe in luck or you can never explain the success of people you don't like. Like most optimists, this one is beginning to sound like an expert, meaning a guy who answers your questions immediately and then sneaks into the books to verify his answer.

Today's Second Lesson gives some expert advice

that cuts through a distorted image of our Judeo-Christian heritage as being a matter of suppressing our personal desires and paging through a catalogue of do's and don'ts toward some self-made solo salvation trip. Like a prompter off-stage, this lesson cues us four times so that we will get the line: *"by faith we understand that the world was created by the word of God . . .; by faith Abraham obeyed when he was called to go out to a place which he was to receive as an inheritance . . .; by faith he (Abraham) journeyed in the land of promise . . .; by faith Sarah herself received power to conceive . . ."*

Our children, our forefathers, you and I are correct. That the only authority, rules, laws that will motivate us effectively so that we will live by them, and lean on them, and believe them are those laws that we, with our whole beings, cannot help but follow because we perceive them as having divine sanction and participating in divinity. In fact, they cease to have even the negative cast of being laws or rules, but are part and parcel of everything we mean when we say they are our God. *"Abraham believed the Lord; and God reckoned it to him as righteousness."* (Genesis 15:6)

The word "believe" is an all-encompassing word! Many mistake belief as something that is comprehended by the mind only. You say, for instance, that you believe the world to be round like a ball, or you may say that you believe the world to be flat like a disc. In either event, all you really say is that you accept one notion or the other as the more likely explanation of the shape of our earth. Whether you believe one or the other, you will go on eating the same sort of meal, choosing the same sort of friends, loving or hating the same people, much as before. Your belief in this situation changes nothing for you. There are people who believe in God much in this way. Sure, they believe in God — so what? Does not every sensible person believe in God? But if someone should suggest that because he believes in God he ought to change his policies of business or labor, he would be quite shocked. A person certainly should be able to believe that daVinci painted the Last Supper, that God created the earth, and that Shakespeare wrote **Hamlet,** without having to change his economics or his politics.

Obviously, if that is what we put into the word "believe," then it is not very important what we believe. But the word does have a much greater depth of meaning.

To believe in God, in the biblical God, pushes the word to its highest point and its widest reach. When the people asked Jesus to describe for them what the works of God were, he replied that to believe in him would be the work of God. By that, he did not mean merely to accept the notion that he was divine. He meant that if we believed in him we would trust him for all things more than we would trust riches or friends. He meant that we would fear him more than we would fear war or cancer. He meant that we would love him more than we would love mother or self. The person who really believed in Christ would fear, love, and trust in him above all things. Now this is more than just a little intellectual excursion of the mind; it is the total surrender and turning around of our lives to Jesus Christ as Savior, friend, and Lord.

In other words, "belief," in this sense, is action, doing something! We can say that we love our wives, but they know whether or not we mean what we say by the things that we do! We can say that we love God, but he knows whether we mean what we say by the things that we do!

By faith in God, Abraham obeyed. Do you see the progression in that statement? Faith in God describes a relationship of trust between a person and his God. Faith is simply believing what God has said, what God has promised; it is the knowledge that what he has said, he will do. Faith is not a series of propositions which are either intellectually believed or not believed. It is, instead, that trust in God which leads one to follow him in whatever situation one may find himself; a trust which waits on the Lord even in times when one is fearful for his life. Faith in God — that is the first priority, a relationship. Then, and only then, is there motivation for obedience to rules. A person can decide to keep a great number of rules regarding right behavior and still not be a person of faith!

Abraham is a person who trusted God, and God accepted that trust as Abraham's salvation. Jesus inferred when he said, "If you love me . . ." it follows naturally that "you will keep my commandments." Relationship of trust, then obedience to his will! Belief is not something we do with our heads. In Jesus' terms, we believe with the whole of our lives or we do not believe.

Once we have appropriated, through faith, the gift of relationship with God that he cared enough to offer us, we begin to care about what God cares about — people!

And it holds true that the real true miracle-worker ✳ today in society is the one who can motivate people to care. No matter what field — business, industry, education, government, sociology, the arts, religion — to motivate workers to care about the customers' satisfaction. In industry — to motivate workers to care about quality of products and executives to care about their responsibility to people and the environment. In education — to motivate students to care about the knowledge that is available to them. In government — to motivate legislators, administrators, and judges to care what the taxpayers get for their money. In sociology — to motivate those who have, to care about what is significant and beautiful in life. In religion — to motivate congregations to care more about true, God-inspired, selfless love than about how imposing their church buildings are. Today's person of genius is the one who can motivate people to care.

Jesus asked Peter, *"Who do you say that I am?"* Peter answered, *"You are the Christ, the son of the living God."* In response, Jesus observed, *"flesh and blood has not revealed this to you, but my Father who is Heaven."* (Matthew 16:13-20) In his book, **The Meaning of Christ,** (Layman's Theological Library, The Westminster Press, Philadelphia, fourteenth printing, 1977) Robert Clyde Johnson says that "the word 'reveal' means to 'unveil' or 'disclose.' To say that something must be revealed is to say that it is not available to our search — or to our research. It must be unveiled *for* us or disclosed *to* us. To say that the meaning of Christ must be revealed by God is to say that only God can do the disclosing or unveiling. Otherwise, his real meaning remains 'veiled' to us." Jesus asked his disciples the question two different ways. The first time he asked, "Who do men say that I am?" And then he repeated the question with one significant word changed, "Who do you say that I am?" The first question was the academic question of reporting other peoples' opinions. The second question of "Who do you say that I am?" cannot be lodged. It cannot be answered with somebody else's answer. It demands our answer.

Let me close with this thought. It has been noticed and often remarked in the world of business that the lower a man is on the executive totem pole, the more he plays the role of being important. Conversely, the higher a man is on this totem pole the less he plays the role. It isn't always true, of course, but to a great extent it seems that the little executive will make greater efforts to seem important — having his secretary screen all calls, and so on. But as often as not, you can call the president of the company and he will see you at your convenience. "Go to the top man with your problem," you're told. "He's always in."

If that advice is good most of the time in the business world, it's good all of the time in the big general world: "Go to the Top Man. He's always in."

Maybe you can't find anyone else to help you with your problem. Maybe the minister is writing his sermon and can't be disturbed. Maybe the priest is out on the streets rescuing people. Maybe the rabbi is speaking at a luncheon. But the Top Man is always in, always ready to help in the ways that are his.

He is the one who is most concerned, and he is the one who has the final authority. So, though his lesser executives are necessary and have their valid functions, when it comes to the really big emergencies, be reassured in knowing that you can get through directly to the Top Man — he's always in.

I don't have to! But once you're in touch with the Top Man, you get to!

Be a blessing!

ISSUES IN
SCIENCE
EDUCATION

PROFESSIONAL
DEVELOPMENT
LEADERSHIP
And the Diverse Learner

Jack Rhoton and Patricia Bowers, editors

National Science Teachers Association
National Science Education Leadership Association

Shirley Watt Ireton, Director
Beth Daniels, Managing Editor
Judy Cusick, Associate Editor
Jessica Green, Assistant Editor
Linda Olliver, Cover Design

Art and Design
Linda Olliver, Director
NSTA Web
Tim Weber, Webmaster
Periodicals Publishing
Shelley Carey, Director
Printing and Production
Catherine Lorrain-Hale, Director
Publications Operations
Erin Miller, Manager
*sci*LINKS
Tyson Brown, Manager

National Science Teachers Association
Gerald F. Wheeler, Executive Director
David Beacom, Publisher

NSTA Press, NSTA Journals,
and the NSTA Web site deliver
high-quality resources for
science educators.

NSTA Press
1840 Wilson Boulevard
Arlington, VA 22201-3000
http://www.nsta.org/

Issues in Science Education: Professional Development Leadership and the Diverse Learner
Library of Congress Catalog Card Number 00-110019
NSTA Stock Number: PB127X3
ISBN 0-87355-186-9
Printed in the United States of America by IPC.
Printed on recycled paper

National Science Education Leadership Association

Susan Loucks-Horsley
1947–2000

For more than a quarter century Susan Loucks-Horsley provided leadership for the science education community. Honoring her achievements and contributions requires one only to pause and reflect on her professional research, books, reports, and presentations. Her accomplishments far exceed in quality and quantity what most of us could only wish to attain. There is another quality of Susan that we must recognize and honor. In Susan's life and work, she always conveyed a freshness of appreciation for the other person. This interest in other people complemented her written contributions and achievements. Susan left the science education community with this deeper and more profound contribution. Personally, she conveyed a belief that, given the opportunity, each science teacher had the potential to improve, and that each teacher wanted her or his students to learn science. Susan let all she touched know that she understood their concerns and recognized their daily struggles to change. She supported their dignity, integrity, and worth as individuals. Susan Loucks-Horsley clearly recognized that the central issue of reform is not educational material; the essential factor is how leaders think and respond to the personal concerns of teachers, how they learn, and what has meaning for them. The foreword she wrote for this book reveals her belief that ultimately it is the individual science teacher who will make a difference in students' lives. Her life made a difference in the lives of others; now we have lost one of our best and brightest. We are left with her inspiration and dedication. Fulfilling her vision passes to all of us. As we look to the future without Susan Loucks-Horsley, we can be thankful for her professional achievements and contributions, and we must be grateful for her personal inspiration and grace.

Rodger Bybee

On the evening of August 8, 2000, Susan Loucks-Horsley died of injuries sustained in a fall.

Contents

Part I.
Professional Development: Implications for Science Leadership

Harold Pratt
The success of any standards-based reform program is dependent on the leader's knowledge of science content and skills in designing, facilitating, and managing an ongoing improvement process. This chapter outlines the characteristics of the best cases of science education reform and the skills and behaviors necessary to a leader's success and addresses the need for a leadership structure that includes teachers and all school personnel in what the NSES call a "distributed leadership."

JoAnne Vasquez and Michael B. Cowan
Professional development programs must provide teachers with the opportunity to become familiar with science content; to develop an understanding of inquiry, assessment, and standards-based lessons; and to design a variety of appropriate learning experiences in alignment with state, local, and national standards. This chapter presents characteristics such as questioning skills and membership in professional organizations that are common to master teachers and addresses the need to move teachers from the mechanical presentation of science units and kits toward the development of a deeper understanding of the content and concepts they are teaching.

Part II. Professional Development and the Diverse Learner

Foreword

Susan Loucks-Horsley

In the early 1980s, alarms were set off across the United States about the deplorable status of education, in general, and science education, in particular. In response, a flurry of activity led to many suggestions about what should be done. In the 1990s, various reform efforts at the local, state, and national levels blossomed, and change began gradually to occur. The *National Science Education Standards* and the *AAAS Benchmarks* emerged after long debates over what it is that students at various grade levels should know and be able to do in science. The notion that "less is more" gradually became a shared value.

Happily, few teachers today would advocate slavishly following a textbook as their science curriculum. Many teachers understand and value inquiry as an outcome for their students and a way of fostering important learning opportunities, and we are moving slowly in the direction of having a scientifically literate population. But, we must not become complacent. Although we have come a long way since the poor status of science education was presented to the American public in the 1980s, there is still a long way to go. Recognition of what our classrooms should look like and what our students should be able to do does not automatically translate into changes in the classroom or with our students. This is due, in part, to a lack of information. However, knowing what needs to be done does not mean knowing how to do it. This is where the critical role of professional development comes in, and it is essential that science leaders—at all levels—take on the challenges of being both the "leaders of learners" and the learners themselves. Unless teachers are being able to practice new ways of learning, teaching, and leading, this reform will fall far short of its potential.

Science teachers are the crucial link between the curriculum and students. Professional development is a concerted effort to help them understand and change their practices and beliefs as they improve the learning experiences they provide for students within their school and district. Professional development can also serve a broader purpose: to help teachers develop leadership and change agent skills. It prepares teachers to take a more informed and focused leadership role in fostering the implementation or improvement of the instructional program. Support for teachers is essential if teaching is to occur as espoused in the *Standards*, and if teachers are to expand their visions to influence others in their schools and districts. The nature of professional development programs in which teachers participate will, to a large extent, determine the changes in students' learning experiences.

As this book suggests, effective professional development programs and initiatives for science teachers have many characteristics in common. They help teachers see their students and classrooms differently as they learn to foster deep

i

understanding of important science concepts, the skills and understanding of scientific inquiry, and an appreciation of the natural world. Effective programs engage teachers in ways that they, in turn, will help their students learn; support collaboration among teachers as they learn and craft learning experiences for their students; and help teachers examine their own practice and become "critical friends" to other teachers. Such programs support teachers over time so that they not only can change their practices, but also can sustain and renew those practices continuously.

Science leaders can broaden their own professional development role by thinking of themselves as designers of learning experiences—much as teachers consider their instructional goals, their students' needs, and the resources and constraints of their school and district, science leaders can craft long-term, multifaceted programs for teachers that reflect current research and the "wisdom" of other professional developers. For example, breaking out of the "professional-development-equals-in-service-workshops-and-summer-institutes" box brings science leaders into contact with a wide array of strategies from which to choose. These include case discussions, action research, coaching and mentoring, and examining student work. They can use student curriculum as a tool for teacher learning, helping teachers go far beyond the "mechanical use" of new curriculum materials as they deepen their understanding of science content, of student thinking, and of teaching strategies. As science leaders broaden their vision for professional development strategies, their designs begin to incorporate and even influence some of the other important elements of systemic reform, such as curriculum, assessment, and the development of a professional community. Examples in this book "push the envelope" of old conceptions of professional learning in ways that can fuel deep and sustainable changes in classrooms, schools, and districts.

This book is written for science leaders at all levels: teachers, science supervisors, science consultants, science coordinators, science specialists, administrators, higher education science educators, and policymakers. The comprehensive presentation promotes understanding of the circumstances in which professional development most influences student learning. It reviews programs in place that work, and it provides a wealth of practical ideas about actions to take in the professional development arena in order to implement and sustain reform in science education.

This is indeed an exciting time to be in science education. As we work together to strengthen our understandings and roles as leaders in the science education community, we at the National Science Education Leadership Association (NSELA) and the National Science Teachers Association (NSTA) welcome you to use the resources in this volume to build programs that enhance and enrich science teaching and learning in our nation's schools.

About the Editors

Jack Rhoton is professor of Science Education at East Tennessee State University, Johnson City, Tennessee. Dr. Rhoton currently teaches science education at the undergraduate and graduate levels, and has also taught science at the elementary, middle, senior high school, and college levels. He has received numerous awards for service and science teaching, and has been an active researcher in K–12 science, especially the restructuring of science inservice education as it relates to improved teaching practices. Dr. Rhoton is the editor of the *Science Educator*, a publication of the National Science Education Leadership Association (NSELA), and director of the Tennessee Junior Academy of Science (TJAS). He also serves as editor of the TJAS *Handbook and Proceedings*. Dr. Rhoton's special research interest is in the area of professional development and its impact on science teaching and learning. He is widely published and has written and directed numerous science and technology grants. He has received many honors including the National Science Teachers Association (NSTA) Distinguished Service to Science Education Award.

Patricia Bowers is the associate director of the Center for Mathematics and Science Education at the University of North Carolina at Chapel Hill, where she teaches undergraduates and provides professional development training for math and science teachers. She also works closely with the UNC-CH Pre-College Program, which recruits underrepresented groups into math and science fields. She has been the project director for numerous grants, including 12 Eisenhower grants, and has received awards for service and science education. Dr. Bowers was a Science, Mathematics, and Reading Coordinator at the system level and worked as a classroom teacher and guidance counselor at the school level. Dr. Bowers is currently president of the North Carolina Science Teachers Association, and secretary of the North Carolina Science Leadership Association. She serves on several committees for the National Science Teachers Association (NSTA), and is a former district director and current board member of the NSELA.

Preface

Jack Rhoton and Patricia Bowers

Nearly every major document advocating science education reform in recent years has focused on science content and concepts to be taught, how science teachers should teach, and guidelines for professional development. The vision of science teaching and learning espoused by school reformers presents a key challenge for teachers' professional development. The vision of practice and standards-based reform advocated by the nation's reform agenda requires that most teachers make a paradigm shift in their beliefs, knowledge, and teaching practices. The success of this agenda will hinge, in large measure, on professional development opportunities that will engage teachers in learning the skills and perspectives called for in the new vision of practice. Because teachers are the crucial link between the curriculum and students, professional development is a major element in developing teacher leadership and change agent skills. It prepares teachers to take a more informed and concerted leadership role in fostering the implementation or improvement of the instructional program, driven by the desire to improve student learning.

Effective professional development also provides occasions for teachers to genuinely address change and renewal and reach beyond the "make and take" and "idea swap" sessions to more global, theoretical conversations that focus on teachers' understanding of content, pedagogy, and learner. For long-lasting and effective change within the science classroom, professional development activities must plow a deeper furrow of inquiry into practice than is normally available to teachers.

Professional development must allow teachers to rethink their notions about the nature of science, develop new views about how students learn, construct new classroom learning environments, and create new expectations about student outcomes. Teachers will need not only to explore new ideas in professional development programs, but also to develop and inculcate habits that will enable them to continue professional development over time.

Even though a common vision is beginning to emerge about what effective professional development should look like, a large number of teachers have not had an opportunity to participate in such professional development in their working environments. However, there is a growing momentum for schools to examine teachers' professional development in light of standards-based reform. This publication positively addresses issues and practical approaches needed to lay the foundation upon which professional development approaches can work to build effective science programs in our nation's schools. In addition, it examines the linkage between professional development and effective science education programs.

The *Issues in Science Education* series shares ideas, insights, and experiences of individuals ranging form teachers to science supervisors to university personnel to agencies representing science education. They discuss how professional development can contribute to the success of school science and how to develop a culture that allows and encourages science leaders continually to improve their science programs.

Using nontechnical language, this text is intended to be accessible to a broad audience. It is written for science teachers, science department chairs, principals, systemwide science leaders, superintendents, university personnel, policymakers and other individuals who have a stake in science education. It will also serve as a supplementary text for university methods course, in elementary and secondary science education.

The 13 chapters in this volume, *Professional Development Leadership and the Diverse Learner,* are organized into two sections. The intent of the book is not to provide an exhaustive coverage of each major theme but, rather, to present chapters that effectively address the issues of professional development. Each chapter in the text illustrates the utility of professional development for practitioners and addresses general issues and perspectives related to science education reform.

Part I of the book, "Professional Development: Implications for Science Leadership," consists of six chapters that deal with program developments within the context of issues that impact the day-to-day work of professional developers, instructional leaders, and science teachers. Part II, "Professional Development and the Diverse Learner," contains seven chapters that address the needs of a greater diversity of learning, including students from different cultural and ethnic backgrounds as well as those with exceptional needs.

Meaningful and sustained change in science teaching and learning is fraught with many challenges and pitfalls. These challenges and obstacles demand effective professional development. The task of developing and sustaining healthy professional development practices is simply too complex for any one person to tackle alone. Therefore, this work is directed at all players in the science education community who have a stake in improving science teaching and learning. Moreover, administrators must create an atmosphere that supports and encourages participation in effective professional development programs. One of the greatest challenges of leadership is to develop a culture that creates "laboratories" of ongoing improvements. The final determinant of success in this effort will be measured through the quality of science programs delivered to our students.

Numerous examples throughout the book illustrate the utility of professional development for practitioners and others interested in the improvement of science teaching and learning. Many of the topics in this book are placed within the context of real world experience and combinations of original research. Some of the concepts covered include: standards-based professional development; the nature of science, assessment and evaluation, leadership, and professional development; strategies for professional development; learning and teaching critical thinking skills; using ENC and ERIC as a resource for professional development; diversity issues in teaching science; and science education in formal and informal settings.

As we honor the memory and life of Susan Loucks-Horsley, we cannot escape the fact that her name is synonymous with professional development. Her many years of service and dedication to the science education community resulted in a body of writing of marked excellence, inspiring each of us to work harder, think deeper and take action on the subject to which she devoted her life—improving science education in our nation's schools. It was for this reason that Pat Bowers and I asked her to write the foreword to this book and to contribute two chapters to this document. We recognized that her works and writings have been influential forces in shaping the thoughts and actions on the direction of professional development in science education. And it will be so for years to come. There was also a human quality that permeated her work. Through my professional collaboration efforts with Susan, I recognized that she not only radiated an unparalleled warmth, glow, and passion for her work, but also was equally dedicated to uplifting each person with whom she came in contact. She was interested in people as individuals and recognized and appreciated the importance and role of each science teacher in his or her struggle and dedication to create effective learning environments for all students. She also worked hard to support teachers in their individual environments. Her memory is destined to linger in our thoughts as we work to fulfill her vision. The science education community will forever be the better for her influence, example, and inspiration.

Jack Rhoton

Acknowledgments

This book would not have been possible without the help, advice, and support of a number of people. More fundamentally, the members of the NSTA/NSELA Editorial Board—Gerry Madrazo, Lamoine Motz, Carolyn Randolph, Susan Sprague, Emma Walton—reviewed the manuscripts and made valuable suggestions for improvement. We could not have achieved our goal without their assistance, and we are grateful. Our appreciation is extended to Shirley Watt Ireton, Beth Daniels, and Anne Early of NSTA Press, for their invaluable help in the final design in which you are now reading. No volume is any better than the manuscripts that are contributed to it; we appreciate the time and efforts of those whose work lies within the cover of this book.

We also want to thank and acknowledge the support, help, and suggestions of the NSELA Board of Directors. Special thanks to Becky Litherland, past president, for her suggestions and guidance in the early stages of the project. The support of President Jerry Doyle and Executive Director Peggy Holliday in the later stages of the project is gratefully acknowledged.

Finally, we would like to credit people who simply made room in their lives for us to do this work. We are indebted to the calm, good-natured support of the East Tennessee State University Division of Science Education office staff: Leslye Culbert and Connie Frances. Each of these individuals did excellent work in word processing and typing the many drafts of each manuscript. And lastly, a special thanks to James Kevin, ETSU adjunct professor, and Chris Bordeaux, ETSU graduate student, for applying their expert editing skills to each manuscript.

Introduction

Jerry Doyle
NSELA President, 1999–2000

The numerous and vexing issues facing the science education leader today have created the need for leadership skills and knowledge that go far beyond those demanded in any previous era. The exceptional leader must be knowledgeable about science as a human endeavor; must be conversant with new developments in learning theory and how they impact classroom instruction; must have practical skills in chemical hygiene and lab safety needed to maintain a safe environment for students and teachers; must have the analytical skills needed to build a comprehensive assessment program and be able to move student achievement scores to higher levels; must be on the cutting edge of recent developments in technology that can be useful in science instruction; must have exceptional people skills and be able to work with a variety of interest groups who care about the science program; must know the structure of the school organization and be able to keep funds flowing toward the science department; must know where to find grant money and write "winning" grant proposals; must be able to create a vision and long-range plan for the science program; and must be able to coordinate a comprehensive staff development program to make that vision a reality.

The exceptional science education leader can master this overwhelming list of "musts" only if key resources are tapped. Pat Bowers and Jack Rhoton have compiled one of these key resources needed in the office of every science education leader. This volume includes an impressive array of pertinent articles from key leaders in the issue domains mentioned previously. It is my belief that this book will make you a more effective science education leader.

The Role of the Science Leader in Implementing Standards-Based Science Programs

Harold Pratt

Harold A. Pratt is the president of Educational Consultants, Inc. and the former executive director of science and technology for the Jefferson County (CO) public schools. He will be the 2001–02 president of the National Science Teachers Association.

If there is one common factor in the best cases, it is the presence of one or more individuals who provide strong leadership for the mathematics or science reform effort...
—Report to the Center for Science, Mathematics, and Engineering Education

Because the goal for science education in the 1990s has been and will continue into the 21st century to be—standards-based reform, the number one question in the science education community is: What is required to accomplish it? According to St. John, who addressed this question in an evaluation report (St. John & Pratt, 1997) to the Center for Science, Mathematics and Engineering Education, when the best cases of reform are examined, leadership emerges as the most important factor.

Although it is not the place of this chapter to provide a detailed description of what is meant by standards-based reform, it can be summarized briefly as the restructuring of the content students learn, the way it is taught and evaluated, and the way the program is supported through professional development—all of which are aligned with a well-developed set of local, state, or national standards. Such a system of reform has often been referred to as "systemic" because all parts of the system are coordinated so that they are all addressing the same major goals and program outcomes.

Although much has been written (Smith and O'Day, 1991; Zucker and Shields, 1995; Knapp, 1997; Consortium for Policy Research in Education, 1995) about the nature of systemic or standards-based reform and what such a comprehensive program would look like if it were in place, not enough has been said about how a district proceeds through the reform process. The literature often seems to imply that improved curriculum, teaching, and assessment just appears from thin air. What is needed is a deeper understanding of the role and function of leadership in the reform effort. The most significant, but often unmentioned, ingredient in the reform of science education at the state and local level is a leader with knowledge and experience who is well placed in the system so that he or she is capable of making the system function in the desirable way. Leaders have much to do: drafting science-education-related policy; coordinating districtwide programs; creating curriculum frameworks; facilitating the selection of instructional materials; and developing assessment policy, procedures, and instruments. Whatever is included in their portfolio, what they know and can do is critical to the success of the local program.

> *The most significant, but often unmentioned, ingredient in the reform of science education at the state and local level is a leader with knowledge and experience who is well placed in the system.*

The leader's knowledge of science is critical. The responsibilities listed in the last paragraph depend, to a large degree, on the nature of the discipline, how they are learned, and how they are best taught. When the major goal of the standards is understanding the subject matter content, the decisions about what science elementary teachers need to learn in their professional development experience, how subject matter is presented in textbooks at all levels, and the nature of the district's science assessment program are all examples of decisions that require knowledge of the content if to be quality decisions that keep the reform on track.

Knowledge of content by leaders is important and necessary, but not sufficient. Leaders should be skilled in designing, facilitating, and maintaining the changes called for in an ongoing improvement process. These include creating a vision of a quality program, designing professional development, managing change, facilitating individuals and groups, organizing groups and tasks, and building the capacity of the system to support the change.

Although most of the literature of reform and systemic change focuses on policy, programs, and practices that the leaders should be responsible for producing, this chapter will emphasize what is known about how leaders bring about these improvements and what the research says about the skills, behaviors, and leadership styles of effective leaders. Finally, this chapter will highlight the concept of distributed leadership as presented in the *National Science Education Standards*.

Importance of Leadership in Standards-Based Reform

The Center for Science, Mathematics, and Engineering Education, the group at the National Research Council (NRC) responsible for developing and supporting the use of the *National Science Education Standards* (National Research Council, 1996), commissioned a study of the best cases of science education reform in an effort to understand the process of reform. The report (St. John & Pratt, 1997) from Inverness

Associates pointed to leadership as a key factor in producing the best cases of reform.

The study found that in the best cases, standards—either local, state, or national—were considered to be policy documents that were not "implemented" but, rather, they became tools for promoting deeper and more reflective approaches to selecting instructional materials, creating assessments, and designing professional development. Policy does not automatically give rise to desired practice. But in the best-case districts, the leaders found ways of using the standards to develop the capacity across all levels of the system to develop and sustain the vision of the standards in improved programs and practices.

The best-case districts have long-term, committed leadership.

In the best-case states and districts, one or more longer-term leaders played a very central role in the reform effort. These individuals typically were energetic and highly committed, with a history of involvement in science reform efforts, who possess multiple skills and knowledge. In addition, they were formally or informally placed in positions of influence where they were charged to bring about change. Although they may not have had true position power due to their place in the district or state formal hierarchy, they had the backing of their superior administrators and/or the influential power based upon their previous experience and successes.

Effective leaders are connected to many sources of support.

The leaders in the best case situations build and draw upon their connections at the local, state, and national level. They typically have been involved with the creation of state and national standards and have years of experience in the National Science Foundation or other externally funded innovative science projects. They were knowledgeable in the important ideas in the research and innovative programs before the standards themselves were written. To these leaders, the standards had more of a reinforcing and clarifying effect on the direction they had already established. They also were well-versed in the process of educational change and how to effect it in their own districts or state.

Effective leaders focus primarily on educational substance.

Another key factor that the study identified was that the best leaders focus primarily on educational substance while functioning well within the political realities of their system. Several writers have noted that standards at all levels are political, as well as educational, documents (Kirst, Anhalt, & Marine, 1997). To the educator, standards identify a vision of quality, teaching, learning, and system support. To those who are politically-oriented, standards represent a means of control over schools. For the political group, standards coupled with large-scale assessments represent tools that communicate expectations, with little attention to the means by which the expectations can be attained. The astute leaders fill this void in the political perspective by

defining and gaining support for the curriculum programs and professional development that provide teachers and students with the opportunity of fulfilling the political expectations. The leaders do this, fully aware that they must mix and blend both
dimensions if they are to be successful and satisfy the politi-
cal expectations placed on them and the rest of the system.

Change requires increased professional development and support and, therefore, budget.

In the best cases, leaders use standards as vision to guide their reform efforts.

The leaders who developed the best cases for standards-based reform used the *Standards* as an overarching strategy for improvement rather than a litany of mandates to be implemented. It is their view—one they are able to communicate to teachers and administrators in their system—that stan-
dards provide a rich vision and resource for the kind of teaching and learning de-
sired. In these cases, the leaders use standards and other policy documents to inform
their local efforts and decisions about their efforts to bring about change. They find
ways of using the assessment teaching, professional development, program, and system standards from the *National Science Education Standards* to fill the void between the mandated content standards and assessment expectations mentioned above.

In the best cases, state and district leaders work not just to build consensus for
specific programs, such as a new set of instructional materials or the availability of
learning technologies, but to build consensus and support for an infrastructure (money,
time, resources, expertise) necessary for the long-term success of their reform effort.
They know that the introduction of standards and other expectations without the
necessary support is an indication that the reform process is more political than educational and more short-term and project-oriented than a long-term sustained effort.
Change requires increased professional development and support and, therefore,
budget.

What Research Says About Effective Leaders

Although leadership is often considered to be more of an art than a science, it is
important to examine the research base for information on the styles of leadership
that leaders must bring to the job. A committee at the NRC recently reviewed the
research about effective leaders in a report entitled *Enhancing Organizational Performance* (Druckman, Singer, & Van Cott, 1997). The research revealed that there
are three, well-known basic skills relevant to effective leaders and one new skill
required in a rapidly changing technological environment.

Technical skills are defined as knowledge of product and services, work operations,
procedures, and equipment. In science education, this would include an understanding of
instructional materials, the ability to facilitate meetings, knowledge of instructional technology, and the ability to interpret educational reports for the public and other administrators.

Conceptual skills include the ability to analyze complex events and perceive trends, recognize changes, and identify problems and opportunities. They also include the ability to develop creative, practical solutions to problems and the ability to conceptualize complex ideas through models and analogies. For the science education leader, this means understanding the role of standards and other policy documents and having the ability to use them as a practical guide to local program development. The leader who understands these documents as being both politically and educationally motivated is operating at the conceptual level. The science educator who can analyze instructional materials not simply by using an evaluation checklist but based upon a deep understanding of the science being presented and how students learn the science at various ages is making maximum use of his or her conceptual skills. The leader who simply follows the lead of other educators in the choice of materials, organization of professional development, and design of curriculum is operating more at the technical or operational level than at the conceptual level. The leader who can synthesize the research on student learning, professional development (adult learning), and the local political climate into a coherent total program that will be accepted by the community and staff must have deep conceptual skills to do so.

Interpersonal skills include understanding of interpersonal and group processes and the ability to understand the motives, feelings, and attitudes of people from what they say and do. Interpersonal skills also include the ability to maintain cooperative relationships with people, oral communication, and persuasive abilities. The effective leader who understands the deep conceptual ideas of science education and has the technical skills to make them work still must involve a wide range of individuals from many diverse roles to implement well-conceived ideas. Skills of tact, diplomacy, and conflict resolution will be constantly demanded of the effective leader in the process of soliciting ideas and suggestions during the formulation of a plan or program and persuading others to approve and implement it.

The leaders who developed the best cases for standards-based reform used the Standards *as an overarching strategy for improvement rather than a litany of mandates to be implemented.*

Self-learning skills are emerging as a new requirement for the 21st century leader. The rapidly changing educational technologies and their implications for student learning and the design of programs requires science education leaders to make decisions with little or no precedent. Faced with the rapid change in many school systems due to shifting political climate, changing student populations, or the introduction of cutting-edge technology, science education leaders must cope with increasing complexity and change with little previous experience or knowledgeable advisors. To cope with such complexity, leaders need the ability to analyze their own learning process and adjust their actions and decisions both to improve their own knowledge and skills and to make decisions that they have never made before. Recent research (Druckman & Bjork, 1994) has identified this self-learning skill as the ability to develop new mental models, learn from mistakes, and change assumptions and ways of thinking within and in response to a changing world.

Behavior of Effective Leaders

Researchers have long sought to discover why some leaders are more effective than others. In addition to the skills outlined above, leadership behavior—those observable actions such as making assignments or facilitating a discussion—are known to be critical to their success and effectiveness. The research synthesized by the National Research Council (Druckman, Singer, & Van Cott, 1997) suggested that there are eight types of behaviors specially relevant to effective leadership.

Clarifying roles and objectives. Subordinates and clients, such as teachers and principals, need to know what work they are to do and the results that are expected. The skill to clarify roles and objectives includes defining job responsibilities, assigning tasks, setting performance goals, and providing support and instructions on how to do the task. As an example, curriculum writing teams who meet without clear instructions, goals, deadlines, and criteria for judging their own work will digress into nonproductive discussions, false starts, and work that is unrelated to the task.

Supportive leadership. A leader who is supportive uses a variety of behaviors to show acceptance and concern for subordinates' needs and feelings. Research from several decades of study has demonstrated that supportive leadership increases the satisfaction and productivity of the people involved. There is some indication that less supportive leadership is necessary when satisfaction with the job and commitment to the task are already high, but even then supportive behavior is effective.

Planning and problem solving. Effective leaders create flexible and practical strategies to meet their objectives. But the planning must be accompanied by the ability to remain flexible, in the event that unforeseen problems disrupt the well-laid plan. Plans are rarely executed fully in the form in which they are originally conceived. The need for problem solving and flexibility in a complex, changing, and political environment should be the norm for effective leaders.

Monitoring operations and environment. Effective leaders use feedback to monitor progress on how well their plans are progressing. The leader who develops and communicates an idea without following and monitoring its implementation will find that good ideas do not implement themselves—people do. Leaders stay in touch with the people and learn from their response to do instructional materials, educational technologies, and innovative teaching strategies. Adjustments are made, plans are altered, support systems improved, and expectations modified—all in an effort to meet the changing environment in which the plan is being implemented.

Participative leadership. The research indicates that decision making improves when other members of the group have information and ideas that the leader does not have and they are willing to cooperate in finding ways to achieve their shared goals. Classroom teachers have knowledge and expertise that central office leaders do not have.

The converse is also true. Curriculum leaders usually possess skills and resources not available to teachers. Only when these different perspectives and kinds of expertise are brought together by a leader who believes in mutual support and participation can effective curriculum teaching and professional development be planned and implemented.

Inspirational leadership. Studies on inspirational leadership indicate it is one of the strongest predictors of a group's commitment and performance. It is especially important in today's complex and changing environment, where major shifts in thinking and strategies on the part of the group are often required. Inspirational leaders stimulate followers to think about problems in new ways and, simultaneously, help them question old assumptions and beliefs that may be no longer valid. Inspirational leadership is more a result of the relationship between the leader and other members of the group and is not simply an innate and intrinsic quality of the leader.

> *Inspirational leaders stimulate followers to think about problems in new ways and, simultaneously, help them question old assumptions and beliefs that may be no longer valid.*

Positive reward behavior. Positive rewards consist of tangible components, such as pay increases, prizes, and recognition or praise for achievement and contributions to the group's goals. Praise is more likely to be effective when it is clearly based on observable contributions and not used by the leaders indiscriminately to control or manipulate.

Networking. Similar to the findings of St. John and the author (St. John & Pratt, 1997) described earlier, research from studies of effective leaders indicates that they develop and maintain networks of people from who they can draw resources, information, and support. In large, complex organizations, internal networks are as important as external networks.

Distributed Leadership in the *National Science Education Standards*

The *National Science Education Standards* recognized the importance of leadership in several standards and suggested a type of leadership referred to as distributed leadership (Bybee, 1993). Program Standard A stated: "Responsibility needs to be clearly defined for determining, supporting, maintaining, and upgrading all elements of the science program." Although all school personnel have responsibilities, clearly defined, leadership at the school and district levels is required for an effective science program (NRC, 1996, p. 211). The *Standards* point out the importance of leadership and distributes the responsibility among a variety of people, including teachers, administrators, and science coordinators.

Teaching Standards F mirrors the expectation that teachers assume a leadership role in the improvement of science programs:

> *Teachers of science actively participate in the ongoing planning and development of the school science program. In doing this, teachers:*

- *Plan and develop the school science program.*

- *Participate in decisions concerning the allocating of time and other resources to the science program.*

- *Participate fully in planning and implementing professional growth and development strategies for themselves and their colleagues* (NRC, 1996, p. 51).

By defining leadership as an individual's ability to work with others to improve science teaching and learning to accomplish the goal of scientific literacy for all students, virtually everyone in the science education community is included. This concept is incorporated in Program Standard F:

- *Schools must work as communities that encourage, support, and sustain teachers as they implement an effective science program.*

- *Schools must explicitly support reform efforts in an atmosphere of openness and trust that encourages collegiality.*

- *Regular time needs to be provided and teachers encouraged to discuss, reflect, and conduct research around science education reform.*

- *Teachers must be supported in creating and being members of networks of reform.*

- *An effective leadership structure that includes teachers must be in place* (NRC, 1996, p. 222).

The messages of the NSES are clear: a) leadership structure and assignment of responsibility are needed for effective programs; and b) teachers are an important part of the leadership structure, so time and support must be provided to make it possible. The location in the system and the role of the individual can vary and be distributed among a variety of people, but we are reminded of what the research outlined earlier in the chapter tells us about the characteristic skills and behaviors of leaders in science education reform.

References

Anderson, R. and H. Pratt. 1995. *Local leadership for science education reform*. Dubuque, IA: Kendall/ Hunt Publishing Co.

Burrill, G. and D. Kennedy. 1997. *Improving student learning in mathematics and science*. Washington, DC: National Academy Press.

Bybee, R. 1993. *Reforming science education: Social perceptions and personal reflections*. New York: Teachers College Press.

Consortium for Policy Research in Education. 1995. *Reforming science, mathematics, and technology education: NSF's statewide systemic initiatives.* (Policy brief). New Brunswick, NJ: Consortium for Policy Research in Education.

Druckman, D. and R. A. Bjork, eds. 1994. *In the mind's eye: Enhancing human performance*. Committee on Techniques for Enhancing Human Performance, National Research Council. Washington, DC: National Academy Press.

Druckman, D., J. E. Singer, and H. Van Cott, eds. 1997. *Enhancing organizational performance*. Committee for the Enhancement of Human Performance, National Research Council. Washington, DC: National Academy Press.

Kirst, M. W., B. Anhalt, and R. Marine. 1997. Politics of science education standards. *Elementary School Journal* 97(4):315–328.

Knapp, M. S. 1997. Between systemic reforms and the mathematics and science classroom: The dynamics of innovation, implementation, and professional learning. *Review of Educational Research* 67:227–266.

National Research Council. 1996. *The national science education standards*. Washington, DC: National Academy Press.

O'Day, J. 1995. Systemic reform in California. In *Studies of education reform: Vol. 2. Systemic reform, case studies*, ed. M. E. Goertz, R.E. Floden, & J. O'Day, 1–38. Newark: Rutgers University, Center for Policy Research in Education.

Pratt, H. 1984. Science leadership at the local level: The bottom line. In *NSTA yearbook: Redesigning science and technology leadership*. Washington, DC: National Science Teachers Association.

School Science and Mathematics. 1997. The factors that contribute to the "Best Cases" of standards-based reform. *School Science and Mathematics* 97(6):316–324.

Smith, M., and J. O'Day. 1991. Systemic school reform. In *The politics of curriculum and testing*, ed. S. Fuhrman & B. Melen, 223–267. New York: Taylor & Francis.

St. John, M., and H. Pratt. 1997. The factors that contribute to the "best cases" of standards-based reform. *School Science and Mathematics* 97(6):316–24.

Zucker, A. A., and P. M. Shields. 1995. *Evaluation of the National Science Foundation's Statewide Systemic Initiatives (SSI) Program.* Second-Year Case Studies: Connecticut, Delaware, and Montana.

Moving Teachers From Mechanical to Mastery: The Next Level of Science Implementation

JoAnne Vasquez and Michael B. Cowan

JoAnne Vasquez is a resource specialist with the Science and Social Sciences Resource Center for the Mesa Unified School District #4, in Mesa, Arizona. Author of numerous journal articles, she has also received recognition for national-level leadership in science education. JoAnne is past president of the National Science Teachers Association and president-elect of the International Council of Associations of Science Education.

Michael B. Cowan is director of science, social sciences, health, and world languages at the Science and Social Sciences Resource Center for the Mesa Unified School District#4, in Mesa, Arizona. He recently served as president of the Association of Science Materials Centers for two consecutive terms.

A grade-level team of teachers is assembled for the inservice training on the new science unit that they are planning to implement this year. As they prepare their notebooks to take the typical procedural notes and the facilitator readies the last of her materials, a ho-hum attitude permeates the room.

"We've been doing hands-on science for years now. Why are we being *required* to come to this inservice before we can teach this new unit," one of the veterans murmurs as she adjusts the stack of papers she is grading.

Another joins in with her teammate: "We should be able to figure it out on our own. I can see training the new teachers, but not us; we know what we're doing."

The workshop facilitator begins the workshop with the usual warm-up activity and then turns around and unexpectedly "dumps" the contents of the science kit onto the table. Styrofoam trays, bottles of shampoo, plastic straws, and dozens of other items empty out of the box. Projecting the learning outcomes from the overhead projector and dividing the participants into groups, the facilitator explains that, using the materials laid before them, they are to design activities that will help their students meet the displayed outcomes. In addition, they must be able to explain what type of assessments they will use to demonstrate that the students have met each of the objectives. After the initial shock and bewilderment, the participants dig into their assignment.

Many districts that have enjoyed a long history of using hands-on, kit-based programs have fallen into the trap whereby the vast majority of teachers have mistakenly come to think of the materials in the science kit as the curriculum. Many go through the mechanics of teaching the required science to their students by proceed-ing through lock-step lessons provided in the teacher's edi-tion, without so much as a thought as to what they are teach-ing, let alone how to integrate the experiences to support other areas of their curriculum. Districts across the nation use a variety of educational terms to describe the nuts and bolts of learning expectations for students. For the sake of clarification, we consider the specific grade and/or course-level goals and objectives as the curriculum to which we refer. The "stuff" provided in the science kits we refer to as instructional materials.

Many districts that have enjoyed a long history of using hands-on, kit-based programs have fallen into the trap whereby teachers have mistakenly come to think of the materials in the science kit as the curriculum.

The misconception that teachers mistakenly accept the cur-riculum for what is included in the science kits they use and disregard specific learning objectives significantly limits the educational value of a science program. Weiss (A. Weiss, per-sonal communication, February 8, 1998) contends that: "If stu-dents aren't going to learn anything with the materials in the kit, then they might as well have fun doing it." Often, teachers and the systems that support them fall into this simplistic prac-tice. Usually, the content of curriculum is painstakingly determined by small groups of administrators, teachers, and community members. The majority of teachers, however, continue their labors, day after day, mechanically guiding students with an almost activ-ity-by-activity monotony through the science kits provided, without addressing the ratio-nale and purpose for such instruction. Students can be observed enjoying the instruc-tional experiences and many times they come away with increased abilities, skills, and enhanced attitudes toward science. Unfortunately, many times they do not reach the in-structional goals intended.

Remarkable as it may seem, most teachers at a technical level of science-kit us-age, going through the motions, do a fairly adequate job of teaching science. After all, students are encouraged to explore new phenomena through established events and activities. It is, indeed, a far cry from the didactic, text-driven approach to in-struction or the shame of no science instruction at all. The challenge for district program supervisors of hands-on, science-kit programs is to recognize when to raise the bar and motivate teachers to transition from a mechanical usage of materials to a mastery level of science instruction.

For many leaders of science education, the understanding and enlightenment of how teachers approach curriculum and the instructional materials provided them comes when they have a one-on-one conversation with teachers who are at the me-chanical level. These teachers are able to explain the rationale for teaching science, list the units they are teaching, and perhaps even state how the objectives for their grade level connect to the kits. It becomes obvious, however, that they lack one important key understanding: Why they are teaching the lessons and providing the experiences that they do.

There is a marked difference between the technical instruction of science and engaging students in the process of scientific discourse. "The research concerning how little is learned when there is no [meaningful] engagement is robust," said Wheeler (1998). "The argument for engagement is best expressed by that common old chant of the 1960s: 'I see…I forget, I hear…I remember, I do…I understand.' I think there is a danger in this view of science inquiry." Wheeler warned that:

> *Unless we know more about the "doing"—what is being done, and how it is being done—this view of scientific inquiry, commonly heard as a call for more "hands-on" activities in students' school science, falls short of reform goals because not all hands-on activities are inquiry-based with the learning outcomes clearly in mind by the teacher* (1998).

All over the United States there are districts, states, and major systemic initiatives working to implement hands-on, inquiry-based science. This, along with the release of the *National Science Education Standards* (National Research Council, 1996), has caused a flurry of reform activity. Those old enough to remember past surges of science education reform recognize how the "alphabet soup" programs, providing recipe-like science curriculum and materials, made a splash in the late 1960s. We can look back and reconstruct what happened to these implemented programs. They were intended to mainly reach the "pipeline" students or those students who had been identified by teachers and counselors as having advanced science-related abilities. These programs guided this select body of students toward becoming scientists and engineers. Despite this focus on the few, all students indirectly benefited from these programs. Unfortunately, the reform efforts were not sustained and programs were not supported sufficiently. Following on the heels of the science reform movement of the 1960s was the "back to the basics" drive for more math, reading, and rote memorization. The curriculum and materials developed to change science education quickly were abandoned and began collecting dust on classroom shelves.

There is a marked difference between the technical instruction of science and engaging students in the process of scientific discourse.

Eventually, many of these materials found their way to the dumpster. Why? Science educators had failed to institutionalize the reform. Teachers all over the country just went through the mechanics of teaching science. They were never introduced or reinforced to understand *why* they taught what they did. If a difference is to be made in the science literacy of the country this time around, the educational system must find ways to facilitate teachers' growth.

The new task of leaders in science education should be taking teachers from the technical presentation of the activities in the science units and kits to developing a deeper understanding of the content and concepts they are teaching. Teachers also need support in designing appropriate learning experiences to help their students achieve appropriate outcomes. These outcomes must be aligned with the *National Science Education Standards* (National Research Council, 1996) as well as state and local standards.

Designers of effective professional development experiences pay close attention to the expressed interests and needs of the participating teachers.

The mastery level of science teaching will come only when the individual teacher recognizes she can reach standards through a variety of instructional avenues. There is no single way to facilitate the students to develop an understanding of, for example, "position and motion of objects (NRC, 1996, p. 123)." There are many ways to design activities throughout the primary grades to achieve this standard, and a teacher in California might do it differently than a teacher in Oklahoma. The important vision here is in understanding what the students are to learn and how to measure whether that learning has taken place.

Educators are often challenged with presenting science experiences to students beyond the mere familiarization of science to effectively knowing the concepts and content of science. This notion applies to teachers' learning of science, as well. Being able to see and orchestrate the big picture of the student's journey to an understanding of the processes and concepts and the connectors between these is the benchmark, which indicates the difference between mechanical and mastery teaching.

The call for inquiry-oriented teachers is not new. Dewey (1933) wrote of the need for teachers to take "reflective action." Zeichner (1983) cited more than 30 years of advocacy for "teachers as action researchers" and "teacher scholars, teacher innovators, self-monitoring teachers, and teachers as participant observers." Like other waves in teaching reform, nothing seems to change but the need to reform. Providing opportunities for teachers to move from just "doing the activities" is the next challenge to science educators and the next task for science reformers to address.

Many educators follow a typical evolution as they first begin to explore, understand, and finally embrace the value of effective science instruction in their classrooms. Normally, this transformation occurs in one of two ways: The first is when teachers become hooked by the whiz-bang discrepant event activities they have seen presented at conferences or in an inservice presented by a "cheerleader for science." Teachers caught in the false comfort that these experiences will result in meaningful science learnings for their children may enthusiastically go back to their classroom and replicate what they have experienced and actually do it quite well. No thought truly goes into why a specific event is being done or where it ties into their learning objectives or even the standards. The second type of science education induction occurs when the teachers are required to move to teaching science using more of a hands-on approach. These teachers will go through the required inservices and will, over time, become quite skilled at what they are doing with their science units. They will even design ways of connecting science into their other curricular areas. Missing from this scenario is what teachers don't have—a feel for inquiry, assessment, and standards-based lessons. These are the structures of knowledge that master teachers possess that can be developed only over time, with careful thought and purposefully designed professional development experiences. These structures must be nurtured, client-driven, and concerns-based. Designers of effective professional development experiences pay close attention to the expressed interests and needs of the participating teachers. Teachers' concerns vary within any given group and will likely change over time (Loucks-Horsley & Stiegelbauer, 1991).

This ability to assess the level of concern of a group came to light quite recently when the authors provided an inservice experience to a group of teachers who were new to a grade level. These teachers were not new to teaching. The experience started off with a two-hour session on developing strategies for using open inquiry. Even though most of these teachers were at the mastery level when it came to facilitating student learning, they approached the inservice at an informational level for this session. The need to know the nuts and bolts of the new science unit being introduced was not addressed appropriately. They had to go through this stage before they were open to considering more of an open inquiry approach to the unit.

Identifying Teachers at the Mastery Level

Here is an example: Imagine two teams of first grade teachers at different elementary schools in the Mesa Unified School District #4, Mesa, Arizona. These teams were both getting ready to implement the Science and Technology for Children (STC) *Solids and Liquids* kit into their required science curriculum for the year. Each team of teachers was required to go through a nuts-and-bolts training session before beginning to teach this kit. It must be noted that Mesa Public Schools has been requiring teachers to teach four science curriculum units per year for the past 15 years. Several teachers in both of these first grade teams had been in the district for at least that long. Each team had one brand-new teacher on the team. In the bigger sense of the word, each team had three experienced veterans and one novice.

A blaring red flag was raised to district-level science leaders when reflecting upon these two experiences in a resource teacher team study session. The difference in needs between the mechanical level teachers and the mastery level teachers was very apparent. Both teams were delighted with the new kit, expressing enthusiasm for the variety of new manipulatives. One team immediately recognized that what they had been doing with properties in math connected right into the development of science concepts about the properties of solids and liquids. This same team saw the avenue for vocabulary development and the opportunity for the first graders to begin to apply their new written communication skills through the use of science logs. But, more importantly, they recognized and verbalized the big unifying concepts and processes of observation, organization, discrimination, sorting, comparing and contrasting, and communication as connectors to developing their students' thinking skills. The other teacher team was able to focus only on the management issues associated with the new curriculum. They could not escape the mechanics of how to implement the new unit.

Most of the people who champion inquiry have a difficult time coming to a common definition for the term.

Bybee (1997) stated "the *National Science Education Standards* are about 'outputs' not 'inputs'." Outputs refer to the identification of the student outcomes and the measurement strategies used to assess whether students have attained them. Inputs refer to the length of school day, teaching days, time devoted to science instruction, and so forth. It is the outputs that master teachers hold as the compass to chart their science instruction.

There is a great deal of rhetoric regarding inquiry-based science. Teachers are being bombarded with the charge to go forth and make certain they are teaching in an inquiry way. Leaders in science education have become a community obsessed with the term. Most of the people who champion inquiry have a difficult time coming to a common definition for the term. Ask 10 "experts" and 10 different responses will be given.

What, then, does the abstractness of the term *inquiry* have upon the teachers in the classroom? The message of one camp in the inquiry debate finds some science educators encouraging teachers to let the students pose their own questions, develop their own investigations, and communicate their results as the mainstay of the experiences in the classroom. "It's easy, it's fun, and you can do it," one can hear them say. This is a message, however, that spells disaster for most novice and mechanical-level teachers, because this type of pure inquiry takes time, skill, limitless resources, and knowledge on the part of the teacher. If the teachers fail at this approach, chances are they will fall back to reading about science and not try any type of investigations. A mastery-level teacher will develop over time the necessary skills to be able to adjust some of the lessons to be an open inquiry approach; other lessons will still be constructed to guide the students to the desired learning outcome. "Master teachers," stated Layman and colleagues, "balance student-directed inquiry with other classroom activities—class discussion, reading, solving problems, elementary activities to introduce skills, i.e., films, tapes and transparencies (Layman, Ochoa, & Heikkinen 1996, p. 34)."

Comparing Mechanical-Level and Mastery-Level Teachers

Teachers enter the teaching profession because they have a desire to communicate knowledge. Teachers in an inquiry-based lesson act as facilitators and resources. They create the environment, which is safe for the investigations to take place; they impart conceptual knowledge, mathematical and technical tools, and general guidelines at optimal moments. These teachers select the learning experiences and adapt and design their lessons to meet the interests, knowledge, abilities, and backgrounds of their students.

"I think I recognized I might be on the track to being a master teacher when I became comfortable with the fact that I didn't have to know it all, but I could figure ways to get the information to help me grow," said Master Teacher Anna Henning. "When maintaining mastery, teachers are constantly upgrading their repertoire of how children learn as new knowledge is published by experts in the field of cognitive sciences (A. Henning, personal communication, September 4, 1998)." Master teachers seek opportunities to fine-tune advanced skills, such as questioning formulation, student facilitation, and reflective improvement strategies. The mechanical teacher is preoccupied with the technical aspects of instructional delivery. That is not to say that they are not concerned about the learning experiences of their students; however, they focus on providing quality learning experiences and do not facilitate students as investigators.

Teachers in an inquiry-based lesson act as facilitators and resources.

Moving Teachers From Mechanical and Mastery Levels of Teaching

How do science education leaders help mechanical teachers become skilled and comfortable with the inclusion of an inquiry-based approach to teaching science? How do science educators and professional developers facilitate an environment where mastery level can occur? Here is the secret: *Time!* Time to grow, time for reflection, time for self-examination, time for peer study groups, time for mentoring by a mastery-level teacher, and time for self-selected professional development experiences devoted to developing a deeper understanding of the content knowledge of the curriculum to be taught.

Time to Grow

Time is a priceless commodity in schools. Teachers are finding themselves pulled in so many ways as they deal with the complexity of the diverse needs of students, burgeoning curriculum requirements, and an ever-shrinking school day. A teacher may teach a unit once a year for only two to three years before being moved to another grade level and must learn a different curriculum. This will completely throw a mechanical-level teacher off base, but mastery-level teachers see the whole picture, and because they have developed a deeper understanding of the content and concepts, their need for technical specifics does not interrupt their vision of good science in their classrooms.

Many practitioners have recognized that most teachers travel through a series of levels of concern with regard to developing new skills and abilities in the classroom. As teachers travel down the path from mechanical to mastery levels of science teaching, they experience some common experiences. The Concerns-Based Adoption Model (1987) was a significant research study on the impact of change on educators. Table 1 outlines the Concerns-Based Adoption Model's levels of concern and possible comments science education leaders may hear as they facilitate teacher growth and promote mastery teaching abilities.

Table 1: Concerns-Based Adoption Model: Levels of Concern

Science Teaching Development	
Awareness	"What is hands-on science?"
Informational	"What types of classroom experiences are you talking about?"
Personal	"What does hands-on science mean to me?" "What will I have to do to be able to teach this way?" "Will my administrator allow me to teach this way?"
Management	"Where do I find the time to fit hands-on science into my school day?" "How do I manage the kids during activities?"
Consequence	"What am I doing to ensure that my students understand the unifying concepts of science?" "How do I facilitate greater student inquiry into my instruction in science?"
Collaboration	"I have a lot of ideas on how to increase the implementation of inquiry into my science instruction." "I can gain a great deal by interacting with others engaged in including inquiry-based science instruction."
Refocusing	"I can access the learning objectives expected to be covered and access the science kit I get and significantly orchestrate new learning opportunities for my students."

Modified from: Hord, S.A., Rutherford, W., Huling-Austin, L., and G. E. Hall. 1987. *Taking charge of change.* Alexandria, VA: Association for Supervision and Curriculum Development.

Teachers who are empowered to design their own professional development and are provided the professional time to implement their desires will benefit significantly from the experiences.

Real mastery levels of teaching science occur as teachers transition from concerns about management to identifying the consequences to students of instruction, curriculum, and the materials used to achieve instructional goals. At collaboration levels, master teachers further enhance their skills by gleaning best practices of others, as well as focusing on what is important as they communicate their own best practices. Finally, at the refocusing level of concern, master teachers move beyond the expected curriculum, see connections to other curriculum areas, and begin to explore new, cutting-edge strategies for instructional delivery.

Time for Reflection

One of the most powerful attributes of human beings is the ability to reflect upon what they have done. Reflective abilities are difficult to cultivate in teachers but can provide powerful benefits. This is not a simple "Gee, how did the day go?" type of experience. Reflection involves deep perception and self-analysis. It incorporates assessing delivery, ability, knowledge, and performance. As teachers become competent and capable of formally reflecting on their impact on student learning and devise strategies for self-improvement, teacher mastery skills blossom and flourish.

There are different strategies to promote reflective practices. A simple beginning is the use of a reflection log. Teachers take time to spend quiet moments reflecting and writing about experiences for the day, including evaluative comments and insights. By keeping a thoughtful reflection log, teachers are empowering themselves to recognize where they are struggling, their successes, and the concepts they need to focus on to enhance understanding, as well as what they might do differently next time around. Having an experienced or master teacher be a mentor for these reflections will give meaning to the process. "Feedback and self-reflection is the breakfast of champions" is the theme of Blanched and Johnson's (1982) popular management book, *The One Minute Manager*. Yet few teachers ever take the time to reflect on their own practice, let alone receive feedback on their reflections from trusted peers.

Time for Self-Examination

It is important to provide the avenues to empower the teachers to self-assess their needs and design their own courses of strategies for developing a deeper understanding. In the minds of many educators, training is synonymous with staff development. Most teachers are accustomed to attending workshop-type sessions in which the presenter is the expert who establishes the content and flow of activities (Sparks & Loucks-Horsley, 1990). Shifting the attitude of professional development to attain mastery levels of teaching involves a transfer from training and "executive control" to self-control. The outcome here is the stimulation of the teachers' deeper conceptual understanding. Teachers who are empowered to design their own professional development and are provided the professional time to implement and pursue their desires will benefit significantly from the experiences. Placing teachers in the role of self-assessors of their professional needs and providing them the resources and time to pursue them provides greater opportunities for teachers to experiment with mastery skills of instruction.

Time for Peer Study Groups and Mentoring by Mastery-Level Teachers

Study groups pertain to "engaging in regular, structured, and collaborative interactions regarding topics identified by the group, with opportunities to examine new information, reflect on their practice, or assess and analyze outcome data" (Loucks-Horsley, Hewson, Love, & Stiles, 1998). To improve student achievement in science, as well as other content areas, schools must weave continuous learning for teachers into the fabric of the job of teacher. Study groups are an excellent means of cultivating collegial schools. Collegial schools that support teachers in study groups are characterized by purposeful, adult-level interactions focused on the teaching and learning of students.

Teaching is a relatively solitary profession. The instructional facilities that house millions of American schoolchildren are not conducive to collaboration. There are few opportunities for educators to gather and meaningfully discuss issues, instructional strategies, and the challenges of teaching. Providing structured blocks of time for team or peer discussion groups can provide a conduit for teachers to learn from each other. As easy as this seems, unfortunately, it is an often-neglected approach in teacher development.

Professional Development Time Devoted to Developing a Science Content Knowledge

One of the challenges of moving from technical to mastery levels of teaching is providing teachers with the opportunity to become familiar with science content so they can facilitate the questions and investigations of the students. Designing learning experiences where teachers are invited to learn from content experts and master teachers can provide the structure to enhance teacher science content knowledge. Most teachers have had at least one or two science content classes in college or in postgraduate work. The element that has been missing in these experiences is the opportunity for teachers to recognize the relevance of the content to what they are teaching. By providing opportunities where the teachers interact with both the content expert and master teacher, they can receive direct examples of how the content they are learning connects with the experiences of the students in their classes. These sessions introduce teachers to the ways activities are designed in the unit to teach the concept, which is relevant to a particular grade level. They also can show the curriculum flow of concepts and content across grade levels. This helps teachers have a deeper understanding of concept development throughout the grades.

> *There are few opportunities for educators to gather and meaningfully discuss issues, instructional strategies, and the challenges of teaching.*

Another key experience that promotes mastery skills of teachers is their belonging to and participating in professional organizations. By reading the latest research in professional journals, they have a wide variety of current information to share with their peers during study group time. They are also challenged to conduct classroom-based action research and look for opportunities to share this as well.

Commonalties Among Master Teachers

Mastery-level teachers seem to exhibit many of the same characteristics:

◆ Science means success—Master teachers have an intuitive feeling for science as an area where all students—regardless of language skills, ethnicity, socioeconomic background, or physical and mental challenges—are able to find success.
◆ Understanding of science content and processes—A deeper understanding of both the content and process of science are common to most master teachers. As new knowledge is gained, they are energized to reorganize and adjust their own thinking.
◆ Mentoring—Being mentored by science education professionals and acting as mentors themselves is common to many mastery science educators. Being a men-

tor to someone else forces one to look at one's own practice as growth is encouraged in others.

- ◆ Collaborative climate—Master teachers take advantage of the professional stimulation provided by a teaching partner or peer team within the school setting who is willing and able to take the time—even if it means four o'clock on a Friday afternoon—for an impromptu discussion as well as organized study group. Being able to talk with one's peers with a feeling of trust is essential to personal growth.
- ◆ Questioning skills—Master teachers, as an art form, use developed questioning skills. They are able to determine by watching and listening to their students' interactions what questions will encourage them to reach for the next level of understanding.
- ◆ Management of events—The ability to know where to include a discrepant-event-type activity that will further ignite the students to move in another direction in their thinking is common to master teachers. They understand "cute" activities must have an instructional purpose and should connect to instructional goals.
- ◆ Accessing research—Master teachers recognize the need for continuous learning through not only reading the latest research by experts, but by conducting their own classroom-based action research as well. Master teachers use these formats of continuous improvement as embedded learning opportunities to improve their instructional and curriculum implementation practices.

If the efforts for improved science education are to be institutionalized through the common national, state, and local efforts at reform, significant efforts must be made. Science education leaders must move teachers beyond the how-to, information-downloading models of instruction to the discovery of new avenues that support the real transformation of the teacher to master facilitator of science learning. This transition becomes apparent upon reflecting on the comments of master teachers who have made the transition from technical to masterful implementation of science curriculum.

"When you move your instruction from being a front seat driver to the backseat, the students will move along the path with you if you facilitate them in the right directions," commented Master Teacher Rosie Magarelli (R. Magarelli, personal communication, August 10, 1998). "You want them to embrace science—not consume it. Get them engaged and go forward, always assessing where kids are and building experiences for them." Magarelli's advice to teachers enhancing their skills and moving toward mastery practices included "focusing on management and questioning. Keep one eye looking forward on the instructional goal in mind and the other in the rear view mirror to assess where you have been."

The path the teacher travels to the mastery level is not an easy one. Like learning to drive a car, at first the new driver focuses on controlling the vehicle, evaluating road conditions, and estimating distances between objects. After a few months of practice, the driver is able to incorporate those skills simultaneously and begin to feel very comfortable with the role of driver. At this point, attention shifts away from the mechanics of driving to identifying and maneuvering your car to get to a specific destination. Mastery-level teachers never lose sight of that destination and recognize there are many routes that they can offer their students toward reaching the ultimate learning objectives.

References

Blanchard, K. and S. Johnson. 1982. *One minute manager.* NY: Morrow.

Bybee, R. 1997. *Reforming science education through the national standards.* Paper presented at the annual national convention of the National Science Teachers Association, New Orleans, LA.

Dewey, J. 1933. *How we think.* Lexington, MA: D.C. Heath.

Driscoll, M., and D. Bryant. 1998. *Learning about assessment, learning through assessment.* Washington. DC: National Academy Press.

Hord, S. A., W. Rutherford, L. Huling-Austin, and G. E. Hall. 1987. *Taking charge of change.* Alexandria, VA: Association for Supervision and Curriculum Development.

Loucks-Horsley, S., P. W. Hewson, N. Love, and K. E. Stiles. 1998. *Designing professional development for teachers of science and mathematics.* Thousand Oaks, CA: Corwin Press, Inc.

Loucks-Horsley, S., and S. Stiegelbauer. 1991. Using knowledge of change to guide staff development. In *Staff development for education in the 90's: New demands, new realities, new perspectives*, ed. A. Lieberman & L. Miller. New York: Teachers College Press.

Layman, J. W., Ochoa, G., and H. Heikkinen. 1996. *Inquiry and learning: Realizing science standards in the classroom.* New York: The College Board.

National Research Council. 1996. *National science education standards.* Washington, DC: National Academy Press.

Sparks, D., and S. Loucks-Horsley. 1990. *Five models of staff development.* Oxford, OH: National Staff Development Council.

Wheeler, G. 1998. *The three faces of inquiry.* Manuscript submitted for publication.

Zeichner, D. L. 1983. *Research on teacher thinking and different views of reflective practice in teaching and teacher education.* Bristol, PA: Falmer Press.

Learning and Teaching Critical Thinking Skills in the Information Age: A Challenge in Professional Development for Science Teachers

J. Preston Prather and Maurice Houston Field
The University of Tennessee at Martin
Center of Excellence in Science and Mathematics Education

J. Preston Prather is a professor of science education and director of the Center of Excellence in Science and Mathematics Education (CESME) at The University of Tennessee at Martin. He is author of numerous journal articles and chapters on topics related to science and mathematics education and has directed several science education grants. Honors include the AETS Outstanding Science Teacher Educator Award, the SAETS John W. Shrum Award for Excellence in the Education of Teachers in Science, the NSTA History of Science Education Award, and Editor Emeritus of the *Journal of Elementary Science Education*.

Maurice Houston Field is a professor of science education and director of the Center for Environmental and Conservation Education at The University of Tennessee at Martin. He is the editor of the *Science Activities Manual: K–8*, an Internet compilation of science lessons, and is the curator of Waterfowl of Chenoa which has on exhibit, as well as in an Internet presentation, pairs of all of the world's species of true geese and shelducks. Honors include a Distinguished Service plaque ('98) presented by the Tennessee Science Teachers Association, Environmental Educator of the Year selection ('93) by the Tennessee Environmental Education Association, and recognition on the cover of *Education* (Summer, 1988) for "Leadership in Science Education."

One of the earliest and most time-honored forms of education is based on development and employment of skills in critical thinking and problem solving. That pedagogical model is commonly called the "Socratic method," in honor of the early Greek philosopher, Socrates, who developed it more than 2,400 years ago. Knowledge is valued in the model, but mastery of factual information alone is not perceived as either a desirable end in itself or the mark of an educated person. Rather, an educated person is one who can examine and understand the ethical, social, personal, and cultural implications of whatever topic might arise. From this perspective, individuals who take pride in the possession of much knowledge but lack the critical thinking skills needed for such understanding would, in fact, be considered quite naive. Having such persons in positions of leadership would be socially undesirable, because unreasoned applications of knowledge could be a detriment to society. The basic purpose of learning, for a Socratic methodologist, is to develop the type of thinking skills required to understand the inherent relationships of ideas and things. Understanding of those relationships is valued for insight into the meaning and worth of knowledge, in the same sense that today's proponents of interdisciplinary curriculum and instruction value an understanding of the inherent connections among academic disciplines and their relationships to learners. The ancient philosophers had a special name for this: They called it "wisdom."

The basic purpose of learning is to develop the type of thinking skills required to understand the inherent relationships of ideas and things.

In the early Greek era as now, however, the great majority of people lacked the time, resources, and/or motivation to pursue sufficient formal education for systematic development of critical thinking skills. Consequently, even though the ideals of critical thinking have persisted for more than two millennia, the focus on knowledge for knowledge's sake has generally prevailed. By the 14th century, education was typically perceived in terms of encyclopedic knowledge, and literature of the era alluded to scholarly types who aspired to learn all there was to know. This did little to foster explorations of multiple perspectives or alternative paths of inquiry, and the concern for acquisition of knowledge eclipsed critical thinking in the human intellectual process.

The advent of the industrial/factory model of education, which has been attributed to the cultural impact of the Industrial Revolution, intensified the problem. By the late 19th century, rapid industrial development had ushered in an era of unprecedented technological productivity. Society valued a strong industrial enterprise as a source of national prosperity and promoted public education as a means to assure a continuing supply of competent employees for the factories. Many educators perceived the industrial tenets of centralization, specialization, and technological efficiency as the best system for school development (Tyack, 1974). Over time, that perception of how and why children should be schooled became a predominant factor in the design of formal education in the United States (DeYoung and Lawrence, 1995).

Lacking the insights of recent research on the psychology of learning, early proponents of the industrial/factory model of education perceived the purpose of schooling in terms of developing efficient means for feeding information into learners and testing to be sure it was remembered. A student was an object of learning. It was widely believed that industrious teaching produced learned and employable students from unschooled children, in much the same way that skillful applications of manufacturing techniques produced useful and marketable objects from raw material. Typically, curriculum planners focused on the amount of material to be covered and teachers graded student performance on the basis of the amount of knowledge acquired.

Rapid increases in development of new scientific and technological knowledge intensified the problem. Science textbooks grew thicker and thicker in the absence of a tradition for critical assessment of information to be included in the curriculum, and the addition of large amounts of disconnected factual information diminished the relevance of the content. This trend resulted in a curriculum that the American Association for the Advancement of Science (AAAS, 1990) decried as "a mile wide and an inch deep."

Questions of what to teach and how to teach are widely discussed topics in professional journals, newspapers, and the halls of government as society seeks ways to improve the quality of science education. The ancient Greek concern about the consequences of unreasoned applications of knowledge is implicit in many current discussions, especially in the area of environmental protection. Knowledge of the inner workings of the atom, for instance, provides a means for generating electricity without many of the undesirable side effects of other methods. However, many people are concerned that applications of that knowledge may produce environmentally intolerable consequences of another nature. Resolution of such issues in a democratic society will require a population with the critical thinking skills needed to identify and understand reasonable options and mandate equitable public policies.

The need for general scientific literacy, however, is accompanied by an equally essential educational imperative to continue to produce an adequate supply of professional scientists and mathematicians needed to maintain continuing scientific and technological development. Therefore, a successful science education program must be directed to two equally essential purposes. First, it must help all students develop lifelong study habits and thinking skills needed to acquire useful scientific knowledge and evaluate its efficacy for problem solving. Second, it must simultaneously encourage those who may find the disciplines of science and mathematics, per se, attractive as career choices and help them prepare to generate new scientific and mathematical knowledge. Promotion of critical thinking skills is conducive to both purposes.

A successful science education program must help all students develop lifelong study habits and thinking skills needed to acquire useful scientific knowledge and evaluate its efficacy for problem solving.

The Concept of Critical Thinking

Skills needed for critical thinking are foundation competencies, Sormunen and Chalupa (1994) declared, but there is no clear definition of critical thinking. However, they concluded, a useful definition appears to be slowly emerging. Earlier models emphasized either a philosophical, process-oriented approach or a psychological, product-oriented approach, they noted, but a hybrid model has emerged that integrates both approaches and imposes a hierarchy of learning. In the hybrid, which they called the educational model of critical thinking, students progress to higher levels of thinking as they translate academic learning into the real world of day-to-day living. In a study of what is needed in the schools, the United States Department of Labor (1991) defined critical thinking skills in similarly practical terms of creative thinking, problem solving, knowing how to learn, reasoning, and decision making.

Dialectical questioning is a typical entry point for criticism for Socratic thinkers. However, McPeck (1981) contended, much more than questioning is involved:

> Critical thinking does not consist merely in raising questions... Nor does it involve indiscriminate scepticism [sic], for that would ultimately be self-defeating, for it leads to an infinite regress. Rather, it is the appropriate use of reflective scepticism [sic] within the program area under consideration. And knowing how and when to apply this reflective scepticism [sic] requires, among other things, knowing something about the field in question. . . . There is, moreover, no reason to believe that a person who thinks critically in one area will be able to do so in another (p. 7).

Critical thinking is not a natural skill, but it can be taught. Children possess a natural curiosity, Meyers (1988) noted, but most require disciplined instruction for development of anything more than haphazard thinking skills. Critical thinking is not rational thinking alone, though that's a part of it, nor is it scientific thinking alone, though there are many overlapping characteristics. It is similarly distinguishable from "'imaginative thinking,' 'sensitive thinking,' 'creative thinking,' and the like (McPeck, 1981, p. 5)." It is complex, multifaceted, and cannot be taught as a separate subject or skill. "'Critical thinking' has an identifiable meaning," McPeck suggested, "but the criteria for its correct application vary from field to field (p. 13)." It is dependent upon the context of thought about something, and it must be learned and taught accordingly.

Critical thinking is not pervasive, and it is not to be applied to all statements. Rather, it is a highly personalized process that involves personal attitudes, commitments, and interests in whatever is being studied. According to McPeck, it is also critically dependent on knowledge of a field and of the connections of that knowledge with other fields. However, Resnik (1987) contended, critical thinking does not necessarily require years of prior drilling on the basics of a subject.

Teachers may use a variety of approaches to encourage students to learn to think critically, but there is no single best way to teach critical thinking skills. The advent of computer-based information technology, however, contributes an important new perspective to the task. Properly used, Pepi and Scheurman (1996) suggested, computers can help to create a meaningful learning environment that will challenge students to move beyond the immediate effects of concrete experiences as they collect information and identify phenomena that can be generalized to other experiences, reflect on those connections, and develop conclusions. Many computer-based programs are available for providing multiple stimuli for students to think about, thereby fostering decision making skills and encouraging independent thought of the type needed for critical thinking (Solomon, 1992; Pepi and Scheurman, 1996).

The Challenge for Science Teachers

Redirection of education to include critical thinking offers opportunities for relating lesson content to meaningful, real-life situations that can help students appreciate the worth of what they learn. It can also create an exciting and fulfilling teaching arena that is conducive to development of lifelong learning skills. In the current era of overstuffed curricula, however, this will not be a simple task. Teaching of thinking skills has always posed a problem, Meyers (1988) noted, "but it is especially acute today, when our culture's output of information far exceeds our ability to think critically about that information (p. xi)." Teaching critical thinking takes time, and science teachers will have to practice the sort of skills they would teach in order to provide that time. Among other things, they must learn to use their own critical analysis to winnow superfluous curriculum content and nonessential instructional activities in order to focus on essential concepts and learning experiences their students need for in-depth understanding and appreciation of science, mathematics, and other subjects. In addition, they must *model* critical thinking in their own teaching, as well as encourage it among students:

> *Students must actively struggle with real problems and issues—and see their instructors doing the same. If the instructor… merely rehearses students in the rediscovery of what is already known, students will acquire little motivation for critical analysis* (Meyers, 1988, p. 8).

The learning environment must encourage open discussion and probing questions as it challenges learners to progress through increasingly complex thought processes in search of useful new information. It must challenge learners to temporarily suspend their own judgments as they criticize options and reflect on new ways of thinking, and it must help them learn to appreciate the important role that their own personal values and interests play in their perceptions.

Given the pressures of the information explosion and the personal nature of thinking skills development, it may appear that teachers face a dilemma. Group instruction, on the one hand, is an efficient means for presenting large amounts of information to classes of students. Individual teacher-student interactions, on the other hand, are more effective for personalized instruction of the type needed for development of critical thinking skills. Fortunately, as Pepi and Scheurman (1996) noted, the integration of computer-based information technology into classroom teaching can help to bridge the gap.

This presents science teachers with a multifold challenge. First, teachers need to develop and model critical thinking skills in their own teaching, beginning with critical assessment of curriculum and instruction as indicated earlier. Second, teachers need to relate lesson content and activities to current topics or issues of interest to their students to provide them a context and incentive for using scientific understanding for dealing with personal and societal concerns. Third, teachers need to be

Most teacher education programs emphasized neither critical thinking skills nor classroom computer applications until recently.

proficient in the use of computer technology and related Information Age resources for both group and personalized instruction. Because most teacher education programs emphasized neither critical thinking skills nor classroom computer applications until recently, many inservice teachers today face an immediate challenge for professional development.

A Perspective on the Challenge of Professional Development

The National Research Council (NRC, 1996) devoted a significant portion of the *National Science Education Standards* to the topic of professional development. Though not addressed specifically, the three challenges for professional development listed above are inherent in the *Standards'* emphasis on "learning science, learning to teach science, and learning to learn (p. 58)." Professional Development Standard A declared that professional development for science teachers "requires learning essential science content through the perspectives and methods of inquiry (p. 59)." Standard B emphasized that professional development "requires integrating knowledge of science learning, pedagogy, and students; it also requires applying that knowledge to science teaching (p. 62)." Standard C avowed that professional development "requires building understanding and ability for lifelong learning (p. 68)."

The *Standards* specifically assumed that "science learning experiences for teachers must... address issues, events, problems, or topics significant in science and of interest to participants (p. 59)" and permit them to "struggle with real situations and expand their knowledge and skills in appropriate contexts (p. 62)." The *Standards* also specified that professional development activities should "create opportunities for teachers to confront new ideas and different ways of thinking... [and] to discuss, examine, critique, explore, argue, and struggle with new ideas (p. 67)." Based on the assumption that teachers tend to teach in the way they were taught, this should help to prepare teachers to relate their own instruction to topics of interest to their own students and, thereby, provide the contextual arena that McPeck (1981) declared essential to teaching critical thinking skills. Clearly, the *Standards* assumed that professional development is a lifelong responsibility for teachers, and it must include a balance of effective content mastery, instructional competency, and critical thinking skills.

The *Standards* also emphasized that professional development must be based on a coherent, long-term plan. Professional development is a complicated matter, the NRC (1996) noted: "However, for an individual teacher, prospective or practicing, professional development too often is a random combination of courses, conferences, research experiences, workshops, networking opportunities, internships, and mentoring relationships (p. 70–71)." Implicit in that observation is a fundamental assumption:

Systematic professional development is a personal responsibility. This places responsibility for effective professional development squarely on individual teachers to identify professional development activities that will meet their specific needs. Proficiency in the use of computer technology, for instance, is an increasingly important teacher qualification. Teachers seeking computer education will find many outstanding programs available, and professional development in this area would appear to be largely a task of locating and selecting an adequate program from a myriad of options. Much more than formal instruction is required, however, including personal persistence in learning-by-doing that may be compared to learning to walk. Others may demonstrate walking, explain what's involved, encourage action, and even hold a child's hand; but a child can learn to walk only by releasing all props and trying it alone—and getting up and trying it again after every fall until she/he becomes proficient at the task. In a similar comparison, maintaining currency in the ever-changing field of computers will require new learning over time, much as a child may learn to run, climb, ride a bicycle, or otherwise fulfill a desire for increased mobility. Consequently, effective professional development in computer education is largely a matter of personal responsibility and persistence.

Ability to teach critical thinking skills is an equally important qualification for science teachers, and professional development in this area is a matter of even greater individual initiative. Teaching of critical thinking has generally not been a priority in the educational arena and, as McPeck (1981) noted, most programs for teaching critical thinking have focused on only a limited perspective of the concept. Some focused on logical analysis and some on other forms of problem solving, he observed, "but perhaps the most pervasive notion...amounts to an unquestioned faith in the efficacy of science and its methods to settle every significant controversy requiring critical thought" (pp. 39–40). Scientific thought involves many dimensions of critical thinking, but it is not inclusive. Critical thinking may be exercised within other areas, as well. However, as John Dewey (1991) noted, scientific reasoning is a conjoint process of analytic and synthetic thinking. This is fortunate for science teachers, whose science preparation constitutes a foundation for learning and teaching critical thinking skills.

Ability to teach critical thinking skills is an equally important qualification for science teachers, and professional development in this area is a matter of even greater individual initiative.

Like computer skills, critical thinking may be learned, in part, from formal instruction, but proficiency is largely dependent on experience through repeated applications. Fortunately for those seeking competency in both computers and critical thinking, the NRC's (1996) assumption that professional development should address problems of significant interest to participating teachers points toward an interesting possibility of using one objective to accomplish the other.

Like computer skills, critical thinking may be learned, in part, from formal instruction, but proficiency is largely dependent on experience through repeated applications.

Using Computer Technology to Learn and Teach Critical Thinking

Preparation for proficient use of computers in science teaching requires practice with a variety of data processing programs, including spreadsheets. By learning to use spreadsheets for study of current issues of interest to themselves, teachers will attain two important benefits. First, they will avoid the tedium of constructing spreadsheets around meaningless textbook examples and simultaneously learn about things of personal interest as they learn to use the technology. Second, it will sensitize them to the affective importance of relating their own teaching to topics of interest to their students.

Use of spreadsheets provides opportunities for the type of critical thinking and reflection needed for in-depth understanding of essential concepts and processes. Spreadsheets also present opportunities for devising activities that integrate mathematics into science instruction in an obvious and meaningful way. A number of spreadsheets that support this premise are available through the Internet. Specific examples, developed for Mac and Windows platforms by Kellogg (1992–95) using Microsoft Excel, include:

1. *Coins*—employs a spreadsheet to find the values of combinations of coins.
2. *Perim/Area*—a spreadsheet program that deals with optimizing area and perimeter.
3. *Circuits*—uses simple circuits to teach Ohm's Law.
4. *Gas Laws*—uses graphics dynamically linked to a spreadsheet relating the variables in the Ideal Gas Law.

Presnall (1997), a high school science teacher, used ClarisWorks to develop the following programs, which are also available on the Internet for Mac and Windows platforms:

1. *Molecular Weight*—allows students to enter the symbols and quantity of elements in a compound and uses a cascading series of logic statements to recognize atomic symbols and report atomic weights.
2. *Trajectory*—enables students to calculate the angle and the distance to a target, based on X and Y coordinates.
3. *Vector Adder*—allows learners to enter the magnitude and direction of up to 10 forces. It then calculates the X and Y components of those vectors, finds the sum of the components, and calculates the resultant of all the vectors.

A Web page on *Spreadsheets, Mathematics, Science, and Statistics Education* (Neuwirth, 1998) presented much useful information for teachers interested in exploring instructional applications of spreadsheets. Topics included (a) recommended books and journals, (b) papers about spreadsheets, (c) example spreadsheets and projects, (d) general resources for spreadsheets on the Web, and (e) Web documents explaining spreadsheet concepts.

The use of spreadsheets can enhance science instruction by helping students learn to focus on the information needed to arrive at a conclusion in an efficient manner. It is also conducive to development of higher-order thinking skills. The efficiency of the process also allows more time for critical thinking and reflection, which will, in turn, contribute to increased depth of teaching and learning.

Practice in preparation of spreadsheets also contributes to the type of professional development for science teachers advocated in the *National Science Education Standards* (NRC, 1996). It requires knowledge and understanding of the science concept to be treated as indicated in Standard A, and permits teachers to struggle with real-life problems in meaningful contexts as indicated in Standard B. It is also compatible with Standard C, which calls for "opportunities to learn and use the skills of research to generate new knowledge about science and the teaching and learning of science (p. 68)." Learning to develop and use computer-based spreadsheets in classroom instruction will enhance the quality of science teaching by enabling teachers to simultaneously introduce scientific concepts and engage students in systematic explorations using research methodology and critical thinking skills. In particular, spreadsheets can make statistical treatment of information a desirable and efficient alternative to the descriptive statistics that might normally be generated. Specifically, the process allows for a more sophisticated, mathematically based conclusion to a hypothesis involving science or science teaching.

Assessment of Critical Thinking Skills Development

Use of spreadsheets is an effective means to promote learning of critical thinking skills, but how to evaluate student performance may be a perplexing problem for many teachers. Nickerson (1984) proposed a solution: Teach writing, too. Writing is a useful vehicle for teaching thinking, he noted, but "another major advantage of writing…is that it yields a tangible product that can be evaluated (p. 33)."

At some point, a critical thinker must synthesize analyzed material and speculate about conclusions. Subsequent reflection on the efficacy of speculations, once articulated, is an excellent way for learners to develop and appreciate their own critical thinking skills. Writing is a time-honored and effective method for making thought visible, Meyers (1988) noted, and it enables a unique form of feedback that is equally useful to the teacher and the student:

Though it is a time-consuming process, sitting down with students to go over papers allows teachers to help the students see more explicitly their own thought processes and thus become more aware of their progress in developing new modes of critical thinking (p. 86).

This approach to evaluation, coupled with the interactive teaching environments discussed earlier, embodies the best principles of close interaction of teacher and student throughout the learning process. It also requires and reinforces independent thinking and decision making and enables teachers to provide formative feedback as students struggle to progress to increasingly higher levels of thinking. Printed reports submitted to the teacher in the traditional manner or through computer communications via e-mail or attachments are equally effective. The important consideration is that the process will require students to articulate their thoughts—and put them out for critical review, first by themselves and then by an instructor. Once they have visualized their thoughts through writing, most learners feel a sense of vulnerability as their work is exposed for all the world to see.

That sense of vulnerability, combined with the sense of ownership that learners typically attach to work that is the product of their own intellectual processes, can be a powerful motivation for developing critical thinking skills. In Piagetian terms, this gives students a real, self-perceived need to know as much as they can about effective thinking. Constructive feedback, provided in a manner that will enable students to reenter the critical thinking process without fear of failure or penalty for prior efforts, can build upon that need to know and help students hone their thinking skills in a manner appropriate to their personal learning style. Requiring written reports for assessment of student progress is, therefore, a potent stimulus for learning that, if nurtured through positive formative assessment by a supportive teacher, can make appreciative scholars and creative thinkers of even the more reticent students. Consequently, integration of writing into science teaching provides a strong motivation for development of clear and effective thought, and it is an effective component of career preparation for entry into the current Information Age employment arena.

Teachers involved in self-directed development of critical thinking skills can also use writing as a vehicle for assessing their own performance. Although the process will not provide the type of feedback they would provide their students, writing will help teachers focus and review their thoughts. It will also enable teachers to lay their work aside for later review from a more detached perspective of a reader. As professional educators, most teachers can learn much through self-assessments of this nature.

Conclusion and Suggestions for Self-initiated Development

As implied in the *National Science Education Standards* (NRC, 1996), systematic professional development is largely a personal responsibility. It is an implicit theme of this chapter that, in the end, effective professional development in computer education and critical thinking is largely a matter of individual initiative and persistence. Much introductory information can be learned from courses and workshops, but mastery of either field is critically dependent upon persistent practice and extensions of what is learned through largely self-directed explorations. This is especially the case with the development of critical thinking skills.

The following publications are recommended as introductory readings for teachers interested in learning and teaching critical thinking skills. After reading and reflecting on the issues and options discussed in these publications, the reader should have a sufficient understanding of the history and scope of the topic to (a) review and evaluate ideas in current publications and (b) select effective professional development activities as needed.

Dewey's (1991) analysis of how people think presented a compelling case for teaching critical thinking. The cultivation of deep-seated and effective habits of discriminating thinking is the business of education, he declared unequivocally, and "since these habits are not a gift of nature (no matter how strong the aptitude for acquiring them …the main office of education is to supply conditions that make for their cultivation (p. 28)." In as much as educators fail in that responsibility, he implied, education fails to emancipate humanity from "the limiting influence of sense, appetite, and tradition (p. 156)."

McPeck's (1981) book on the relationship of critical thinking and education, like Deweys', promotes the development of thinking skills as a fundamental purpose of education. However, McPeck emphasized an essential relationship of content knowledge to effective critical thinking and contended that "there is no…reason to believe that a person who thinks critically in one area will be able to do so in another (p. 7)." He also emphasized the fact that those who would teach critical thinking skills must first be proficient in those skills. Those teachers, in turn, are an essential source of leadership. There are many unresolved and untested dimensions surrounding the relationship of critical thinking and education, he concluded, and "whatever the final verdict about these issues, I would be greatly surprised if it involved teachers who were nor themselves critical thinkers (p. 162)."

Nickerson (1984) summarized the kinds of thinking taught in most programs: "The enhancement of thinking ability is…a major objective of the educational process," he declared, but "unfortunately, many students graduate from high school without acquiring the ability to deal effectively with intellectually demanding problems (p. 28)." His comprehensive breakdown of thinking skills programs according to categories is especially informative for teachers seeking a concise overview of the scope of the topic.

Sormunen and Chalupa (1994) discussed research in critical thinking skills, with emphasis on developing evaluation techniques. Critical thinking is a teachable skill, they concluded, and students who undergo instruction on thinking critically generally do better on assessments than those who do not receive instruction. Their review and criticism of current testing practices and tests is especially informative.

Requiring written reports for assessment of student progress is a potent stimulus for learning that, if nurtured through positive formative assessment by a supportive teacher, can make appreciative scholars and creative thinkers of even the more reticent students.

Ruchlis (1990), a former science teacher, presented a challenging introduction to and explication of the basic principles of critical analysis, using a large number of real-life examples. This book is a stimulating introduction to the problems facing teachers who would teach critical thinking skills amidst the flood of information that characterizes the Information Age. Teachers like to learn from other teachers who have "been there," and for that reason this book is recommended as a source of inspiration and encouragement to teachers who may feel overwhelmed by the challenge of teaching critical thinking. There are many problems, he emphasized over and over again, but teachers have a good foundation to build upon. Clearly, he concluded, there is reason for optimism:

> *The many sources of error in reasoning described in this book may leave some people feeling much too skeptical about the body of knowledge we possess. They may wonder how much of it is really true. Such an attitude is not realistic, because we would never accomplish anything if every fact and conclusion had to be checked and verified before decisions were made. Fortunately, most of the thinking we do in solving everyday problems is very effective and needs no basic overhaul* (Ruchlis, 1990, p. 232).

References

American Association for the Advancement of Science (AAAS). 1990. *Science for all Americans: Project 2061*. New York: Oxford University Press.

Dewey, J. 1991. *How we think*. New York: Prometheus Books.

DeYoung, A. J., and B. K. Lawrence. 1995. On hoosiers, yankees, and mountaineers. *Phi Delta Kappan* 77:105–112.

Kellogg, D. 1992–95. *Spreadsheets*. Available: http://cesme.utm.edu/resources/other/SS/Spreadsheets.html.

McPeck, J. E. 1981. Critical thinking and education. New York: St Martin's Press.

Meyers, C. 1988. *Teaching students to think critically*. San Francisco: Jossey-Bass.

National Research Council. 1996. *National science education standards*. Washington, DC: National Academy Press.

Neuwirth, E. 1998. *Spreadsheets, mathematics, science, and statistics education*. Available: http://sunsite.univie.ac.at/Spreadsite/spreaded.html

Nickerson, R. 1984. Kinds of thinking taught in current programs. *Educational Leadership* 41(1):66–76.

Pepi, D., and G. Scheurman. 1996. The emperor's new clothes: A critical look at our appetite for computer technology. *Journal of Teacher Education* 47:229–236.

Presnall, G. 1997. *The Greg Presnall collection*. Available: http://cesme.utm.edu/resources/other/presnall/presnall.html

Resnick, L. 1987. *Education and learning to think*. Washington, DC: National Academy Press.

Ruchlis, H. 1990. *Clear thinking: A practical introduction*. Amherst, New York: Prometheus Books.

Solomon, G. 1992. The computer as electronic doorway: Technology and the promise of empowerment. *Phi Delta Kappan* 74:327–329.

Sormunen, C., and M. Chalupa. 1994. Critical thinking skills research: Developing evaluation techniques. *Journal of Education for Business* 69:172–177.

Tyack, D. 1974. *The one best system.* Cambridge, MA: Harvard University Press.

United States Department of Labor. 1991. *What work requires of schools: A scans report for America 2000.* Washington, DC: US Department of Labor.

Bringing About School Change: Professional Development for Teacher Leaders

Josephine D. Wallace and Catherine R. Nesbit
University of North Carolina at Charlotte
Carol R. Newman
Charlotte Mecklenburg Schools

Josephine D. Wallace is an associate professor and director of the Mathematics and Science Education Center, College of Education, at the University of North Carolina at Charlotte. Her research interests are focused in two areas: cognitive science involving the examination of students' conceptions and structures of knowledge in science through the use of concept maps, and teacher leadership development in the area of science. Dr. Wallace has been awarded a number of national and state-funded grant projects to support the professional development of teachers in science.

Catherine R. Nesbit is a science educator and associate professor in the Department of Reading and Elementary Education, College of Education, at the University of North Carolina at Charlotte. She has worked extensively with research in professional development for teacher leaders in science.

Carol R. Newman is the director of the Grants Development Office of the Charlotte-Mecklenburg School System in Charlotte, North Carolina. She has extensive involvement with teacher professional development. Her expertise includes the areas of team building, working with adult learners, developing teacher leadership skills, and other areas of professional development.

As public education in America crosses into the next century, four national reports—*Everybody Counts* (National Research Council [NRC], 1989), *Professional Standards for Teaching Mathematics* (National Council of Teachers of Mathematics, 1991), *Science for All Americans* (American Association for the Advancement of Science, 1989), and *National Science Education Standards* (NRC, 1996)—call for dramatic reform in science and mathematics education. When implemented, these reforms will change *what* and *how* students learn, as well as the role teachers play in the school reform movement. This paradigm shift in teachers' roles is echoed in national education reform reports (Carnegie Commission on Teaching, 1986; Holmes Group, 1986). Pellicer & Anderson (1995) stated that if reforms are to take place in the entire school, teachers must assume a variety of leadership responsibilities. Leadership responsibilities may include teachers working with their colleagues in improving instruction in each classroom in the school. Instead of being receivers of change, these teacher leaders will themselves become key decision makers, empowered to be the creators and genuine owners of the reform, and will encourage their fellow teachers to do the same.

To prepare teacher leaders to take on these new roles, professional development programs must provide interactive learning environments where teachers deepen their understanding of science and mathematics content and pedagogy and sharpen their leadership skills so that they can develop and implement unique plans for reform that suit the climate of their schools. Research on adult development and the stages of teacher growth indicate that passive, one-size-fits-all approaches to professional development will not produce the needed changes in our schools. If the end result is to help teachers become change agents for schoolwide reform in science and mathematics education, we have to start designing professional development programs for teacher leaders differently.

Research on adult development and the stages of teacher growth indicate that passive, one-size-fits-all approaches to professional development will not produce the needed changes in our schools.

Current research (Carey, Frechtling, & Westat, 1997) reports the need for effective teacher leader professional development programs that result in dissemination at the school level. In order to achieve schoolwide results, Darling-Hammond & McLaughlin (1995) called for a new kind of professional development that includes problem solving, brainstorming innovative ideas, and generating school plans collaboratively. Other factors to be included are knowledge about leadership styles and skills for team building, resolving conflicts, decision making, building visions, and problem solving (Loucks-Horsley, Hewson, Love, & Stiles, 1998) and the opportunity to practice these same leadership skills (Pellicer & Anderson, 1990). O'Connor and Boles (1992) reported that teacher leaders need to have a good understanding of school politics and the change process, as well as the following skills: communication with adult learners, group dynamics, and how to conduct and organize workshops. Hatfield, Blackman, Claypool, & Master (1987) identified teacher leaders' need for the following attributes: flexibility, patience, and the ability to command respect. In addition, they noted the importance of knowing how to work with others and how to communicate well. Research reported by Zinn (1997) identified four key factors within the educational arena that support new teacher leadership: (a) a climate that is supportive of teachers as key decision makers (Bennis, 1989; Garmston, 1988; Leithwood, 1992; Pellicer & Anderson, 1995); (b) principals or other administrators who are supportive (Barth, 1988; Conley, Schmidle, & Shedd, 1988; Hanson, Thompson, & Zinn, 1993; Lieberman, 1988; Pellicer & Anderson, 1995); (c) teachers supporting each other (Bolman & Deal, 1994; Bredeson, 1995; Wasley, 1991); and (d) a supportive relationship with colleagues, such as central office personnel (Lieberman, 1995; Darling-Hammond, 1995).

Informed by teacher leader research, North Carolina implemented an initiative for teacher leader professional development. Programs were used that included critical elements and strategies to develop and support the teachers in their new leadership role of bringing reform to the entire school. The North Carolina Mathematics and Science Education Network (MSEN) conducted these statewide professional development programs for elementary school reform in science and mathematics and the U.S. Department of Education's Fund for the Improvement and Reform of Schools and Teaching (FIRST) funded a three-year grant for this project. The FIRST project sponsored 15 professional development programs designed and implemented at eight university sites involving 180 school leadership teams, representing 360 elementary teachers in all. The two-teacher teams agreed to lead their staffs in making schoolwide change. Teacher leaders assumed different roles depending on the needs of their school. These roles included classroom role model, workshop facilitator, grant writer, resource lab person, and curriculum innovator. The professional development programs used a standards-based approach that included hands-on/minds-on strategies and activities that extended over time to prepare these teacher leaders for their new roles. Carey, Frechtling, & Westat (1997) referred to this approach as "best practices" in professional development. Each of the 15 FIRST programs had a similar framework but varied in the amount of time and emphasis placed on content, pedagogy, and leadership skills. However, within this variance, four critical elements and related strategies were a part of each program.

What elements should be included in professional development programs to create teacher leaders who have the skills to bring about whole school reform—reform that impacts and is reflected in every teacher's classroom? This question will be addressed in this chapter. The learnings come from the North Carolina FIRST initiative and focus on one of the 15 programs that were implemented across North Carolina.

Critical Elements of Professional Development Programs for Teacher Leaders

From the onset of the FIRST project, the planners realized that merely declaring a teacher "teacher leader" would never bring about the desired results. They understood that creating teacher leaders who would reform science and mathematics education at the school level required extensive professional development. The challenge was to design a comprehensive professional development program that would give teachers the skills needed for their new role. The professional development model used to support science and mathematics reform and teachers' new leadership roles focused on the following four key elements: 1. Designing and implementing long-term professional development; 2. Building teachers' capacity for shared decision making; 3. Creating a supportive environment for the teacher leaders; 4. Incorporating assessments. To implement these, the program included a series of strategies. (See Table 1.)

Table 1: Critical Elements and Strategies Needed to Develop and Support Teacher Leaders

1. **Designing and Implementing Long-Term Professional Development**
   Strategies Used:
   > Build a multiphased professional development program.
   > Create time for reflection.

2. **Building Teachers' Capacity for Shared Decision Making**
   Strategies Used:
   > Administer a needs assessment.
   > Design a school improvement plan (SIP).
   > Allow for review of professional development activities.
   > Process leadership content and practice leadership skills.

3. **Creating a Supportive Environment for the Teacher Leaders**
   Strategies Used:
   > Provide principal support.
   > Allow time for two-teacher team collaboration.
   > Include time for teams of teacher leaders to problem solve with other teams.
   > Include project staff support during implementation phase.

4. **Incorporating Assessments**
   Strategies Used:
   > Conduct formative assessment.
   > Conduct summative evaluation.

Critical Element 1: Designing and implementing long-term professional development.

Teacher leaders experienced professional development that created a community of learners and provided time for the reforms to take hold.

Strategies:

Build a multiphased professional development program.

The professional development program was one-and-a-half-years-long. The teacher leaders participated in approximately 30 days of professional development, including preassessment sessions, a summer institute, academic-year follow-up sessions, and a final workshop the following summer. Preassessment sessions provided the teacher leaders with a vision of elementary science and/or mathematics teaching according to the national standards. In addition, the sessions included the opportunity for the teachers to assess the needs and strengths of their school's science or mathematics programs. The summer institute included opportunities for the teacher leaders to increase their skills and knowledge of content, pedagogy, hands-on/minds-on instruction, and leadership strategies. Academic-year follow-up sessions provided a supportive environment for teachers to share successes and challenges they encountered as they implemented reforms in their schools and the opportunity to make revisions to implementation plans when needed. The summer workshop offered a final opportunity to cover needs and concerns of teacher leaders, as well as to make future plans for implementation of reforms at their schools.

Create time for reflection.

Traditional staff development experiences often do not include time for analysis and reflection. However, in the FIRST program, reflection was viewed as an essential strategy that helped teacher leaders integrate science or mathematics reforms with their prior knowledge. In addition, they had the time to plan how they would present the reforms to their school staffs, and this reflection allowed them time to take into account the unique circumstances of their individual school settings.

Traditional staff development experiences often do not include time for analysis and reflection.

Critical Element 2: Building teachers' capacity for shared decision making.

The professional development leadership programs directly involved the teacher leaders in decision making. At the same time they developed their own decision making skills, they also learned how to foster shared decision making with their school peers.

Strategies:

Administer a needs assessment.

Teacher leaders administered an assessment to their school's entire faculty and administration to identify the strengths and weaknesses of their mathematics and science programs. The results of this assessment identified needed changes at the school. The assessment also ensured that staff members participated in the decision making process by identifying specific changes for their schools. The assessment instrument was modeled after the National Science Teachers Association's School Science Program Guidelines for Self-Assessment and was developed by the University of North Carolina MSEN (Franklin, 1990). It provided a picture of the science or mathematics program at each school by asking the teachers what was going on currently and what should be going on. These two questions helped identify the strengths and weaknesses in four areas: science or mathematics curriculum, instructional practices, student assessment, and the school environment.

Design a school improvement plan (SIP).

Based on the results of the needs assessment, each teacher leader team developed its school's plan for mathematics and/or science reform. The SIPs included identified needs with objectives and strategies for addressing these needs. Most teacher leaders took the completed working draft SIPs back to their school staffs for input, discussion, and revisions so that the final product would reflect the ideas of the entire faculty. All but four of the 183 teams completed SIPs. The results of the needs assessment formed the basis for all the SIPs and, in that sense, involved input from the school faculty. However, at least half of the teams provided opportunities for discussion and feedback from their faculties, in addition to filling out the needs assessments (Franklin, 1993).

Allow for review of professional development activities.
The teacher leaders had numerous opportunities to critique and change the professional development activities, which ensured that the activities would assist them as they implemented their SIPs. Depending on the decisions made by the teacher leaders, the professional development program included varying amounts of time for content, pedagogy, and leadership skills. Through an ongoing process of review, the professional development program served as a model for shared decision making and evolved as a vehicle to develop committed teacher leaders who would bring about science and/or mathematics reform. In turn, teacher leaders also allowed their school staffs to critique the professional development activities that they offered as part of their SIPs.

Process leadership content and practice leadership skills.
Paramount to bringing about change at the school level was the knowledge of how to work with teachers at their schools to introduce new reform ideas, concepts, and pedagogy, as well as the knowledge of how to serve as a facilitator who could increase teacher ownership, involvement, and investment. Sessions on leadership content focused on areas such as team building, stages of adult development, teacher development, learning styles, and workshop presentation skills. In addition to leadership content, the teacher leaders experienced opportunities to practice leadership skills by presenting reforms in mathematics and/or science to the other teacher leaders.

Critical Element 3: Creating a supportive environment for the teacher leaders.
A supportive environment during each phase of the program fostered fuller implementation of the reform initiatives at the school level.

Strategies:
Provide principal support.
Because the principal's commitment to the project was crucial to the outcomes of the project, his or her involvement was essential throughout the professional development program. In each phase, the principal participated in full-day or partial-day activities in which the teacher leaders and the principals had time to discuss, plan, and solve issues related to implementation of the SIP. With advice from the principals, the teacher leaders gauged the readiness levels of their school staff and determined the most appropriate strategies to use. Areas of principal support reported as most valuable by teacher leaders included supplying resources, release time, space, encouragement, and praise. One teacher leader described her principal's support with the following comment: "Well, he attended our workshop and participated in all the activities....And because he was there actually doing it with us, other teachers responded well to it (Franklin, 1993, p. 45)."

Allow time for two-teacher team collaboration.
A key aspect in the project design was to identify two teacher leaders per school who together made up the leadership team. This allowed the teacher leaders to provide ongoing support for one another back at their school as they implemented their SIP. An additional support mechanism that the professional development program used was formal and informal peer coaching. The teacher leaders used formal peer coaching when they conducted five school-based observations of each other in which they focused on an area related to their leadership role. This focus area was one they wanted feedback on and one they had identified during a preobservation conference. After they observed each other, they held follow-up conferences to share their feedback. These formal peer coaching sessions were described by one teacher leader: "The person who did our leadership session…showed us how to go about improving our leadership skills…. The other teacher leader (at my school) was a tremendous support and we practiced leadership with each other (Franklin, 1993, p. 74)." The teacher leaders also practiced informal peer coaching with each other when they shared, discussed, analyzed, and reflected upon problems and solutions in an informal, nonevaluative manner.

Include time for teams of teacher leaders to problem solve with other teams.
The professional development program schedule included time for teacher leaders to discuss problems and successes they experienced as they planned and implemented their SIPs. One teacher leader described the support she received from other teacher leaders in this way: "I think one of the pluses in it [professional development program] was how we were able to share with teachers…. We can sort of get together and share, maybe something that I'm doing can help you and maybe something that you're doing can help me (Franklin, 1993, p. 73)." One problem that most teams encountered was how to engage the "resistant" teacher. Sharing successful strategies helped the teacher leaders build on each others' strengths, plan appropriate action, and prepare themselves with the skills necessary to bring reform to their school. As each team shared its problems with the other teams, they realized that they often had the same problems experienced by others. This problem solving helped the teachers feel less isolated by providing them with a climate where they shared encouragement, solutions, and successes.

Include project staff support during implementation phase.
Project staff provided ongoing support during follow-up sessions to address the teacher leaders' needs. This included school site visits, telephone calls, workshop presentations at the school, and one-on-one discussions.

Critical Element 4: Incorporating assessments.
The professional development programs included ongoing assessments of teacher leaders' needs and successes.

Strategies:

Conduct formative assessment.

Ongoing assessments identified the teacher leaders' needs and the successes of the professional development program. Throughout development and implementation of the program, the project staff used the needs of the teacher leaders to refine and guide the program design. The program included assessments done on both a daily and monthly or bimonthly basis through the use of small-group discussions, comment cards, and journals. Specifically, teachers gave daily feedback on the program's effectiveness in helping them implement their SIPs. In addition, the Concerns-Based Adoption Model (Hall & Hord, 1987), which details teachers' stages of concern when implementing an initiative, was presented as part of the professional development sessions to help the site coordinators respond to the teacher leaders' changing concerns. Other techniques, such as Focus Group Interviews and Home Groups, were used. The Focus Group Interview technique gathered perceptions of six to eight teacher leaders at one time as they progressed through the staff development process. Home Groups collected assessment data by providing teacher leaders with time to talk informally together in small groups for the purpose of evaluating the progress of the professional development program. The key to the successful implementation of the Home Group technique was allowing teachers enough time together in their groups to develop a trust level that fostered open sharing of their needs.

Conduct summative evaluation.

The summative evaluation measured the project's impact on the school level because this was the desired outcome of the project. Several stakeholders involved in the project—the teacher leaders, their principals, and other teachers at their schools— gave feedback and perceptions regarding the success of the project. Three different data-gathering methods were used (Franklin, 1993.):

a. SIPs and Progress Reports. *At the end of the project, the team of teacher leaders reviewed the SIPs and rated each objective in terms of (a) whether or not it was accomplished and (b) the degree to which it was accomplished. Thirty percent of teams (52 schools) from programs across the state rated their objectives as "exceeded" or "accomplished." Fifty-eight percent (101 schools) rated their objectives as "nearly accomplished" or "in progress."*

b. Pre- and Post-Program Assessments. *At the beginning and end of the project, randomly selected teachers at the schools rated the science and/or mathematics program at their school. Thirty statements that characterized an effective program related to science and/or mathematics curriculum content, instructional practices, student assessment techniques, and the school environment were given achievement ratings. Forty-two percent of schools from programs across the state showed increases of 10 percent or more on their ratings. Given that these randomly se-*

lected teachers were not those directly receiving the professional development, these results show the project's positive impact on the entire school, not just on the teacher leaders' classrooms.

c. Interviews and Narrative Comments. *At the end of the project, the teacher leaders, other teachers at their schools, and the principals responded verbally and in writing to open-ended questions describing project-related changes they had seen in their schools following project implementation. Across all respondents from programs across the state, the most frequent change cited was increased use of a hands-on approach to teaching mathematics and science. Other changes mentioned were increased positive attitudes toward mathematics and science for both students and teachers and the increased availability of resources for teaching mathematics or science.*

Conclusion

This chapter describes critical elements from the FIRST initiative and answers the question of how to design effective teacher leader professional development programs. Having defined the key elements, the challenge centers on the balance of those elements. The question becomes: How much time should be devoted to content and pedagogy versus leadership? Content and pedagogy need professional development time or else the teachers may not have the required knowledge of the discipline or know how to best deliver it. If, on the other hand, content and pedagogy take up too much time, and not enough time is given to the leadership aspects of their new role, then teacher leaders may not have the necessary skills to influence other teachers' practices. Of course, how much attention needs to be given to content and pedagogy versus leadership skills depends on the skills, expertise, and experiences that the participating teachers bring to the professional development program in the first place. In order to provide the teachers what they need, a needs assessment should be given at the beginning stages of the program design. In addition, the climate of the schools where the teacher leaders will be working, the principal's orientation, and the district's priorities may all play a role in how well a newly-defined teacher leader can help bring about changes.

Although most professional development programs in the fields of science and mathematics provide subject content and pedagogy, they often leave out the development of leadership skills and teacher leaders who can translate the reform into other teachers' classrooms in their school. One of the unique features of North Carolina's FIRST initiative was the inclusion of a leadership development component that gave teachers an additional tool to change science and mathematics instruction not only in their own classrooms, but in the classrooms throughout their schools.

References

American Association for the Advancement of Science. 1989. *Science for all Americans.* New York: Oxford University Press.

Barth, R. S. 1988. School: A community of leaders. In *Building a professional culture in schools*, ed. A. Lieberman, 129–147. New York: Teachers College Press.

Bennis, W. 1989. *Why leaders can't lead.* San Francisco: Jossey-Bass.

Bolman, L. G., and T. E. Deal. 1994. *Becoming a teacher leader: From isolation to collaboration.* Thousand Oaks, CA: Corwin Press.

Bredeson, P. V. 1995. Role change for principals in restructured schools: Implications for teacher preparation and teacher work. In *Educating teachers for leadership and change*, ed. M. J. O'Hair & S. J. Odell, 25–45. Thousand Oaks, CA: Corwin Press.

Carey, N., J. Frechtling, and Westat, Inc. 1997. *Best practice in action: Follow-up survey on teacher enhancement programs.* Washington, DC: National Science Foundation, Division of Research, Evaluation, and Communication.

Carnegie Commission on Teaching as a Profession. 1986. *A nation prepared: Teachers for the 21st Century.* Hyattsville, MD: Carnegie Forum on Education and the Economy.

Conley, S. C., T. Schmidle, and J. B. Shedd. 1988. Teacher participation in the management of school systems. *Teachers College Record* 90(2):259–290.

Darling-Hammond, L. 1995. Policy for restructuring. In *The work of restructuring schools: Building from the ground up*, ed. A. Lieberman, 157–175. New York: Teachers College Press.

Darling-Hammond, L., and M. W. McLaughlin. 1995. Policies that support professional development in an era of reform. *Phi Delta Kappan* 76(8):597–604.

Franklin, M. E. 1990. *Mathematics and science education network: Elementary school science and mathematics program assessment.* Chapel Hill, NC: University of North Carolina, Mathematics and Science Education Center.

———. 1993. *Statewide improvement in elementary mathematics and science education through peer teacher training* (Final Report of Project R168D00258-92). Chapel Hill, NC: University of North Carolina at Chapel Hill, Mathematics and Science Education Network.

Garmston, R. 1988. Empowering teachers: Some practical steps. *Thrust* 18(2):21–24.

Hall, G. E., and S. M. Hord. 1987. *Change in schools: Facilitating the process.* Albany, NY: State University of New York Press.

Hanson, L. J., M. M. Thompson, and L. F. Zinn. 1993. *Perceived behaviors of elementary school principals which promote teacher leadership.* Unpublished manuscript, University of Northern Colorado, Greeley.

Hatfield, R. C., C. Blackman, C. Claypool, and F. Master. 1987. *Extended professional roles of teacher leaders in the public schools.* Unpublished manuscript, Michigan State University, East Lansing.

Holmes Group. 1986. *Tomorrow's teachers: A report of the Holmes Group.* East Lansing, MI: Holmes Group.

Leithwood, K. A. 1992. The move toward transformational leadership. *Educational Leadership* 49(5):8–12.

Lieberman, A. 1988. Teachers and principals: Turf, tension, and new tasks. *Phi Delta Kappan* 69(10):648–653.

———. 1995. Practices that support teacher development: Transforming conceptions of professional learning. *Phi Delta Kappan* 76(8):591–596.

Loucks-Horsley, S., P. W. Hewson, N. Love, and K. Stiles. 1998. *Designing professional development for teachers of science and mathematics.* Thousand Oaks, CA: Corwin Press.

National Council of Teachers of Mathematics. 1991. *Professional standards for teaching mathematics.* Reston, VA: NCTM.

National Research Council. 1989. *Everybody counts: A report on the future of mathematics education.* Washington, DC: National Academy Press.

———. 1996. *National science education standards.* Washington, DC: National Academy Press.

O'Connor, K., and K. Boles. 1992. *Assessing the needs of teacher leaders in Massachusetts.* Paper presented at the annual meeting of the American Educational Research Association, April. San Francisco.

Pellicer, L. O., and L. W. Anderson. 1995. *A handbook for teacher leaders.* Thousand Oaks, CA: Corwin Press.

Pellicer, L. O., L. W. Anderson, J. W. Keefe, E. A. Kelley, and L. McCleary. 1990. *High school leaders and their schools: Volume II. Profiles of effectiveness.* Reston, VA: National Association of Secondary School Principals.

Wasley, P. A. 1991. *Teachers who lead: The rhetoric of reform and the realities of practice.* New York: Teachers College Press.

Zinn, L. F. 1997. *Supports and barriers to teacher leadership: Reports of teacher leaders.* Unpublished doctoral dissertation, University of Northern Colorado, Greeley.

Building Capacity for Systemic Reform in Mathematics and Science Education: A Focus on a Develop-the-Developer Model

Karen J. Charles and Francena D. Cummings

Karen J. Charles is a senior program specialist with the Eisenhower Consortium for Mathematics and Science Education at SERVE. In this role, she has served as the coordinator of the Technical Assistance Academy for Mathematics and Science Services, a professional development institute for staff developers, and as coordinator of professional development activities for the Consortium. Honors include the Tandy Technology Scholar Award, First Union Back Outstanding Young Educator Award, and NC Region VII Science Teacher of the Year.

Francena D. Cummings is the director of the Eisenhower Consortium at SERVE, an educational organization focused on improving learning through research and development. In this role, she has responsibility for developing and implementing a plan to improve mathematics and science reform in the southeastern states. For a significant part of her career, she has provided a variety of technical assistance to school improvement initiatives in Maryland and Texas. Honors include Teacher of the Year and national president of the National Council on Educating Black Children.

D o you know this department chair?

During the 1995–96 school year, I was not only a high school mathematics teacher, but also a slightly reluctant department chairperson. My style of leadership was challenged only by having to put out the largest fire first. Most of the department meetings were spent making announcements. Of course, I had to rush through because half my audience became bored stiff while the other half dashed off to an emergency doctor's appointment or athletic practice. Though I was given a job description, my basic duties amounted to counting textbooks and issuing supplies. I didn't know how to do much more than this. But I had a desire to see my fragmented, disjointed department transformed into a cohesive group of colleagues that would pool their talents and resources to meet the challenges facing our students. I realized that I knew mathematics, but I did not know effective professional development strategies with which to engage my staff.

—Veronica King (personal communication, April 1998)

Or, can you identify with this staff developer?

I was a schoolteacher for 30 very good years; but in 1994, I left my 4th grade classroom to become education coordinator of a new elementary science reform initiative involving the University of Alabama at Birmingham and six local school systems. The project director and I were expected to work with hundreds of dynamic teachers and their school systems' curriculum specialists. We were Lucy and Ethel, wrapping pieces of candy that sped by faster and faster on the conveyor belt. Many pieces were getting away! We believed that we had been good classroom teachers, but we had to become professional development consultants...quickly!

—Joan Dawson (personal communication, April 1998)

These are *real* educators with *real and immediate needs.* In the field of education, the transition from classroom teacher to staff developer is not uncommon. What is uncommon is that any type of support might accompany this transition. Most teachers and staff developers have not encountered staff development classes in education course work (at any level) nor is there an abundance of inservice workshops dedicated to the development of staff developers. This begs the question: Where do staff developers and other educational leaders learn this craft and find the follow-up support necessary to experience ongoing personal professional growth to sustain themselves? Further, how might professional development programs be designed to help staff developers deepen their content and pedagogical knowledge regarding teaching and learning science and mathematics?

The Eisenhower Consortium for Mathematics and Science Education at SERVE (referred to herein as the *Consortium*) recognized the real needs of these real educators and designed the Technical Assistance Academy for Mathematics and Science Services (TAAMSS; referred to hereafter as the *Academy*) as a vehicle to build regional capacity for systemic reform. This chapter provides an overview of the Academy, highlighting features of the design, some evidence of changes in participants who were involved, and lessons learned from the Academy experience.

Designing the Academy

Context Setting

According to the National Education Goals Panel report (1991), U.S. students will be first in the world in science and mathematics by the year 2000. To a great extent, this goal is the focus of systemic reform in mathematics and science. In simplest form, *systemic reform* means aligning policies and programs of a system to support the development and implementation of standards in mathematics and science for the improvement of teaching and learning for all students. Standards-based reform calls for schools and teachers to replace the practice of transmitting knowledge and facts with active engagement that promotes deep understanding, critical thinking, and authentic learning. According to McLaughlin and Talbert (1993), this approach—teaching for understanding—requires classrooms in which students and teachers develop knowledge collaboratively, where facts are challenged continually in discourse, and where teachers as well as their students engage in learning and inquiry. New roles for teachers and learners require rethinking skills and developing new support systems for teachers—new forms of support for professional growth and change.

The ideas advanced by McLaughlin and Talbert are representative of those found in current reform documents such as the *National Science Education Standards* (NSES; National Research Council, 1996), *Science for All Americans* (American Association for the Advancement of Science, 1989), and the National Council of Teachers of Mathematics Standards (NCTM) *Curriculum and Evaluation Standards for School Mathematics* (1989) and *Professional Standards for School Mathematics* (1991). These ideas are wonderful and challenging; however, according to a recent report from the National Commission on Teaching and America's Future (1996), wonderful ideas tend to stop short of the desired outcomes.

Wonderful curriculum ideas fall flat in classrooms when they are not understood or supported by the rest of the school. And increased graduation and testing requirements create only greater failure if teachers do not know how to reach students.

On the whole, the school reform movement has ignored the obvious: what teachers know and can do makes the crucial difference in what children learn. And the way school systems organize their work makes a big difference in what teachers can accomplish. New courses, tests, and curriculum reforms can be important starting points, but they are meaningless if teachers cannot use them well. Policies can only improve schools if the people in them are armed with the knowledge, skills, and supports they need. Student learning in this country will improve only when we focus our efforts on improving teaching.

> *Wonderful curriculum ideas fall flat in classrooms when they are not understood or supported by the rest of the school.*

The message from this passage is that teachers and teacher competence must be at the heart of any efforts to change teaching and learning. This is especially true in mathematics and science classrooms because current mathematics and science reform challenges the views many teachers hold about who can learn these subjects and what is involved in teaching them. Increased student diversity provides still another challenge: to address a variety of learning styles and individual differences.

Most districts, local schools, and state educational agencies rely on professional development as a primary strategy to help build both organizational and individual capacity to implement and maintain change. However, in many cases, professional development activities offered are too short and episodic and lack intensity and follow-up. Further, the nature of the professional development design is not sufficient to build skills and knowledge for the support of continuous improvement. The preceding thoughts were ever on the minds of the Consortium staff when the Academy was envisioned. The challenge was to think and plan conceptually for a holistic approach to professional development.

In many cases, professional development activities offered are too short and episodic and lack intensity and follow-up.

Goal Setting

The Consortium has the mission of improving mathematics and science education, and the Academy was chosen as a vehicle to reach more science and mathematics professionals across the southeast. How could this happen? The Academy was designed as a means to build both individual and organizational capacity to support those professionals who have some responsibilities for designing, conducting, and supporting professional development for mathematics and science educators.

Seventy-five educators from six southeastern states (Alabama, Florida, Georgia, Mississippi, North Carolina, and South Carolina) accepted the invitation to participate in the Academy. The one major criterion for acceptance was to have solid content knowledge in the areas of mathematics and/or science. Prospective Academy members also needed to embrace a variety of approaches to learning, for example, effective questioning, problem posing, etc.

The design of professional development is a complex process and the Consortium staff kept this in mind, stringing together the various themes and topics that informed our work. All activities had to align with the major goal of building capacity through creating a develop-the-developer model to support the delivery of professional development and technical assistance to local districts. As a result of extensive thought and lengthy discussion of Academy goals, the journey was charted. In keeping with the notion that "less is more," the following concepts informed our work:

- ◆ Everyone can learn.
- ◆ Learning requires active participation.
- ◆ Everyone comes with a wealth of expertise.
- ◆ Context matters.
- ◆ Significant issues must be continuously identified and addressed.
- ◆ Community building is important for the learner.
- ◆ Questions are our friends.
- ◆ There is no need to reinvent the wheel; use existing strategies and resources.
- ◆ Problem solving is our intent.

Making Change, a simulation game about the change process, was a tool used to aid participants in thinking about their work and identifying their expectations. Because everyone can "win" when playing *Making Change*, the activity became a central part of the Academy design and inspired our theme, *The Wins of Change*. In this model of win-win, student benefits (a message from *Making Change*) were the bottom line. The major Curriculum resource was *Facilitating Systemic Change in Science and Mathematics Education: A Toolkit for Professional Developers* (Regional Education Library Network, 1995; hereinafter referred to as the *Toolkit*) because materials in the Toolkit focus on change as related to mathematics and science education. In particular, there is a focus on initiating, planning and managing change.

Planning the Academy

Table 1 (p. 55) lists the overall goals and objectives of the Academy. These goals were established prior to the first Academy meeting. While recognizing the value of participant input, the best data from regional work and from effective research were used to get started. A structure was then created that provided for input into the decision making process for the Academy. Each state team (a multipurpose structure devised for members of each state to interact as needed) appointed a state facilitator to meet with the Consortium staff between sessions to review and revise upcoming agendas based on both team and individual needs and concerns. Also, participants provided a wealth of written input at each session; this was used to create activities, design experiences, and invite specialists. The "good teachers" invited the "students" into the learning process by outlining the anticipated journey and then asking for suggestions for vehicles that would move the process along.

Doing the Academy

What was to become the first phase of the Academy, 1996–1997, included four sessions, TAAMSS I-IV. Participants were offered a unique opportunity to partner in a long-term professional development experience that would include not only participation in an ongoing professional community, but also support in their individual roles back home. Each four-day session was held in a comfortable environment, providing an atmosphere where participants could concentrate fully on their Academy experiences and easily network with colleagues from across the region. Table 2 (p. 56) represents a glimpse of the content provided in the Academy sessions. While discussion is limited to the details of the sessions, summaries are included.

The Academy Journey

The road map for the Academy journey featured a clearly marked route: the four sessions mentioned in *Doing the Academy*, with several roadside stops. Each segment of the journey focused on the major content. The roadside stops highlighted some behind-the-scenes thinking and learning from the journey. The discourse that emerged was very important, and attempts to capture the essence of this process were made through sharing the "journey talk." The journey talk was guided by the action that occurred along each segment of the trip: What worked? What needed to be changed? What has been learned? Are the needs of the participants being met? This process was a way of addressing continuous improvement.

TAAMSS I

TAAMSS I was crucial to the success of the Academy because it was the first public platform to convince participants of their roles in capacity building for mathematics and science. To develop the right focus, finding the right blend of content, process, and affect would be the challenge. The session began with activities designed to build community through data collection around personal needs and interests. It then moved to *engaging* participants with the Toolkit, a curriculum resource used throughout the Academy. Activities from the Toolkit reinforced many of the TAAMSS I goals: to experience reflective thinking and collaborative problem solving in staff development sessions; to draw on each others' professional experiences; to actively engage in acquisition and construction of knowledge; and to develop a community of learners committed to systemic reform in mathematics and science education. Because commitment to systemic reform requires understanding the big picture of change in education, the challenge was to assist participants in developing new skills and knowledge that would enhance their understanding of systemic change. Conveying the interconnectivity of all Academy activities was particularly important in establishing and implementing a vision of successful learning by all students. A necessary strategy was to find an approach to help participants think systemically about improving mathematics and science education. As mentioned earlier, the simulation game, *Making Change,* not only focused participants on the implementation of systemic change, but also created a high-energy environment in which a learning community could begin to form.

Since many of the participants were unknown prior to initiating the Academy, activities that would build knowledge about self were elected as starting points. A personality styles inventory based on self-assessment, True Colors (Lowry n.d.) was implemented. After reflecting through this new lens (Am I blue, orange, green, or gold?), participants wrestled with a problem presented that involved using their new knowledge to create teams that could effectively and creatively complete a given task. Two years later, people are still using what they know about personality from both True Colors (Lowry, n.d.) and Gregorc's (1982) *Style Delineator: A Self-Assessment Instrument for Adults* (in a subsequent session) to build effective teams, to assign tasks, to design workshops, and to facilitate meetings. The information is relevant to their work and has been used to create better understandings of teammates, coworkers, and clients.

Roadside Stop I: Understanding Change

Community building was imperative during the first segment of the journey. Recognizing that affect is a crucial part of the learning community, the heart was the target, attempting to tap the emotions of the participants and to tease their readiness for change. Affect reigned when participants engaged in substantive activities that spoke to human needs and diversity. The structures that enabled people to connect were established. An environment to promote learning through collective aspiration was

Table 1: Academy Goals

To build capacity for systemic reform in mathematics and science education.
To scale-up the dissemination of exemplary mathematics and science materials.

Content Pedagogical Focus Session Goals	TAAMSS I Understanding Change Engage	TAAMSS II Curriculum Delivery Explore	TAAMSS III Workshop Design Explain	TAAMSS IV Facilitation Skills Apply
	1. Increase participants' understanding of systemic reform.	1. Explore the use of the planning grid used to design all Academy sessions.	1. Provide a forum for regional stakeholders to discuss the impact of TAAMSS on the field of professional development.	1. Showcase their presentation skills and knowledge.
	2. Develop community and an emerging network.	2. Experience and reflect on the components of good lessons.	2. Enhance presentation skills through training in workshop design.	2. Apply content and staff development standards to work-related situations.
	3. Enrich strategies by both the acquisition and construction of knowledge.	3. Math and science delivery through leaders, such as Mary Budd Rowe.	3. Explore exemplary lessons and materials that reflect the Toolkit lessons.	3. Enhance reflection practices.
	4. Explore a variety of methods to draw on professional expertise.	4. Dissemination as it relates to professional development.	4. Reflect on previous experiences and making connections.	4. Celebrate success.
	5. Experience activities promoting reflective practice and thinking and problem solving.	5. Understanding change in individuals, schools, and entire systems.		5. Continue networking.

Table 2: A Sampling of Features and Activities from Each Academy Session

Many activities referenced in this table were either modified from or inspired by the resource *Facilitating Systemic Change in Science and Mathematics Education: A Toolkit for Professional Developers.*

Recurring Components	TAAMSS I	TAAMSS II	TAAMSS III	TAAMSS IV
Toolkit Resources for Professional Development	The Change Game Adult Learners Team Building A Model Lesson: Pendulums	Dissemination CBAM: Concern-Based Adoptions Model	A Model Lesson: Soaring with Science	A Model Lesson: Them Bones Team Building Take III Facilitation Skills A Model Kickoff
Math/Science Content Standards	Pendulum I	Son of Pendulum: Focus on Curricular Approaches	Third International Math/Science Study CAAMP: Computer Applications Math Manipulatives Program Science and Assessment.	Problem Solving Hands-On Science Math Quest Forensics
Adult Learning/ NSDC Standards	There's a Song in My Heart Listening Posts	Action Planning Team Building Take II	Workshop Design	Developing a Professional Portfolio Reflective Teaching Grant Writing Parental Involvement Staff Developers:
Equity	Family Science Connected Math Project	Considerations for developing a sense of fate control in students	Appreciating Diversity: A gardener's perspective	Designing Our Future The Equity Continuum: A call for action
Reflection	True Colors Southern Voices Red-Black Game State Team Meeting	Gregorc Learning Style Delineator State Team Meeting	Hello Gorgeous State Team Meeting State Team Presentation	Stretch for Excellence Presentation Debriefs Graduation Celebration

created. Together, participants reflected on where they were in their staff development journeys and where they wanted to go. Activities like *A Song in my Heart*, *Southern Voices,* and *Making Change Happen* were great for the trip.

Within the safety of the community, participants began to realize that improving might require changing. If they were to become better staff developers, improvement may not include refining a current skill. It may necessitate deep change—rethinking what was being done and how it was being done. It may take reexamining goals and outcomes in the light of new ideas, approaches, and strategies. It may take abandoning current yet comfortable skills in favor of innovation and risktaking. Could quality learning experiences that would help the participants change continue to be provided? What features of the design would get the learners where they wanted and needed to be?

TAAMSS II

In TAAMSS II, the agenda featured the usual components as shown in Table 2. The recurring themes of standards-based lessons, change, and equity are the components that continued to serve as the compass for the Academy design. With the constant emphasis on systemic change, it was vital to recognize the importance of individual change to system change. The mechanism used to guide the participants in their understanding of change was the Concerns-Based Adoption Model (CBAM). The CBAM framework allowed reemphasis with participants on the importance of understanding how individual concerns fit into the big picture of working systemically to implement changes in mathematics and science reform.

Although science and mathematics content is not a primary focus for the Academy, there is always an effort to focus on some aspect related to effective teaching and learning of these disciplines. In session II, activities to show content specialists multiple ways to think about curriculum were designed, providing new ideas that could easily be transferred to their clients. For example, the writings of Rowe (1978) helped shape a pendulum activity (a revisit to TAAMSS I) that featured not so much the science of pendulums as the different emphases teachers could take in presenting the concept: process skills, discovery, problem solving, or content. Depending on one's purpose (or emphasis), the pendulum lessons can shape up very differently. This was truly an "aha" for the staff developers as they reflected on their own particular biases in presenting content. Rowe suggested that this type of personal reflection concerning one's own approach to curriculum is critical to student success when she wrote:

> But curriculum is not a static thing. We change our conceptions of what content and emphasis should prevail as we accumulate experience and try to foresee the kinds of futures in which our children will have to operate. Will what we do develop sufficient flexibility and sufficient mental and emotional fluency to put them in command of their fates rather than make them victims of circumstance (p. 23)?

Do educators want to create students who will be consumers of knowledge? Or should students be the knowledge makers?

This very powerful statement gets to the heart of the equity issue that continues to be a challenge in making science for all children a reality. Do educators want to create students who will be consumers of knowledge? Or should students be the knowledge makers? Rowe provided a challenge through her query of whether to provide nurturing and challenging experiences to students such that they begin to see the possibilities for controlling what and who they become. Rowe clearly supported the notion that science programs can make a difference in how children perceive themselves in relationship to what happens in their environment. Providing opportunities for students to control variables in the context of a science lesson provides a start.

Roadside Stop II: Approaches to Content Delivery

Would the participants value a revisit to the pendulum lesson? This was a dominant thought while reflecting on the second segment of the journey. Professional Standard B (NSES) says that: "Professional development for teachers of science requires integrating knowledge of science learning, pedagogy, and students; it requires applying that knowledge to science learning (National Research Council, 1996, p. 62)." Like teachers, staff developers must ask some basic questions about curriculum delivery. Moreover, they should engage in discourse about a variety of curricular approaches. With regard to curriculum approaches, it was discovered that the group varied in its thinking about curriculum (when pushed) but most often, they had not given a lot of conscious thought as to why they do what they do. While beliefs about curriculum approaches were a very basic platform, it was an important topic of focus for the clients.

As mentioned in the section on Planning the Academy, input from state facilitators and participants guided the design of TAAMSS II–IV based on information gathered during TAAMSS I. For example, during TAAMSS I, participants asked specific questions about the structure of the activities they were experiencing. They learned at TAAMSS II that the key format embedded in all Academy sessions was: engage, explore, explain, and apply (EEEA; See Table 3). These four words not only provided the design format for all Academy experiences, but also continued to serve as the key components of all model lessons for students and of all model workshops for staff developers. As a key tool of the Academy, they provided a framework from which to build constructivist experiences for all learners. Participants received an EEEA grid for every session presented at TAAMSS II to further reinforce this concept. Immersion into workshop design would be the next stop.

TAAMSS III

The Wins of Change continued to strengthen the network as TAAMSS III focused on workshop design. In a previous survey, participants selected workshop design as a criti-

Table 3: What is Effective Science Education?

1. To revisit the pendulum activity. 2. To relate the pendulum to a variety of instructional strategies. 3. To model modifications to the activity.

Time	Focus	Activity	Material\Tools
5 min	Engage	"Just a Swingin": Set up the activity, show the slides, play the music.	Slides/projector, tape/player
20 min	Explore	Distribute materials/questions and direct participants to solve the problem presented; work in groups of four.	Pendulum packs various questions
20 min	Explain	Ask participants to display data in a chart or table design; have them gather where their question is posted and share data.	Chart paper, markers quiz questions for facilitators
20 min	Apply	Distribute puzzles and ask participants to discuss implications of instructional strategies; share group ideas.	Puzzle modified jigsaw
10 min	Debrief	Participants facilitated discussion of reactions/responses to modifications presented; evidence of standards, equity, problem solving, and constructivism.	Questions

cal content piece for their professional growth. To honor the commitment to their input, advice was sought from the National Staff Development Council (NSDC), whose leadership suggested a consultant. With her input, an agenda for TAAMSS III was designed around NSDC's *Standards for Staff Development* (1995), the principles of adult learning, and the EEEA grid that was now the cornerstone. This idea had been purposefully initiated through the activities of earlier academy sessions with the hope that participants would make the connection. TAAMSS III was opened with Hello Gorgeous, a light-hearted reflection activity enhanced by the Supremes singing in the background "reflections of the way things used to be." Physical clues of previous TAAMSS activities were demonstrated, and participants were asked to think about how the activity had caused them to see things differently. Without ever knowing it, their collective and shared memories about personal and professional changes and about how they were helping their clients think differently about curriculum set the stage for the intense introduction to workshop design that was to follow. Reinforcing previous concepts of understanding change and approaches to content delivery in math and science content sessions sprinkled throughout TAAMSS III. Manipulatives, such as cuisinaire rods and paper airplanes, helped explain how experiences build knowledge.

During the next several days, participants not only examined and sharpened their conceptual workshop design skills, but also enhanced their technical skills with after-hours sessions on computer software applications for electronic presentations. In "completing the package" for the workshop designer, it became necessary to augment the pedagogy with the latest technology tools available for adding a professional touch to presentations.

Roadside Stop III: Workshop Design

Designing ways for participants to discover for themselves the threads connecting Academy sessions was always a challenge. Did the opening activity, Hello Gorgeous, invite them to continue community building? Could their world be tapped into by observing their choices of creative presentations? Yes, the strategy worked. Without the tedium of a typical review session, participants revisited their past Academy experiences in order to prepare themselves for the next lesson—workshop design.

Concern existed that there was more direct delivery of information in this session as would be expected when the intent was to "explain." Participants became acquainted with the NSDC standards for staff development and began to realize that staff development was a distinct field of study, with its own content standards and pedagogy. Would this information alone enhance their transition from teacher to staff developer? Perhaps not. Fortunately, a seasoned staff developer was found whose two-day presentation modeled a constructivist approach workshop design. She skillfully led the participants through a series of highly interactive and reflective experiences that mirrored expressed convictions about the role of constructivism in staff development. Indeed, seeing and hearing change began through the discourse that emerged in both formal and informal structures. The Academy was reinforcing

Fosnot's (1989) contention that educators build community dissecting and reflecting on their experiences to build new knowledge. For the first time, many realized (constructed) that some former skills were not suited for this journey. In keeping with the journey metaphor, staff developers were advised to pack for a trip then to remove some of the items in their "suitcase" with the promise that more than enough would remain. All bags were lightened during TAAMSS III as preparation began to disclose what old stuff was selected for keeping and what new stuff was selected to add. Would the newly designed travel bags be enough support through TAAMSS IV?

TAAMSS IV

Across the southeast, staff developers specializing in mathematics and science were already content specialists. Time and again, however, by their own admission, they lacked facilitation skills—considered by many to be the art of helping *someone* learn *something* without getting in the way of either. Development and extension of these skills provided the glue that bonded the Academy and supported its design. The basis of what the learner knew (in their case, content), combined with their prior knowledge, could begin to help them construct new knowledge (the pedagogy of staff development). It was no secret that by seeing this concept modeled, they would, in turn, use it with their clients (teachers), who would then incorporate its use with their clients (students).

Academy members were responsible for most activities presented at TAAMSS IV. It was time for them to showcase their presentation skills and knowledge, *apply* content and staff development standards, enhance their reflection practices, and celebrate their success. The design of TAAMSS IV had to be the right blend of standards-based challenges, purposeful rigor, and opportunity for success. Participants were given two choices. They could opt to join a six-member team and codevelop a general session (1.5–2 hours) for the whole group to observe and critique. The Consortium staff predetermined group presentation topics and offered these choices: A Model Kickoff (a large-group tone-setting activity), A Model Lesson, Facilitation Skills, Equity, and Team Building. Recognizing and responding to varying levels of comfort and confidence in Academy members, a second option was developed. Groups of two could opt to design and deliver a mini-session (one hour) on a topic of their choice (content and pedagogy aligned with Academy practices.) To develop presentations, often across many miles, each group—large and small—worked with a Consortium partner and created its activity with, of course, the EEEA grid and a presentation checklist developed around lessons learned from workshop design and adult learning principles. As their products came together with remarkable polish, participants recognized in themselves and in each other their growth and increased capacity for effecting change in science and mathematics education.

Roadside Stop IV: Facilitation Skills

As the Consortium began its work in the southeast, these questions were asked: Who provides services, resources, and support for staff developers? Do they want prepackaged workshops to deliver to clients, or would they prefer extending their own skills of innovation and development? The more questions asked, the louder the responses. Their biggest needs were resources and materials on which to base and create their own presentations, multiple opportunities to upgrade their facilitation skills, and avenues through which to exchange ideas with other staff developers. The personal bias of the Consortium staff was affirmed: Give a man a fish and he eats for a day; teach him to fish and he eats for a lifetime.

While an atmosphere of celebration prevailed at TAAMSS IV, the most serious and, perhaps, most gratifying activity was the presentation debrief. Participants completed observation checklists during each presentation and were assigned to critique and debrief one of the presentation teams. How would they respond to the feedback from their colleagues? Had a safe enough environment been created for this kind of risk taking? The Consortium was pleased to see that by this time, the Academy community had developed such a strong sense of trust that the questioning that occurred during the debriefings was thought-provoking yet nonthreatening. Participants were asked to discuss and even defend various components of their activities and everyone learned.

Looking Back at the Journey: Are We There Yet?

The Academy supports a cadre of professional development providers from across a six-state area by giving them opportunities to learn through networking with others in similar roles and through confronting challenges and solving problems together. They represent a cross-section of the education community: university staff, classroom teachers, local school and district administrators, agency directors, field-based curriculum specialists, and representatives from informal science entities. The goal was to "build capacity" of this diverse group to address mathematics and science reform in the southeast.

How to build capacity is among the major issues to be addressed in the design of effective professional development for mathematics and science reform. Capacity building consists of the following components or dimensions: developing people who can work with teachers and others to support their learning and teaching; supporting systems for professional development providers; exploring and applying a knowledge base of professional development theory and practice; supporting subcultures in which professional development can flourish; and influencing policies, resources, and structures that make professional development central rather than a marginal activity (Loucks-Horsley, Hewson, Love, and Stiles, 1998). As the Academy emerged and began to offer opportunities for participants, these principles were embraced and used to guide the design of the Academy, as well as a way to look back at effectiveness.

Phase I of the Academy was fertile ground for learning about this develop-the-developer model. For example, it was learned that the Consortium is in a unique position to convene participants across state lines to dialogue about mathematics and science reform. The major challenge was finding the right blend of pedagogical and general content knowledge of mathematics and science, knowledge of learners, and content and pedagogical knowledge of professional development. From the participants it is known that their existing knowledge of professional development theory and practice was deepened. This was evident through their performances, through conversations, and through visits to their work sites. The Consortium followed some of them on this eventful journey from being seasoned teachers to becoming novice staff developers, from novice staff developers to becoming neophyte staff developers, and from neophyte staff developers to becoming polished and effective staff developers. As more is learned about their work in local sites, the nature and level of further impact of the Academy can be determined. The greatest evidence of effectiveness came through the willingness of over 50 percent of the Academy members to sign up for Phase II of the Academy.

Moving Forward

It is probably premature to say that the goal of building a cadre of staff developers who are able to scale-up efforts to address reform in the southeast has been reached. Nevertheless, it is believed that a few lessons have been distilled that can be communicated to other reformers about the Academy initiative. These lessons include the following:

Leveraging is a powerful process. The Consortium has learned how to leverage resources among partners by continuous communication with them about the value of what participants are learning and how they use it in their work. It has also been discovered that some individuals face time constraints with their commitment to the Academy, while a few others continue to justify the cost of their involvement to their supervisors. (Participants pay only their travel to Academy events.)

Reliability and quality matter. Over 80 percent of Academy members have requested and received a variety of technical assistance from Consortium staff as they continue their work as regional service providers. This additional support is an extension of TAAMSS and was promised to Academy members in return for their commitment to their own professional development. In return, the Consortium made every effort to follow through on the commitments it made to Academy members. Recent interviews with all participants reveal a high level of transfer of skills and knowledge, with specific examples of modifications and adaptations of tools and resources (…teach a man to fish…). Also, they continue to comment on the usefulness and currency of tools they receive from the Consortium.

Building a culture for change is important in achieving systemic reform. Attempts to promote change through developing a critical mass of leaders who can provide leadership at the local level were made. However, these participants have an awesome task of getting the participants back home to join in the battle to make high quality professional development a priority.

Nurturing makes a difference. This diverse group of staff developers necessitated a high level of differentiation in the amount of nurturing that was provided for participants. Working individually with participants as they designed and delivered services allowed the Consortium an opportunity to serve as personal consultants and/or critical friends. In essence, quality interactions among Consortium staff and colleagues advanced the skills and confidence of the participants.

Reaching across state lines is beneficial. Quality time to engage in conversation across state lines is a nonevent for most of the Academy members. However, the advent of the Academy gave members a reason to network. Getting to know each other in the context of talking about their work through a professional development lens opened up new ideas for sharing resources. More importantly, it served to break down the feeling of isolation and improved the chances for collaboration.

As the two-year commitment to Academy participation wound down, Consortium staff and Academy members revisited the journey known as TAAMSS. Jointly, they proposed that designing a second phase to the Academy and extending the journey could further sustain the personal and professional growth experienced by all participants. Fifty members elected to continue their affiliation with the Consortium and TAAMSS and, together, are creating "The Academy—Phase II." These are 50 educators who believe that all children can learn, that philosophies must change to respond to the growing diversity in southern schools, and that a personal commitment to change is currently challenging them. With a core of staff developers in each southeastern state having access to the training and resources that the Consortium can provide, capacity building can be a reality. One final thought from the Mathematics Department chair:

> *As a result of sitting down with professionals from all levels of education to discuss issues that are of importance to all stakeholders, I have seen the necessity of coming out of the classroom and collaborating with colleagues next door. Through our participation in the Academy, we are discovering how to provide better staff development, which can change the way that teachers think.*
> —Veronica King (personal communication, April 1998)

References

American Association for the Advancement of Science (AAAS). 1989. *Science for all Americans.* New York, NY: Oxford Press.

Gregorc, A. F. 1982. *Style delineator: A self-assessment instrument for adults.* Columbia, CT: Gregorc Associates.

Fosnot, C. T. 1989. *Enquiring teachers, enquiring learners: A constructivist approach for teaching.* New York: Teachers College Press.

Loucks-Horsley, S., P. W. Hewson, N. Love, and K. E. Stiles. 1998. *Designing Professional Development For Teachers Of Science And Mathematics.* Orchard Park, CA: Corwin Press.

Lowry, D. (n.d.) *True Colors: Keys to successful teaching*. Corona, CA: True Colors.

McLaughlin, M. W., and J. E. Talbert. 1993. Introduction: New visions of teaching. In *Teaching for understanding*, ed. D. K. Cohen, M. W. McLaughlin, & J. E. Talbert. San Francisco: Jossey-Bass.

Mundry, S. E., and L. P. Hergert, eds. 1990. *Making change*. Andover, MA: The NETWORK, Inc.

National Commission on Teaching and America's Future. 1996. *What matters most: Teaching for America's future*. New York: Teachers College, Columbia University.

National Council of Teachers of Mathematics. 1989. *Curriculum and evaluation standards for school mathematics*. Reston, VA: NCTM.

————. 1991. *Professional standards for teaching mathematics*. Reston, VA: NCTM.

National Education Goals Panel. 1991. *The national education goals report, building a nation of learners*. Washington, DC: Author.

National Research Council. 1996. *National science education standards*. Washington, DC: National Academy Press.

National Staff Development Council. 1995. *National staff development council's standards for staff development*. (High school, middle school, and elementary school level editions). Oxford, OH: National Staff Development Council.

Regional Educational Laboratory Network. 1995. *Facilitating systemic change in science and mathematics education: A Toolkit for professional developers*. A Product of the Regional Educational Laboratories.

Rowe, M. B. 1978. *Teaching science as continuous Inquiry: A basic*. NewYork: McGraw-Hill Book Company.

The Precollege Program: A Collaborative Model of Student Enrichment and Professional Development in Mathematics and Science

Patricia S. Moyer
George Mason University
Eric D. Packenham
National Science Teachers Association

Patricia S. Moyer is an assistant professor of mathematics education in the Graduate School of Education at George Mason University, Fairfax, Virginia. She conducts research on teachers' and students' uses of representations in mathematics, and preservice and inservice teacher development. She is a former coordinator of the UNC-Chapel Hill Pre-College Program.

Eric D. Packenham is the program director of the Building a Presence for Science initiative at the National Science Teachers Association. His work is to end the isolation of classroom science teachers while also helping to bring standards-based teaching and learning into schools in participating states and helping teachers implement the National Science Education Standards (NSES) in conjunction with state science standards.

National organizations have called for major reform in the teaching and learning of mathematics and science. The release of the Third International Mathematics and Science Study (TIMSS) challenges educators in the United States to teach mathematics and science in new and different ways (Pursuing Excellence, 1996). In *Failing Our Children: Implications of the Third International Mathematics and Science Study* (National Science Board, 1998), the National Science Board declared the critical importance of reaffirming the commitment to improving mathematics and science performance in our nation. Findings in the TIMSS report encouraged mathematics and science teachers to add depth to instruction in these subjects. Lane (1996), director of the National Science Foundation (NSF), reported that teachers in other countries are expected to teach a narrow range of subjects and have more time for planning and collegiality, enabling them to investigate topics in greater depth.

It is not only the depth to which subjects are taught, but the way in which instruction occurs in our nation's classrooms that is of concern. The National Council of

Teachers of Mathematics (NCTM, 1989) called for major reform in the way in which mathematics is taught. Mathematics educators were encouraged to redirect the focus of mathematics instruction away from the memorization of facts and algorithms. Meaningful mathematics instruction recognizes the need for students to construct knowledge through their active involvement in mathematical situations and their appropriate use of mathematical tools. Terms in the *Professional Standards for Teaching Mathematics* (NCTM, 1991), such as explore, communicate, construct, conjecture, and investigate, imply the notion that students are involved in doing mathematics. Similarly, the National Science Teachers Association (NSTA) charges that students should be doing science. This requires teachers of science to plan the teaching and learning interactions in their classrooms in entirely new ways. In an NSTA press release, Workosky (1998) cited Gerry Wheeler, executive director of NSTA, who stated: "In the process, teachers assume new roles as coaches, getting students actively involved in their own learning."

As leaders in mathematics and science education design professional development for teachers, it is important to view that role as one of a facilitator, instead of a trainer.

The professional development of teachers plays a key role in the mathematics and science teaching and learning occurring in the nation's classrooms. As leaders in mathematics and science education design professional development for teachers, it is important to view that role as one of a facilitator, instead of a trainer. Much of current professional development in mathematics and science relies on fragmented, piecemeal experiences, where teachers attend a one-week workshop with an expert who espouses new ideas and classroom strategies. These experiences offer participants no time for planning, no opportunities to implement new pedagogy, and no support as teachers experiment with new materials, technology, and methodology in their classrooms. A successful model of professional development redirects these worthy efforts into a strategic plan with clear, coherent, long-term goals. In this way, professional development can systematically provide schools with direction and focus on individual and system development.

An example of this model of systematic reform is the University of North Carolina Mathematics and Science Education Network (UNC-MSEN) and more specifically, the MSEN Precollege Program. The mission of MSEN is to provide leadership for teachers in North Carolina in the area of professional development, with a particular emphasis on the inclusion of under-represented groups in mathematics and science. MSEN accomplishes this through its 10 Centers and its six Precollege programs, located on university campuses throughout the state. These centers and programs operate in cooperation with local education agencies (LEA) that participate in the program voluntarily and provide financial and material support. Continuing teacher education is offered on and off campus through courses and institutes. It is this collaborative network of resources that has enabled MSEN teachers and students to attain continued success.

Precollege Program Structure

In 1986, the MSEN Precollege Program piloted four university sites in North Carolina. In its initial years of operation, the program's mission was to increase the number of historically under-represented students in mathematics and science by providing enrichment opportunities for students in grades 6–12. Today, the North Carolina State Legislature funds MSEN as a part of UNC's outreach programs serving public schools surrounding the universities. The scope of the program has broadened to include all students pursuing mathematics- and science-based majors and careers, preparing students for the new millennium. However, students in the program are predominantly minorities, with 87 percent African American. The program recruits students of average to above-average ability who have not been sufficiently exposed to mathematics- and science-based courses and careers. During the 1997–98 academic year, the Precollege Program served over 3,000 students in North Carolina through its academic year enrichment and summer enrichment programs.

An important benefit for Precollege Program teachers is the link the program offers to the professional development opportunities provided by the centers, which occur as summer workshops, Saturday Academies for Teachers, and other projects, courses, and institutes. Both Precollege teachers and other professionals are recruited to participate through the Precollege Program, the center's Web page, and the LEAs. These professional development opportunities provide Precollege teachers with valuable resources, up-to-date pedagogical knowledge, and opportunities for collegiality and collaboration.

At each university, a Precollege Program coordinator oversees the operation of enrichment programs. Each participating school has a Precollege Program teacher or teacher team that offers academic enrichment classes at the middle school level and academic enrichment clubs at the high school level. The rich resources of UNC offer opportunities for students to participate in internships, Saturday academies, summer programs, and other academic-year enrichment programs. On the university's campus, students have access to university faculty, research laboratories, libraries, computer labs, and other facilities.

Another vital component of the program's success is the Parents Involved for Excellence (PIE) Clubs. PIE Clubs exist at each participating school and provide leadership and support for the school's Precollege Program. Through a series of monthly meetings, parents plan and assist in the implementation of quality educational programs at the local and school-system levels.

Three important characteristics embedded in the Precollege Program structure reflect powerful ideas with important implications for the design of current professional development models. The first characteristic is the focus, not on counting heads or administering attitude surveys but on obtaining substantive results. Critical results that remain a central issue are: (a) What academic changes can be observed in students as a result of their participation in program initiatives? (b) What instructional changes can be observed in teachers as a result of their participation in professional development? The second characteristic is thinking systematically. The Precollege Program is mindful of the interconnectedness of each of its components. Programmatic changes at one level may impact the entire system. This systematic thinking allows center directors and Precollege Program coordinators to continuously reevaluate the quality of program offerings and the impact of these offerings on the teachers and students they serve. A third characteristic is providing teachers and students with programs that utilize a model of constructivism. Current research (Cobb, 1994; von Glasersfeld, 1987) on how learning occurs indicates that individuals do not passively acquire knowledge through transmission but that these knowledge structures are actively constructed in the mind of the learner. This educational theory is cognitively oriented, viewing learners as active participants, constructing knowledge by reorganizing their current ways of knowing. It is critical to apply constructivist models of teaching and learning in student programs and teacher professional development experiences. By remaining mindful of these characteristics—focusing on student and teacher results, thinking systematically, and using a constructivist model for instruction—the Precollege Program provides effective professional development for teachers and successful enrichment programs for students.

> *It is critical to apply constructivist models of teaching and learning in student programs and teacher professional development experiences.*

Teacher Professional Development Initiatives

Professional development for teachers is essential to improve mathematics and science education. Teachers need time to cultivate their knowledge, thinking, and ideas throughout their teaching careers. Their school day should allow time for interaction with their colleagues to share, plan, and implement strategies.

The Precollege Programs and the Centers for Mathematics and Science Education have combined efforts to offer a number of professional development initiatives for Precollege Program teachers. The following examples come from the Center for Mathematics and Science Education at UNC-Chapel Hill and are similar to other initiatives offered throughout the state at other centers.

The *Technology Tools Project* is a statewide project supported by NSF. Its goal is to establish 10 university training centers in North Carolina to instruct teachers in the application of current technologies to mathematics and science instruction. The Tech Tools Project includes two years of professional development with coursework throughout the summers and regular workshops throughout the academic year. During the 1997–98 academic year, teams of two teachers from each of the schools participating in the MSEN Precollege Program took part in the project. Each team included a Precollege Program teacher and a mathematics or science teacher from the same school. Teachers received over $350 in materials for their classrooms. This project enhanced Precollege Program instruction, enlarged the network of professional collaboration at the teachers' schools, and fulfilled the state's technology requirements for teachers.

Another project that tied technology with mathematics and science was the *Mathematics and Science Technology Tools Project*, supported by Eisenhower funds. Participants during the 1997–98 academic year were teachers of mathematics and science in grades 3–12. The goal was to model the activities of a restructured classroom heavily based in technology as a tool for instruction. Teachers learned through direct involvement how to restructure their classrooms to make them more student-centered and project-oriented.

Teachers need time to cultivate their knowledge, thinking, and ideas throughout their teaching careers.

Teachers received approximately $350 in materials to replicate this learning environment in their own classrooms. Classroom observations indicated that teachers were successful in implementing the new technology, creating a dynamic and interactive environment for student learning.

The *Middle Grades Mathematics Tools and Technology Project*, supported annually by Eisenhower funds, is subject-specific for middle-grades teachers. Its goal is to model NCTM-based (NCTM, 1989) instruction for participants in the use of a variety of mathematical tools appropriate for the middle grades. Participants receive over $300 worth of mathematics manipulative materials for their classrooms, along with professional development in the use of manipulatives, calculators, and computers for mathematics instruction. Through classroom observations, follow-up instruction, and teacher interviews, participants receive continuous support as they implement the new materials and pedagogical strategies into their classrooms. Project participants have become leaders in mathematics. They have written successful grants for additional materials and interdisciplinary projects, provided school systemwide professional development for other teachers, and presented during the program's summer institutes and at the North Carolina Council of Teachers of Mathematics State Conference.

The center also offers professional development experiences in nationally acclaimed programs, such as the *Great Explorations in Mathematics and Science* project, the *Gender/Ethnic Expectations and Student Achievement* project, and the *Activities Integrating Mathematics and Science* project. These program offerings enrich teaching and learning by providing models of hands-on instruction, the integration of mathematics and science topics, inquiry-based approaches, and strategies for reaching all students. Teachers who participated in these professional experiences have been successful in providing increased student involvement in the doing of mathematics and science in their classrooms.

There are common threads of effective professional development throughout the programs offered. Arbuckle and Murray (1989) noted several characteristics of effective science and mathematics professional development programs: (a) collegiality and collaboration; (b) experimentation and risk taking; (c) use of available knowledge bases;

(d) participant involvement in appropriate aspects; (e) time to participate and practice; (f) leadership and sustained support; (g) appropriate incentives and rewards; (h) application of knowledge about adult learning and change; (i) integration of individual, school, and district goals; and (j) integration of science and mathematics professional development with other professional development and organizational development activities. These characteristics are preeminent in each of the professional development projects offered through the centers, as well as the structure of the Precollege Programs. Maintaining a focus on each of these characteristics in the development of program initiatives has created a network of support for teacher and student learning in mathematics and science.

Student Initiatives and Results

Aligning professional development with student outcomes has produced significant benefits for students, as seen throughout the Precollege Program components. At the middle school level, students participate in elective academic enrichment classes that include hands-on experiences in mathematics and science labs, experiential learning through field trips, individualized and group tutoring, role model mentoring, and counseling on course selection and career choices. At the high school level, students participate in academic enrichment clubs that provide career counseling, achievement test preparation, college campus tours, leadership seminars, and academic support through links with the university's study skills centers. This ongoing support for students in grades 6–12 provides them with the content knowledge, the confidence, and the exposure to college entrance requirements that enables students to successfully enter college. In the 1996 MSEN Status Report surveying high school seniors, 98 percent of those in the Precollege Program reported that they planned to attend a four-year institution, with 87 percent having been accepted to a four-year institution at the time of the survey. In a survey of the last four cohorts of Precollege Program graduates, over 95 percent of students surveyed reported that they were currently enrolled in college. In the class of 1994, 97 percent of program students participated in the survey collection. Of those students, 99 percent were enrolled in college, with 65 percent enrolled in a major in a mathematics- or science-related field. These are significant results when one considers that only about 30 percent of the general college population is enrolled in mathematics- or science-related fields.

Saturday Programs

Throughout the academic year, students participate in Saturday academy sessions on UNC's campus that support their content knowledge in mathematics and science through hands-on investigations. Saturday classes include science labs, mathematics, career awareness, and communications/technology. Special-focus Saturday sessions include topics in testing preparation for the SAT, PSAT, and ACT, as well as career fair sessions where students have opportunities to interact with professionals from mathematics- and science-based fields. University faculty, scientists, and precollege teachers who have participated in MSEN professional development offerings teach in these Saturday sessions. The broad intent of Saturday academy is to expose students to ideas that may stimulate their career interests and support concepts that may be missing from the regular school curriculum. A majority of Precollege Program students indicate that their goal is to major in a mathematics- or science-based field in college, with approximately one-third of these in medicine.

UNC's nationally recognized health professions schools participate as MSEN partners. One specialized program for students interested in medical careers is the "3000 by 2000" Saturday program, funded by the UNC School of Medicine. Saturday sessions familiarize students with the medical school, laboratories, and careers in medicine. Students participate in interactive lectures by clinical faculty, lab exercises, case studies, discussion groups, and tours.

Summer Programs

Students at each grade level select from a number of summer program offerings. Summer Scholars, funded by NSF, was a four-week summer opportunity for students entering grades 6–8. The summer program allowed instructors to go into greater depth in a variety of topics and gave students the opportunity to design mathematics and science projects. Middle school students in the Summer Scholars Program participated in field trips to businesses, museums, college campuses, and scientific laboratories. Collaboration with on-campus resources enabled each Summer Scholars Program to provide unique offerings for students. For example, in the past four years, cooperation with the UNC-Chapel Hill Department of Chemistry resulted in the annual "Chem Magic Show," a program that taught students how seemingly magical tricks could be explained through chemistry.

Summer opportunities for high school students combine the experiential opportunities found in middle school programs with the rigor necessary for students to prepare for careers in research. The Exploring Science Program, for students entering grades 8–10, allows students to explore their interests in the fields of science in challenging and interactive sessions. Topics include biology, chemistry, physics, mathematics, research methods, and computer applications of research. Students begin a science project during the summer program; are mentored during the school year by Precollege Program teachers; and, upon completion of the project in the spring of the year, receive a $200 scholarship from the Burroughs Wellcome Foundation.

The "3000 by 2000" Health Professions Partnership Initiative, funded by the Robert Wood Johnson Foundation, offers a summer opportunity for high school students that complements the academic year Saturday session experiences. Students in grades 9 and 10 participate in Summer Experience I, a four-week institute exploring career options in the health professions by shadowing health professionals in different disciplines and participating in weekly health professions seminars. Students in grades 10 and 11 participate in Summer Experience II, a six-week project-oriented experience where students participate in a laboratory research project or other health-related science project.

The most intensive and rigorous program for Precollege students and teachers is the Precollege Research Experience Program (PREP), funded by NSF. Students in grades 11 and 12 and classroom teachers compete for selection as paid summer interns on the university's campus. Selected interns conduct an eight-week research project under the direction of a university faculty preceptor. Participants write a quality research paper worthy of publication, design a project display, and present their findings at a research symposium. In the 1998 summer PREP program, 12 students and five classroom teachers selected for this competitive project conducted research in archeology; geography; molecular biology and biotechnology; physics and astronomy; environmental science and engineering; computer science; biology; pathology and laboratory medicine; biochemistry and biophysics; pharmacy; laboratory and animal medicine; and pediatrics and pathology.

There are numerous opportunities for student involvement and enrichment that occur throughout the year. Some of these events include: leadership retreats, where high school students are involved in leadership training experiences; Central Intercollegiate Athletic Association Tournament High School Day, a college recruiting day for high school juniors; and MSEN Day, a statewide competition in mathematics, science, and other academically-related topics.

Parental Involvement

The Parents Involved for Excellence (PIE) Clubs are one of the most important components of this systemic model. In addition to the PIE Club at each of the participating schools, parents are involved at the regional and state level in the long-range goal setting of the program. Parents actively participate in securing grant funds, locating and serving as role-model speakers, and providing guidance and direction for the program's state advisory board. Parents are active in the communications of the program, assisting in the development of school web pages, writing articles for news releases, participating in television broadcasting, and maintaining school newsletters. Parents meet regularly at the school level, as well as send representatives from each school for districtwide planning meetings. The parent organization maintains the program's connection with the public, challenges the program to continue its visionary direction, and demands student achievements and results in all program activities.

As a part of its mission of continuing education, the Precollege Program offers workshops for parents to update them on options and opportunities that exist for their children in preparation for college. Parents participate in seminars and learn about the uses of technology and how to support their children in mathematics and science throughout their middle and high school years. Parents particularly enjoy workshops that assist them in locating funding sources for educational support and those that provide in-depth information on the college application process. An important goal in each of these seminars is to develop parents' awareness of the many opportunities that exist for their children in the fields of mathematics and science.

Conclusion

The Precollege Program consistently offers high-quality programs for teachers, students, and parents. The interconnectedness of all parts of the program and a focus on student and teacher results has contributed to the program's 12-year success record. One-shot programs that give teachers and students a boost are not enough to make lasting change. For student results to occur, teachers and students need continuing enrichment and professional development in a system that is interconnected with long-range and holistic goals. Collaboration needs to exist between the university community, the public school community, the business community, teachers, parents, and students. All stakeholders need opportunities to contribute their opinions and visions so that, through experimentation and risk taking, common goals can be set and achieved. There needs to be appropriate leadership at different levels, with time for participants to practice what they are learning in an atmosphere of ongoing support. Finally, the mathematics and science learning that occurs needs to be woven like a thread throughout each and every aspect of the program. This can lead to a successful model of student enrichment and professional development in mathematics and science for everyone.

References

Arbuckle, M. A., and L. B. Murray. 1989. Effective professional development. In *Facilitating systemic change in science and mathematics education: A toolkit for professional developers*, 2–25. Andover, MA: The Regional Laboratory for Educational Improvement of the Northeast and Islands.

Cobb, P. 1994. Constructivism in mathematics and science education. *Educational Researcher* 23(7):4.

Lane, N. 1996. *On release of the curriculum analysis aspect of the third international mathematics and science study*. East Lansing, MI: US TIMSS National Research Center.

National Council of Teachers of Mathematics (NCTM). 1989. *Curriculum and evaluation standards for school mathematics*. Reston, VA: NCTM.

———. 1991. *Professional standards for teaching mathematics*. Reston, VA: NCTM.

National Science Board. 1998. *Failing our children: Implications of the third international mathematics and science study*. (Report #98-154). Arlington, VA: National Science Foundation.

National Center for Education Statistics. 1996. *Pursuing Excellence: A Study of U.S. Eighth-Grade Mathematics and Science Teaching, Learning, Curriculum, and Achievement in International Context* Washington, D.C.: National Center for Education Statistics. Available: http://nces.ed.gov/timss

von Glasersfeld, E. 1987. Learning as a constructive activity. In *Problems of representation in the teaching and learning of mathematics*, ed. C. Janvier, 3–18. Hillsdale, NJ: Erlbaum.

Workosky, C. 1998. *NSTA applauds NAGB for setting high standards for science student performance* Arlington, VA: National Science Teachers Association. Available: http://www.nsta.org/pressrel/

LEARN North Carolina:
A Teacher-Directed Model of
Technology Integration

David J. Walbert

David Walbert is research and communications coordinator for LEARN North Carolina, where he edits a statewide magazine for teachers and assists in the development of professional development modules. He has a Ph.D. in history from the University of North Carolina at Chapel Hill.

The Learners' and Educators' Assistance and Resource Network of North Carolina (LEARN NC) is a program of the School of Education at the University of North Carolina at Chapel Hill (UNC-Chapel Hill). The LEARN NC Web site, located at http://www.learnnc.org, is a one-stop collection of professional development opportunities and learning resources provided free of charge to North Carolina teachers and students. These resources are designed and created by educators themselves, who use the Web site to share classroom materials and ideas, learn technology skills, and build connections with educational organizations. Now in its second year of operation, LEARN NC has over 6,000 participating educators in 96 of North Carolina's 100 counties and is the only statewide program of its kind in the United States. Although LEARN NC's primary goal is to deliver content, using technology only as a medium, professional development, particularly in the use of technology, has been an important effect of the program's implementation in the state's public schools. This chapter will examine LEARN NC's history and mission, some challenges that have arisen in implementing a statewide, teacher-driven educational program, and how they have been met.

A state of connectedness

In September 1995, the Public School Forum of North Carolina (the Forum) issued a report, *A State of Disconnectedness* (1995), on mathematics and science instruction in the North Carolina public schools. After a year-long study, the Forum found that although North Carolina students had improved academically with respect to children in other states, they still lagged "far behind" in the areas of mathematics and science. The problem, the researchers found, was not a lack of resources for teachers; on the contrary, a great variety of resources, both government and private, existed to support mathematics and science instruction. There were, however, few points of connection between these resources; the resulting situation was the "state of disconnectedness" to which the report's title referred. If the state was to make "real progress" in mathematics and science education, the researchers concluded, "there must be more collaboration, communication, and coordination between and among the myriad of government and private entities involved in policy making, training and resource delivery in the K–12 mathematics and science arenas (Public School Forum of North Carolina, 1995, p. 4)."

This report spurred University of North Carolina System President C. Dixon Spangler to ask the state's schools of education to address these issues. UNC-Chapel Hill's School of Education was chosen to coordinate these efforts and to develop an electronic performance support system for North Carolina teachers. Such a system would facilitate communication between the state's educators and the Department of Public Instruction, using information technology to help teachers create reliable curriculum resources for their classrooms. This support system, which would become LEARN NC, was broadly conceived as a partnership of the UNC-Chapel Hill School of Education, which would administer the program; UNC-Chapel Hill's Institute for Academic Technology, which would develop and maintain the program's technological side; the North Carolina Community Colleges, which would contribute ideas and resources; and the state's public schools. Public schoolteachers and administrators were more than just the program's market; they were made full partners in its development. Educators from six pilot school systems, representing a broad range of technological resources, were surveyed to learn what they would want from an instructional support system.

As a result of these discussions among educators, which continued throughout the academic year 1995–1996, a consensus emerged as to the kind of Internet-based service that would most benefit the state's teachers and students. LEARN NC would consist of a package of resources for teachers and students, available via the World Wide Web. In order for these resources to reach the greatest number of classrooms, the system must be built on a least-common-denominator standard, a level of technology accessible from hardware and software available in every school system; otherwise, information technology would only widen the gap between haves and have-nots. All resources should relate to the North Carolina Standard Course of Study, the state's new prescribed curriculum, and the quality of the resources must be assured, so that the material on the Web site would be appropriate for North Carolina classrooms. Lastly, the system should not simply create extra work for teachers; it should be easy to use and should facilitate more effective teaching rather than simply providing a technological distraction in the classroom.

The most important piece of LEARN NC's package of resources is a lesson plan database, a library of lesson plans submitted by teachers around the state. Teachers seeking ideas for their own classrooms can search this database by grade level and subject area to find a plan that meets their needs. Although some plans are designed to bring technology into the classroom, most simply find new and creative ways to teach traditional subjects like science and writing. To ensure quality, each lesson must pass a triple peer review. First-year teachers and veterans alike can then use the plans to infuse their teaching with new ideas. In addition, the process provides them a rare opportunity for professional publishing. While other professions encourage inventive and experienced people to share their knowledge and ideas with colleagues, the K–12 teaching profession provides few formal opportunities for practicing teachers to publish their ideas and learn from one another. LEARN NC's Lesson Plan Database allows teachers to share their best work with their colleagues across the state.

The K–12 teaching profession provides few formal opportunities for practicing teachers to publish their ideas and learn from one another.

Encouraging collegial interaction is also the primary goal of a second piece of LEARN NC's package, the online discussion forums. Through these forums, educators can post news, questions, or topics for discussion to a kind of electronic bulletin board. Contributors to a forum can exchange classroom ideas, notify colleagues of professional development opportunities, and discuss important issues in education. Discussion forums, unlike chat rooms, are asynchronous—that is, participants need not be online simultaneously. Teachers with busy schedules can read postings to a forum and respond at their own convenience.

A third online resource is a library of links to other Web sites relating to K–12 education. Like online search engines such as Yahoo®, LEARN NC's Web link library helps Internet users to find Web sites that match their interests. But LEARN NC's library is unique in that it indexes only educational sites, so that its contents will be both safe for students and useful to teachers. In addition, to make the collection relevant to North Carolina classrooms, much of its content is North Carolina-specific. The library provides links to state historic sites and museums, for example, but a teacher searching for field trip opportunities will not be overwhelmed by lengthy lists of sites in South Dakota or New Hampshire.

The final major piece of the package of resources is designed to be used directly by students. A series of multimedia curriculum resources—databases of images; sound; and, sometimes, video—links classrooms across the state to museums, exhibits, historic sites, and other educational facilities. One of the first resources takes students on a virtual field trip to UNC-Chapel Hill's Morehead Observatory; in 1999, students will be able to use the computers in their classrooms to control the Observatory's telescope and perform their own astronomical research.

Each of these four resources was designed to address the concerns of the educators in LEARN NC's pilot teams and the lack of connectedness among the state's K–12 education community. LEARN NC's resources are collaborative; they are designed and created by the educators who will use them. All resources are correlated to the North Carolina Standard Course of Study; an online map of the curriculum is provided on the Web site, with links from each goal and objective to relevant instructional plans, and both instructional plans and Web links can be searched by grade level and curriculum area. All resources are reviewed by experienced educators to ensure quality and appropriateness of content. The Web site itself is designed to be as user-friendly as possible, with a simple design that allows pages to be read quickly with even a relatively slow Internet connection.

LEARN NC's pilot phase, the 1996–1997 academic year, allowed technology-savvy educators to design, test, and implement these resources. The program became operational in September 1997, when the first teachers were formally trained in the use of the Web site. By the fall of 1998, all of the state's 117 public school systems were using and contributing to LEARN NC's online resources, and the program had over 6,000 participating educators. In addition to the original package of resources, the K–12 Curriculum Program, LEARN NC is now developing a series of online courses for inservice professional development and a preservice component that will allow prospective teachers to use LEARN NC's resources to build teaching skills. LEARN NC also made connections with some 20 partner organizations that share content with LEARN NC and its participants. In the 1998–1999 academic year, it is expected that LEARN NC will reach an additional 15,000 teachers and will continue to create links within North Carolina's education community.

Technology as a means, not an end

Although LEARN NC has always had the goal of integrating technology into the classroom, it is primarily about educational content. Internet technology is the means by which this content is delivered, but is never an end in itself. Often, political campaigns and computer industry advertising portray the Internet as a panacea for American education. In practice, this notion often results in initiatives that graft new technology uncomfortably onto traditional classrooms and curricula without a clear idea how it is to be used. LEARN NC's philosophy is that such grand claims for the power of technology insult educators by implying that they can be effectively replaced by computers or that teaching and learning are not fundamentally difficult and challenging work. Instead, LEARN NC sees the Internet, like all technology, as merely a tool—albeit a very powerful one—which, in the hands of skilled educators, can play an important role in improving K–12 education.

Teachers have responded quite positively to this view of technology and have been more willing to accept technology into their classrooms when it is offered in this way. Although the participants in LEARN NC's pilot program were already proficient with computers and the Internet, this has not been generally true of the several thousand educators who joined LEARN NC in its first year of operation. Many of these educators previously had lukewarm or negative attitudes toward using the Internet as a teaching tool but have been attracted to the educational resources LEARN NC provides. As a result, LEARN NC has proven an effective vehicle for technology training. This is particularly important for North Carolina teachers, who must complete inservice training in educational technology in order to renew their certification.

LEARN NC has also helped administrators who were unsure how to provide this training. Several school systems have awarded teachers a continuing education unit (CEU) for completing the required six hours of training in the use of the Web site and submitting a lesson plan for online publication. This model of technology training places the lesson plan—the design of educational content and the opportunity to share one's ideas with colleagues—at the center of the training. As a result, many teachers who only recently could not use a Web browser have now become authors of Web-based instructional resources.

Although LEARN NC's resources are all shared via the Internet, not all require the use of technology in the classroom. Instructional plans, for example, may be technology-dependent, technology-rich, or technology-free. Most of the plans require no computer use at all, but teach traditional topics in traditional but innovative ways: a high school chemistry experiment on making alloys, for example, or an eighth grade lesson in which students learn the principles of cartography by mapping their school campus. Technology-rich plans, the second largest group, use computers, the Internet, or other technology as learning tools, but can be adapted for a classroom with limited technology. An example is a fifth grade lesson on climate, in which students use the World Wide Web to research the climates of various cities in the Western Hemisphere; after assembling and analyzing this information, they videotape television news-style weather forecasts for the cities they researched. Although the Internet simplifies the research for this project, students could also use a library; similarly, although being on camera is certainly exciting to fifth-graders, students could perform their weather forecasts for their classmates without videotaping them.

> *It may be that students, like their teachers, learn most effectively to use technology when they are using it for a directed, practical purpose.*

Relatively few lesson plans are actually dependent on technology. A seventh grade unit on diet, for example, requires students to use a computer-generated spreadsheet to compile nutritional data and analyze their dietary needs. This project requires too many calculations to perform by hand; indeed, part of the lesson's goal is to show students the value of computer spreadsheets for large-scale mathematical analysis. But even in such technology-dependent plans, technology is nearly always a medium for learning rather than the primary end goal of the lesson. (The exceptions are plans addressing the computer area of the standard course of study, which do teach primarily computer skills.) It may be, however, that students, like their teachers, learn most effectively to use technology when they are using it for a directed, practical purpose, as a means rather than as an end in itself. If this is so, LEARN NC's classroom resources can be greatly effective in making students, as well as teachers, comfortable with information technology.

Ensuring teacher participation: training

Training, more than any other factor, has been vital to generating and maintaining teachers' interest in LEARN NC. This would be true of any technology-centered program, but is particularly important for LEARN NC. Whereas most education initiatives need only win over administrators to be implemented, LEARN NC is almost entirely teacher-created; although the architecture of its Web site can be maintained by its staff, educators design and submit the vast majority of its resources. If teachers were simply required by their school systems to submit lesson plans, the quality of LEARN NC's resources would be dubious, and even teachers who wanted to use them would find them of little use. Not only the success but the very existence of the program, therefore, depends on active and voluntary teacher participation, and teachers are much more willing to participate when training has made them comfortable with the technology. Training also ensures quality of content; although lesson plans are reviewed before being approved for publication, reviewers' jobs would be greatly complicated if teachers submitting plans were unfamiliar with the Web site or even with basic browser use.

The original model of training was a train-the-trainer model. At regional training sessions, LEARN NC staff trained two or more administrators from each school system, who became LEARN NC coordinators for their system and were responsible for registering and training teachers. This model assured an element of local control and flexibility to LEARN NC's network of educators. A statewide program with potentially 80,000 participants could quickly grow distant from the educators it served; local coordinators could serve as a first-line help desk and pass teachers' comments and suggestions along to LEARN NC's office. In addition, local control of teacher registration and training had the very practical effect of saving the program money. When LEARN NC launched its operational phase in September 1997 and began formal training of teachers, the program had only three full-time staff members and its total budget for the 1997–1998 academic year was approximately $1 million. These resources simply were not sufficient to train thousands of teachers or to deal with requests for help. Even as LEARN NC's staff has expanded greatly in its second year of operation, local coordinators continue to be vital to the success of the program.

As training progressed, however, this model of training had to be refined. The original plan for training called for school systems' representatives to attend a half-day information session, followed by a two-day training session. Although the combination of information and lengthy training session ensured that coordinators were thoroughly comfortable with the Web site, its resources, and the registration process, it proved too cumbersome and too time-consuming for busy administrators. By the end of 1997, educators across the state were familiar with LEARN NC, and the information sessions proved unnecessary. As word of the program spread, moreover, school systems began to complain that they had not been offered a fair chance to join. In response to this growing demand, the original first-year cap of 40 school systems (counties) was lifted in January 1998, and plans were made for all of the state's 117 public school systems to be brought on board by the end of the academic year. The two-day training session proved too cumbersome not only for attendees but also for LEARN NC's trainers, who were now trying to reach some 70 school systems in three months.

A second problem with the original training model arose from the need for qualified attendees. To give the project legitimacy and to ensure that teacher training could proceed smoothly, it was asked that attendees be assistant superintendents. Administrators at this level, however, were often too busy to attend a two-day training session or (as it turned out) even a one-day session. Although the educators who attended in their place were often highly skilled and motivated, some were drafted at the last minute by their superintendents and given little idea of what they would be doing or why. Not surprisingly, although many draftees were won over by the end of the training session, teacher training has proceeded poorly in districts whose coordinators did not volunteer for the position. As LEARN NC became better known throughout the state, this problem became rarer, and media and technology specialists volunteered to become coordinators and trainers.

Although many were won over by the end of the session, teacher training has proceeded poorly in districts whose coordinators did not volunteer.

In addition, although superintendents were told that the representatives they sent must already be proficient with computers and the Internet, some attendees lacked basic computer skills. The original two-day training format allowed these people to achieve the necessary proficiency in navigating LEARN NC's Web site, but such a wide range of abilities proved difficult or impossible to accommodate in a single eight-hour session. By the spring of 1998, LEARN NC's staff and trainers had adopted a more insistent tone in their requests that only technology-proficient educators be sent to the training sessions, but these calls were not always heeded. Although the vast majority of LEARN NC's coordinators have been both skilled and enthusiastic, these qualifications have proved difficult to enforce, and occasional problems have continued into the present.

A third, and more serious, problem with the train-the-trainer model of administration has been guaranteeing that teachers would, in fact, be trained at the local level. Interestingly, this model has been most successful in school systems of moderate size. Two or three coordinators—those who attended LEARN NC's training sessions—could train all the teachers in a small system. But coordinators in a district with several thousand teachers must train additional trainers, and the extra level of administration is perhaps more than they have time to handle. On the other hand, small systems often have few computers and Internet connections available to teachers, which makes hands-on training difficult. To remedy these problems, LEARN NC has hired 34 regional trainers who will assist coordinators with teacher training. The regional trainers will hold day-long Saturday training sessions at schools, community colleges, or universities during the 1998–1999 academic year, with a goal of reaching 10,000 additional teachers. The combination of additional trainers with well-equipped venues for training should help LEARN NC reach teachers considerably more quickly than would otherwise be possible.

Despite the need for adjustments, however, the use of local coordinators to train and register teachers has been extremely successful during LEARN NC's first year of operation. The school system coordinators have, as a group, surpassed anyone's expectations in training teachers, and the system of local control has allowed LEARN NC to reach many times more teachers than would have been possible from a small central office. The need for flexibility, constant evaluation, and adjustment should not detract from what has proven an inexpensive and effective means of providing professional development and linking teachers statewide.

Linking the state

Despite the warm reception LEARN NC has received in the state's public schools and the early success of the program in collecting both participants and resources, several important challenges have emerged in managing a statewide educational program. These challenges relate to LEARN NC's original charge to build connections among the state's many educators and educational organizations, and solutions to the problems are still evolving.

The connection between LEARN NC's online resources and the North Carolina Standard Course of Study, for example, has made LEARN NC an important link between teachers and policymakers, but it also poses technological problems. Interestingly, linking new resources to the standard course of study is a far more tractable problem than keeping old resources current. Each instructional plan on the Web site is indexed to several specific goals and objectives of the standard course of study; teachers can reference goals and objectives from lesson plans and vice-versa. When teachers submit plans, they specify the relevant goals and objectives to allow this referencing. But as the state updates the standard course of study at a rate of one curriculum area per year, these links will need to be updated as well. To date, no automated means of updating these links has been found. Someone, therefore, will have to manually check each of the thousands of lesson plans in LEARN NC's databases and revise the listed goals and objectives—up to a dozen per plan—to fit the new curriculum. This task could require hundreds of hours of work each year but is absolutely necessary to maintain LEARN NC's relevance to North Carolina classrooms.

A second challenge has been the creation of links among educational organizations. Since the beginning of 1998, LEARN NC has been working actively to build partnerships with these organizations. Some partner organizations, such as university departments, museums, and observatories, provide content for LEARN NC's Web site in the form of multimedia resources and instructional plans. Several dozen cutting-edge lesson plans written by educators working for the state's Department of Public Instruction now reside on LEARN NC's Web site, where they can be freely accessed by teachers. The North Carolina Teacher Academy, a statewide professional development program, now uses LEARN NC in its technology training and assigns teachers to produce technology-rich lesson plans for LEARN NC. Other partners require special services to meet the needs of particular groups of students. The ABC Technology Consortium, a group of schools in five North Carolina counties that use a curriculum rich in technology to reach low-performing students, has helped LEARN

NC to create a special database of instructional plans that include student activity components; these lesson plans will be available to all participating LEARN NC teachers, as well as to members of the ABC Consortium.

A third problem, a technological one, relates to the need for a least common denominator standard for LEARN NC's Web site. Even as schools acquire computers with faster processors, modems, and Internet connections, many teachers prefer to access LEARN NC from their homes through Internet service providers that can often be painfully slow. Simplicity of design and reliance on text rather than images for communication have minimized the time needed to access the LEARN NC Web site. Images and other memory-intensive files in lesson plans, for example, are stored separately so that teachers can scan the plans quickly and download only those files they wish to see. But the need to minimize connection time also limits the kind and quantity of information that can be transmitted. Multimedia resources with sound and video, for example, would be relatively inexpensive to produce with current technology and could be of great value for classroom instruction; but few schools could, as yet, access such resources reliably. The least-common-denominator standard also affects the organization of the Web site. Users must be able to move quickly from the LEARN NC homepage to specific resources via a minimum of links, because each intervening page may take up to half a minute to load. At the same time, each page should be easily navigable, with as few options as possible to avoid confusion. But as the number and variety of resources on the Web site grow, it becomes increasingly difficult to keep the Web site user-friendly and easily navigable yet still accessible from a 14K modem. It would be nice to say that this problem will be solved by faster and cheaper technology, but the desires of the technology-rich will always clash with the needs of the technology-poor. Balancing the two will be a continuing challenge and will require sensitivity to the needs of educators, as well as creative solutions.

The the desires of the technology-rich will always clash with the needs of the technology-poor.

Finally, there is the problem of continued training for participating teachers. The original plan required six hours of training per teacher per year to keep participants up-to-date on changes in the LEARN NC Web site. As the design and content of the Web site have evolved over the past year, the need for continued training has remained clear; only the most technology-savvy teachers are comfortable with unexpected changes, and there is a concern that too much or too rapid change will alienate some users. At the same time, however, teacher training requires a great investment of time and resources, both by LEARN NC and by local school systems, and annual training sessions will likely prove impractical. LEARN NC has attempted to get around this problem in various ways, none entirely satisfactory. The primary means of communication with teachers is through the school system coordinators, who receive monthly email notices about changes in Web site design, content, and policy. To what extent this information is passed on to participating teachers, however, is impossible to know. Announcements can also be made directly on the Web site's homepage, but if a teacher does not use LEARN NC in a particular week, he or she may miss an important announcement. Third, the LEARN NC User Manual, designed as a training aid and reference for teachers, is updated periodically and can be downloaded from the Web site, but so large a document is often impractical for Web transmission. Some districts, moreover, find the cost of photocopying the manual prohibitive, and LEARN NC cannot afford the cost of printing and distributing manuals to tens of thousands of teachers every four to six months as the Web site changes. As a result, while the manual is an effective training tool, it is not the best means of communication with teachers who have already been trained. Unlike a commercial software package, which may be updated at the will of the company that produces it but must be deliberately purchased by users, LEARN NC must be updated for all users at once. Although the Web site must continue to change, improve, and grow in order to remain useful and relevant in classrooms, the need for change poses problems that will have to be solved in the coming months and years.

Conclusion

The success of LEARN NC is a result of its constant focus on the teachers who use its services. Asking teachers to recommend, design, and create resources has guaranteed that they can use them, while careful training has guaranteed that they will use them. LEARN NC has also proven to be a successful means of integrating technology into the curriculum, in large part because its goal is to treat technology as a means of improving public education rather than as an end in itself. The program's focus on educators and educational content has made it, after only one year of operation, the state's largest independent educational program and the only statewide program of its kind in the country. As a result, LEARN NC is well on its way to meeting its original mission of linking educators and educational organizations statewide by facilitating collaboration, peer support, and exchange of resources.

As LEARN NC continues to grow, adding preservice and inservice professional development, as well as expanding and improving its curriculum resources, the limits of this free, voluntary, teacher-directed approach will be tested. Participation may reach a plateau after the first wave of technology-friendly teachers has been trained; local and state administrators may have to find money for improved user-end technology to make LEARN NC more widely accessible to teachers and students; and the system of locally-controlled, hands-on training may have to be further revised to accommodate the needs of 80,000 teachers across North Carolina. Nevertheless, LEARN NC's early success proves the value of a teacher-directed approach in improving public education and can serve as a model to other organizations.

References
The Public School Forum of North Carolina. 1995. *A State of Disconnectedness: An Examination of Mathematics and Science Instruction in the North Carolina Public Schools*. Raleigh, North Carolina: The Public School Forum of North Carolina.

Teaching Science to Diverse Learners:
A Professional Development Perspective

Paul Rowland
Center for Excellence In Education , Northern Arizona University
Donna Montgomery
College of Education, East Tennessee State University
Greg Prater
Center for Excellence in Education, Northern Arizona University
Sam Minner
Division of Education, Truman State University

Paul Rowland is an associate professor of curriculum and instruction at Northern Arizona University in Flagstaff, Arizona. He has special interests in the areas of environmental education and curriculum theory.

Donna Montgomery is an assistant professor of special education at East Tennessee State University in Johnson City, Tennessee. She has conducted various inservice and professional meetings on techniques to include students with disabilities in regular education classes.

Greg Prater is a professor of special education at Northern Arizona University in Flagstaff, Arizona. He is also the principal investigator of the Rural Special Education Project, a school-based teacher preparation program located in Kayenta, Arizona.

Sam Minner is the head of the division of education at Truman State University in Kirksville, Missouri. His interests include issues of hegemony in school settings and critical theory.

Jill wonders how she will get through the sixth grade. Her science teacher, Mr. Thomas, seems like a nice man, but she has many doubts about her ability to succeed in his class. She does not like science and rarely raises her hand or actively participates in classroom discussions. She prefers to sit in the back of the room and remain silent. Though she has been told by previous teachers that she has the ability to succeed in science and even had early dreams of becoming an engineer or a chemist, the pressures she feels in the class are simply too great. She hopes that Mr. Thomas will allow her to continue to sit in the rear of the room and remain quiet, perhaps not even participating.

Donald is also in Mr. Thomas' sixth grade science class. As a member of the Navajo tribe, Donald's traditional view of the world is sometimes very different from that taught by his teacher. The tension resulting from this dissonance is considerable. He has talked to his parents and his grandparents about some of the ideas discussed in the class and their thoughts have been helpful. However, sometimes he is confused during and after classroom discussions, yet he is hesitant to ask many questions. The fact that he is the only Navajo person in the class does not help. He has dreams of becoming a scientist and he knows that he will have to do well in science and mathematics if his dream is to become a reality.

By the end of the second grade, Richard very much disliked school. He doubted his ability to learn new things and worked hard to simply avoid being noticed by his teachers and his classmates.

Richard is not in Mr. Thomas' science class at present, but is scheduled to begin the class next week. Richard has had a difficult time in school. It was hard for him to learn to read and compute mathematics, making science even more difficult. By the end of the second grade, Richard very much disliked school. He doubted his ability to learn new things and worked hard to simply avoid being noticed by his teachers and his classmates. While in the third grade, he was referred for possible placement in a special education class and was ultimately placed in a program for children with learning disabilities. There, he received individual attention and experienced some degree of success. In recent years, he has been mainstreamed into some regular classes. This year, he will be in Mr. Thomas' regular science class. He has many doubts about his ability to succeed in that class. He is anxious about it and knows that is not a good way to start.

Jill, Donald, and Richard are not real students, but composites of students that teachers have known over the years. They represent the changing demography of learners in today's schools and the considerable challenges and opportunities faced by the educators who teach them. The fictional science teacher described above appears to have a challenging year ahead of him. Will he find a way to engage Jill in the class and increase her confidence? How can he help Donald reconcile the varying philosophical and scientific ideas presented in the school with the traditional ideas taught in the home? Can he meet Richard's individual needs, given the considerable and equally demanding needs of the other 23 children in his class? Though challenging, his task is hardly unique; indeed, his situation is similar to that of a large number of science teachers throughout the nation. The degree to which Mr. Thomas and thousands of teachers like him succeed in effectively teaching science to *all* students is a critical variable in their ultimate academic success, the strength of today's schools, and the overall health and vitality of the nation.

In this paper, the focus is on the many challenges science educators face when attempting to effectively teach diverse learners. Also included are implementation ideas for the classroom that will enable science educators to meet these challenges. The breadth and scope of the diversity among American students today is incredible, and there are many topics that could have been included. However, this paper will focus on three types of diversity: gender diversity, ethnic diversity, and diversity of cognitive ability.

Teaching Science to Students of Both Genders

The differential experiences and treatment of boys and girls in science classes have been well documented and widely discussed. Early research in this area found that girls enrolled in fewer science classes in school (Kahle & Lakes, 1983; National Science Board, 1989), reported less initial interest in science-related careers (Hewitt & Seymour, 1991), and demonstrated a much greater lack of confidence in their ability to succeed in science classes than their male counterparts (American Association of University Women, 1992). Adding to these problems were the many sex-stereotyped and cultural factors negatively affecting girls and their study of science. For example, some research suggested that the behavior and personal characteristics associated with many successful scientists (e.g., independence, high task commitment, a high level of self-confidence, being comfortable working in isolation, etc.) were traits most commonly associated with males. Girls and women often receive strong cultural messages that such traits are unfeminine and inappropriate. The result of these factors and others was a significant under-representation of women in science careers. In 1988, only about three percent of all engineers were women and only about six percent of all scientists were female. Though some evidence suggests that more girls are enrolling in science and technology classes and more are meeting with success in those courses ("Computer Classes," 1998; Martin, Sexton, Wagner, & Gerlovich, 1997), significant problems remain. More recent attention has been focused on methods and programs to encourage girls to enroll in science classes, actively participate in them, and seriously consider careers in science-related fields.

Teachers who believe that science is the domain of males undoubtedly provide that message powerfully and often to the students in their classes.

Suggestion and Recommendations for Science Teachers

The American Association of University Women (AAUW) was among the first professional groups to provide educators with recommendations regarding how to increase the level and quality of girls' participation in science. Their recommendations included: revision of teacher preparation programs to focus on the differential needs and treatment of girls and the establishment of new policies and/or support of existing policies ensuring that women are provided with equal opportunities to work in key educational positions, such as science department chairs and science curriculum coordinators. The AAUW also recommended that schools develop strong mentorship programs, pairing female students with successful women scientists, and work to ensure that the contributions of women scientists are included in science curricula.

Pollina (1995) reported on 10 successful techniques designed to encourage girls to enroll in science classes and more actively participate in science experiences. Her ideas ranged from a revision of the language science educators use (e.g., moving from masculine metaphors such as "tackling" problems) to more inclusive language (e.g., let's examine this problem from all sides before we draw any conclusions) to making sure that females are frequently provided with opportunities to be in control of technology.

Science educators need to be aware of the possible differential treatment of boys and girls in their classrooms.

Many researchers interested in gender issues and science highlight the importance of the expectations teachers have toward their students. Teachers who believe that science is the domain of males undoubtedly provide that message powerfully and often to the students in their classes. In most classrooms, teachers retain a very high degree of power in terms of which students are called on, the kinds of questions they are asked, the types of activities they are encouraged or asked to complete, and the type and degree of feedback provided to learners. If boys receive preferential treatment in these areas, it is possible that many girls become discouraged, come to doubt their ability to succeed, and assume passive roles in science classrooms. We doubt that any teacher would purposefully and consciously behave in such a sexist and unprofessional manner. However, studies have found that many teachers are simply *unaware* of the differential treatment they provide to the girls and the boys in their classes (Sadker & Sadker, 1994). Gender bias appears to be a highly pervasive, even insidious, classroom dynamic. Still, good teachers can take some steps to counteract classroom gender inequities. They may videotape themselves and specifically examine the tapes for examples of gender bias and inappropriate differential treatment. Alternatively, they may ask a trusted colleague to observe them and specifically look for gender bias and examples of sexist deportment.

Science educators need to be aware of the possible differential treatment of boys and girls in their classrooms. Unfortunately, many science teachers have not been well prepared for inclusive teaching in regards to gender issues. A significant number of preservice teacher preparation programs do not include such information. This should change, and informed teachers should assist those responsible for teacher induction to include gender-related topics in those programs. Teachers need to investigate mentoring programs for female students, pay close attention to gender equity issues in terms of who is appointed to important positions in schools, be aware of the language used during instructional activities, and attend to the degree boys and girls are given access to and control of technology. However, perhaps no issue is of greater significance than the attitudes of science teachers toward gender equity. It is strongly recommended that science educators read about gender-related issues and science, carefully think about these issues, and discuss them with trusted colleagues. Attitudinal changes often precede changes in behavior. The heightened awareness of gender issues such reflection may cause will do much to promote gender equity in many science teachers' classrooms.

Teaching Science to Ethnically Diverse Learners

The ethnic identification of a student, whether self-identification or identification by another, is a critical variable in how a student interacts with others. If most learning takes place as a result of interactions between a learner and others, then it seems equally clear that ethnic identity is a very important component in learning and teaching. Atwater (1994) suggested that U.S. schools have become and will continue to be more diverse as a result of numerous social factors, including desegregation, immigration, and differential birth rates among ethnic groups in our nation. The concerns and problems faced by ethnically diverse students are very real in America, and a host of reports indicate that these students are at a clear disadvantage when it comes to learning. Ethnic minority students drop out of school more frequently than white students. They are more likely to live in poverty, more likely to attend a violent and poorly-funded school, and more likely to be taught by inexperienced and/or poorly-prepared teachers (Delany-Barmann & Minner, 1997). Considerable evidence exists that ethnic minority students also have special problems in the area of science. A disproportionately low number of ethnic minorities enroll in science classes; a relatively low number experience success in those classes; and, consequently, a relatively low number of them are employed in scientific careers (Davidman & Davidman, 1996).

The ethnic identification of a student, whether self-identification or identification by another, is a critical variable in how a student interacts with others.

Some ethnic minority students hold worldviews inconsistent with traditional Western views of science, and this sometimes inhibits their ability to succeed in science classes and their teachers' ability to effectively instruct them. For example, some Native American students are not comfortable handling or even looking at some animal specimens due to cultural beliefs and traditions. A teacher's insensitivity to these student beliefs could be disastrous and lead to a host of instructional and learning problems.

Suggestions and Recommendations for Science Teachers

Because some members of ethnic groups evidence values and behaviors that influence performance in science classes and have different ideas about what constitutes scientific knowledge (indeed, what constitutes truth), what can and should science educators do to appropriately engage them and support their high achievement? An example targeting a specific ethnic group may be instructive.

In a review of the literature on science education for Native Americans, Rowland and Adkins (1995) suggested that good science teachers were concerned with two major issues: relying on good instructional practices in science generally and connecting science to native science, especially by recognizing the Native American connection to earth.

In examining the first theme, Rowland and Adkins noted that instructional practices, such as cooperative learning, active/experiential/hands-on activities, integrat-

Some ethnic minority students hold worldviews inconsistent with traditional Western views of science, and this sometimes inhibits their ability to succeed in science classes and their teachers' ability to effectively instruct them.

ing science with other subjects, and creating connections between science concepts and traditional ideas in the culture, appeared to promote engagement of students and their subsequent high levels of achievement in science classes. If these practices are familiar to most science educators, it should be no surprise. Good science teaching that recognizes the centrality, importance, and individuality of each student is at the heart of the past several decades of science education reform. The same variables are also at the heart of improving science education for ethnic minority students.

When teaching ethnic minority students, comparative discussions about science concepts (e.g., this is how scientists think the world works...how does this compare with other culturally-based explanations of the world and, when they differ, how may they be rectified?) may help foster tolerance of alternative ideas and epistemological philosophies. A good example of this approach to science instruction is the Native Science Connections Research Project (NSCRP), funded by the National Science Foundation. NSCRP Director Dr. W. Sakiestewa Gilbert, of Northern Arizona University, is developing a science curriculum merging traditional Western science with the cultural knowledge of several tribes. Other good sources of information regarding this approach to science instruction may be found in books by Bentley, Ingham, & Mo (1997); Carey (1993); and Petty (1994).

Teaching Science to Children With Disabilities

Prior to 1975, many children with disabilities were excluded from participation in regular classes, including science education classes. The prevailing sentiment among educators was that students with disabilities could not benefit from regular classroom experiences and, indeed, could require so much attention that nondisabled learners would suffer. In an early survey pertaining to the interest of science teachers in accepting disabled learners into their classes, Mabry and Olin (1972) found that only about 22 percent of junior high science teachers and about 16 percent of high school science teachers felt that disabled students should be permitted to enroll in regular science courses. Teachers cited safety concerns and a lack of training concerning preferred methods of teaching learners with disabilities as the most critical reasons supporting their position. Though elementary level teachers were much more willing to accept students with disabilities into their classes than their counterparts at the secondary level, even that group doubted the wisdom of devoting much time to teaching science concepts to that special population. A third grade teacher in the study commented: "I really don't see how handicapped children would use that information. They need lots of work in basic subjects, like reading and spelling, and everyday living skills, like cooking and self-care." The situation has not improved much in recent years. Norman, Caseau, & Stefanich (1998) surveyed several hundred science teachers and found that, as a group, they had little or no direct experience in teaching students with disabilities, were not aware of best practices associated with teaching that population, had a very limited awareness of the resources available to help them effectively teach these students, and held highly stereotypical views of what students with disabilities could and could not do. Fortunately, the teachers in this study also indicated that they were quite receptive to receiving additional training regarding disabled youngsters.

Educational practices for students with disabilities dramatically changed in 1975. Public Law 94-142 (the Education for All Handicapped Children Act) was passed by Congress and required that schools make more powerful efforts to educate students with disabilities. The law has sometimes been referred to as a Bill of Rights for children with disabilities, and a variety of advocacy groups, parent associations, and professional organizations have used the law to substantially increase the involvement of children with disabilities in regular classrooms, including science classes. Though the legislation is extremely complex and has been revised several times, two elements of the law are of particular importance to science educators: the least restrictive environment (LRE) component of the law and the requirement that all students with disabilities be provided with an individualized education plan (IEP). The LRE component of the law stipulates that students with disabilities should be placed in the least restrictive educational setting consistent with their needs and abilities. The absolutely least restrictive setting is defined in the law as the regular classroom. According to the federal law, if a student with disabilities can participate in a regular class and be successful there (including a regular science class), that is where he/she should be educated. All students with disabilities are also required to have an IEP, which stipulates the goals and objectives for that child each year. Regular classroom teachers, including science teachers, often play key roles in the development of IEPs.

Though a legal basis for including many youngsters with disabilities in science classes now exists, many problems remain. Students with disabilities receive little science instruction, special educators know little about science or how to teach it, and science teachers know little about youngsters with disabilities.

Suggestions and Recommendations for Science Teachers

There is a common saying among special educators that *all* teachers are special education teachers; indeed, science educators now teach and will continue to teach many students with disabilities. Students with disabilities are more frequently enrolling in introductory and advanced science classes in American schools; consequently, the teachers in those classes must endeavor to provide them with the highest quality instruction. Though there are many steps science educators could take to prepare themselves for this work, we have targeted three important ones: professional development activities, use of preferred instructional practices, and collaboration.

Though virtually all science teachers have students with disabilities in their classrooms, a very low number of them have had any preservice or inservice preparation for such work. As a result, many science teachers continue to hold highly stereotypical notions about learners with disabilities and preferred methods of teaching them. With approximately 12 percent of all students in American schools having a disability, it is imperative that science educators make some attempts to learn more about this population. Many opportunities exist for formal and informal professional development work in this area. Teachers may attend meetings of professional organizations devoted to the welfare of students with disabilities or individual sessions at science education meetings devoted to these students' specific learning modifications and accommodations.

Learners with disabilities are not a homogeneous group, and it is a mistake for teachers to assume that all of them will learn the same way.

The Council for Exceptional Children (CEC) is the largest professional organization concerned with individuals with disabilities, and many local, regional, national, and international CEC meetings are held each year. Likewise, the National Science Teacher's Association, the Association for the Education of Teachers in Science, the School Science and Mathematics Association, and others occasionally include a session concerning students with disabilities at their annual meetings. Another good resource is the ERIC Clearinghouse for Science, Mathematics, and Environmental Education at The Ohio State University, which maintains a very large database of information pertaining to science instruction, including resources pertaining to students with disabilities.

Learners with disabilities are not a homogeneous group, and it is a mistake for teachers to assume that all of them will learn the same way and will equally benefit from any specific instructional strategy. However, many researchers have found that students with disabilities often do quite well when the instruction is activity-oriented rather then heavily didactic or textbook-based. Fortunately, there is general agreement that such an approach is effective for nondisabled learners as well. In thinking about ways to engage students with disabilities in science, teachers should attempt to plan lessons involving a variety of hands-on activities, experiments, and demonstrations.

It is difficult for science teachers to keep up-to-date with the ever-increasing advances in scientific knowledge and remain up-to-date in the areas of human learning and pedagogy. To know one's subject is critical in science. For a teacher, it is also critical to effectively instruct learners in that content. To do both equally well seems impossible at times. One solution to this dilemma is for science and special educators to form close professional collaborations for the benefit of the students they both serve. For example, we have known science teachers who routinely meet with special educators to review the performance of disabled learners and to attempt to devise approaches and techniques to more powerfully engage them. Other science and special education teachers occasionally team teach classes. Special education teachers may recommend specific classroom modifications for students with disabilities, including such simple things as preferential seating, to much more complex approaches, such as collaborative learning activities and peer tutoring programs. The combined expertise and commitment of science and special education teachers will address many of the needs of students with disabilities in science education.

Conclusion

The national vision is to make American students first in the world in mathematics and science. However, this is hardly the only important goal of American public education. Americans have stated very forcefully that their schools must also address difficult issues, such as sexism, racism, equity, and social justice. It is often within schools that our national debates concerning these matters have been played out.

At one time, only male students were routinely permitted to enroll in some programs of study. Women were literally barred from enrolling in these programs or, more frequently, were very strongly discouraged from doing so. This has changed and continues to change in our schools. Not that many years ago, ethnic minority students were segregated and provided with second-class facilities, poorly-prepared teachers, and extremely low levels of funding. Once again, Americans forcefully said that schools should and could do better, and they have. A few decades ago, students with disabilities were routinely excluded from schools. Parents with sufficient resources enrolled their sons and daughters in private schools, but many parents lacking such resources simply kept their children at home. Today, all American children may attend public school.

Schools have become more inclusive. The demography of students in the nation's schools has changed and will continue to do so. There is no doubt of that. Many individuals have suggested that these matters are "problems" or "barriers" for teachers to overcome. Such language is often suggestive of the stereotypically negative attitudes some educators have held regarding diverse learners. Being a girl in a science class should not be a problem for her. Her achievement and success in science should be unrelated to her gender. Being black, Hispanic, Asian, or Native American should not be a barrier to learning science. Again, students' ethnic identification should be unrelated to their chances for success in science classrooms. The same goes for students with disabilities. The problems or barriers related to diverse learners are not student problems. They are almost always instructional (or teacher) issues, and good teachers take the time to carefully think about them. Mere reflection is not enough, however. Good teachers then take action. They plan and deliver lessons ensuring that girls are actively engaged in learning and are encouraged to achieve. They are attentive to the cultural backgrounds of their students and think of those differences not as problems to overcome, but as differences to enrich and diversify the classroom environment. They learn ways to include students with disabilities in lessons and attempt to capitalize on their learning strengths. When science teachers behave this way, changes in what they do instructionally and how they do it are required. However, though very important, these changes are much less critical than the internal changes good teachers experience when they acknowledge the key role they play in effectively teaching all learners in their classrooms and work hard to achieve that goal. When that occurs, all learners have an excellent chance of achieving high levels of scientific competence.

In the introduction of this paper, readers were introduced to Jill, Donald, and Richard. All three students were anxious about their ability to succeed in their science class. Though Jill's gender, Donald's ethnic identity, and Richard's disability should be considered when their teacher plans science lessons and activities, what must be done to support their learning is not all that much different than what the other students in the class also need. Good instructional practices and respect of the individual learner will do much to support their growth.

References

American Association of University Women (AAUW). 1992. *How schools shortchange girls: The AAUW Report.* New York: Marlow.

Atwater, M. 1994. Research on cultural diversity in the classroom. In *Handbook of research on science teaching and learning*, ed. D. L. Gabel. New York: MacMillan.

Bentley, M., D. Ingham, and X. Mo. 1997. *Science timelines: A multicultural resource.* San Francisco: Mimosa.

Carey, S. 1993. *Science for all cultures: A collection of articles from NSTA journals.* Arlington, VA: National Science Teachers Association.

Computer classes aren't just for boys anymore. 1998. *Education Week* 21(January 21):1.

Davidman, L., and P. Davidman. 1996. Teaching science with a multicultural perspective in secondary teacher education. In Proceedings *of the National Association for Multicultural Education*, ed., C. Grant, 210–223. San Francisco: Caddo Gap Press.

Delany-Barmann, G. and S. Minner. 1997. Development of a program of study to prepare teachers for diversity. *Equity and Excellence in Education* 30(2):78–85.

Hewitt, N., and E. Seymour. 1991. Factors contributing to the high attrition rates among science and engineering undergraduate majors. *Report to the Alfred P. Sloan Foundation*, April.

Kahle, J., and M. Lakes. 1983. The myth of equality in science classrooms. *Journal of Research in Science Teaching* 20:131–140.

Martin, R., C. Sexton, K. Wagner, and J. Gerlovich. 1997. *Teaching science for all children.* Needham Heights, MA: Allyn & Bacon

Mabry, J., and C. Olin. 1972. *Teaching science to handicapped children: The opinions of regular classroom teachers and parents.* Paper presented at the meeting of the Council for Exceptional Children, March. Louisville, KY.

National Science Board. 1989. *Indicators-1989: Women and minorities.* Arlington, VA: National Science Foundation.

Norman, K., D. Caseau, and G. Stefanich. 1998. Teaching students with disabilities in inclusive science classrooms: Survey results. *Science Education* 82:127–146.

Petty, C. A. 1994. *Waterdrum science: Science through American Indian arts and cultures.* Chino Valley, AZ: Larchmere.

Pollina, A. 1995. Gender balance: Lessons from girls in science and mathematics. *Educational Leadership* 53(1):30–33.

Rowland, P., and C. Adkins. 1995. Teacher education for teaching science to American Indian Students. *Journal of Navajo Education* 12(3):31–35.

Sadker, M., and D. Sadker. 1994. *Failing at fairness: How America's schools cheat girls*. New York: Scribner.

Leadership in a Multicultural World: Transforming Today's Science Classrooms

Deborah J. Tippins
University of Georgia
Sharon E. Nichols
East Carolina University

Deborah J. Tippins is a professor of science education at the University of Georgia. She has written numerous research articles and chapters concerning science teachers' beliefs, multicultural issues in science teaching, and the use of reflective tools in science teacher education. An innovative teacher and scholarly researcher, she has received several awards, including the NSTA Gustav Ohaus Award for Innovations in College Science Teaching and the NARST Early Career Award.

Sharon E. Nichols is an associate professor of science education at East Carolina University, where she serves as graduate coordinator. Her work has focused on sociocultural aspects of elementary science teaching, reflection in teacher education, and feminist critique of science education. Together with Dr. Tippins, she is involved in a longitudinal study of science teacher education professional development in collaboration with science education professors at West Visayas State University in the Philippines.

For the most part, the science teaching profession has and continues to be represented by individuals of middle-class, white backgrounds; more exclusively, males predominantly teach science at secondary and postsecondary levels. This poses problems as demographic changes indicate that groups historically referred to as minority populations are becoming more dominant in communities and schools across the country (Snyder & Wirt, 1998). Nationwide assessments conducted by the National Assessment of Educational Progress since 1969 have reported higher scores in science by white students as compared to black and Hispanic students (Campbell, Voelkl, & Donahue, 1998). In response, many states have pressed for teacher accountability policies as a way to ensure that teachers develop instructional practices that will improve the academic performance of all students. Accordingly, the need has grown for teachers to receive professional development and curricular guidelines that can help them effectively address multiculturalism and issues of equity in science classrooms.

Over the past decade, several major documents have been published in attempts to address the teaching of science and bridge science performance gaps across all ethnic and gender groups. Deeply embedded in these documents, however, are assumptions that undermine the conceptualization of equitable and multicultural science teaching practices. The publication of Project 2061's *Science for All Americans* (American Association for the Advancement of Science, 1989) was one such example. Although the intent of this document was to promote the notion that all students could and should participate in learning science, it failed to examine underlying reasons why females and minority students had not been participating and succeeding in sciences. Also, the document raised debates about science teaching as a representation of a universal way of knowing that denies the contributions of non-Western science. More recently, the *National Science Education Standards* (National Research Council, 1996), a document intended to provide guidelines for science education reform, has been criticized for its superficial treatment of multiculturalism and equity as an "invisible" discourse (Rodriguez, 1996). Rodriguez pointed out that whereas the *Standards* featured numerous pictures showing females and minorities as active participants in science activities, the written text did not articulate any theoretical or empirical bases for its recommendations for changing how diverse learners experience science in classrooms. Educators must take care to observe implicit assumptions reflected in curricular guidelines and reform documents that influence how teachers think about the goals and outcomes of science teaching practice.

Despite the intents of science education reform documents, such as the *Standards*, to enhance science teaching nationwide, teachers must make sense of science teaching practice with regard to their local schools and community contexts. Professional development leaders are challenged to ensure that teachers have opportunities for professional development that can provide them with the skills, resources, and knowledge necessary to help diverse learners gain literacy in science.

The purpose of this chapter is to assist professional development leaders as they work with teachers to address issues of multiculturalism and equity in science education. In the sections that follow, several themes highlight assumptions that are essential for leaders to consider as they envision directions to be taken in professional goals and activities. Vignettes containing fictional accounts created by the authors accompany each thematic section to illustrate what these assumptions might mean in practical terms. Given that teachers (including professional development leaders) may have backgrounds quite different from the students they teach, the themes and vignettes may serve an important role in bridging cultural and social gaps that might not otherwise be perceived by practitioners. Ultimately, the authors hope this chapter provides professional development leaders and teachers with tools to help them articulate and critique their own practices of multiculturalism and equity in science teaching and learning.

Assumptions of Multicultural Practice and Perspectives
Assumption #1: The Iceberg View of Culture
In recent years, the cultural dimensions of science and science teaching have come to occupy a much-enhanced position within the science education community. There

is an explicit recognition that science is a social practice that is fundamentally cultural in nature. However, there is little agreement about the very meaning of culture. Similarly, in today's science classrooms that are located in multicultural communities, diverse accounts of *what counts as science* prevail. It is not surprising that educators struggle with applying the concept of culture to science teaching; it is a concept that is dynamic and ever-changing in nature.

The *Iceberg View of Culture* is one model that is useful in developing multicultural perspectives of science teaching and learning. The model uses an analogy of an iceberg, where the tip of the berg, visible above the surface of the water, constitutes only a small portion of the total surface area. The larger portion of the iceberg remains hidden below the water's surface. When using this model to consider multicultural practice in science classrooms, it is the "tip of the iceberg" that usually receives emphasis. The tip of the iceberg, in this context, consists of items that reflect an appreciation of different cultures—items such as the fine arts, literature, famous scientists, games, traditions, scientific inventions, and the foods of particular groups of people. If science educators are to truly prepare students through science to live in an increasingly diverse world, they must move beyond the mere appreciation of culture. It is necessary to consider the many different aspects of culture below the tip of the iceberg that directly influence how children learn science (e.g., patterns of group decision making, approaches to problem solving, relationship to animals, ordering of time, conceptions of past and future, theories of disease, conceptions of beauty).

There is an explicit recognition that science is a social practice that is fundamentally cultural in nature.

The following vignette illustrates what happens when a third grade teacher is unaware of aspects of culture below the tip of the iceberg:

Mark Hamilton knew that the students in his third grade class were excited about the insect unit he had introduced earlier in the week. For the past two months, they had worked diligently, with the help of several parents and volunteers from the local nursery, to plan and build a school butterfly garden. Mark had used the newly completed garden as a centerpiece for developing lessons for the insect unit. He leaned back in his favorite chair, eager to read his students' first journal entries of their observations and reflections in the butterfly garden. As Mark read Sarah's journal entry, he became increasingly perplexed: "My teacher says butterflies are beautiful and we should be careful not to hurt them. He says that there are many kinds of butterflies that make the world beautiful. My dad says that Mr. Hamilton only thinks butterflies are beautiful because he buys his food at a grocery store—but me and my dad, we know better."

In this vignette, Mark Hamilton, a well-intentioned teacher, recognized the importance of connecting science to real-world experiences. He viewed the butterfly garden as an ideal opportunity for students to develop firsthand knowledge and appreciation of insects. What he failed to consider was the lived experiences of students that rest below the tip of the iceberg. For many years, Sarah's family has made a living from their small farm on the outskirts of the community. The vegetables from the garden and fruits from the orchard keep food on the table, but only when her family is successfully able to eliminate insect pests such as butterflies. A professional development leader in science must be aware of the need for teachers to look below the tip of the iceberg and help them recognize and utilize the unique cultural knowledge and experience that all students bring with them as they enter the science classroom.

Assumption #2: Pipeline Goals for Science Education
In 1987, the National Science Foundation (NSF) published a report featuring a "pipeline" chart that dramatically illustrated the decline of student interest in pursuing advanced science and engineering degrees. The study depicted a population of 4 million high school sophomores having a cohort of 750,000 students indicating an interest in studying science and engineering. As seniors, only 590,000 from this same group would declare a continued interest; following college, only 206,000 would graduate with baccalaureate degrees in science and engineering. From this group, the researchers estimated that only 61,000 would pursue graduate degrees, with a mere 9,700 ultimately completing doctorates in science and engineering fields. This picture pointed toward serious shortfalls in terms of having a work force prepared to deal with the increasing demands of a future technologically-reliant society. More critically, the pipeline dilemma raised questions about what factors contributed to this problem and whose interests were implicated in this picture.

Initially, the solution to the pipeline dilemma was a matter of removing barriers that prevented females and minorities from participating in science. Barriers were evident in academia, as women in sciences consistently held more positions as assistant professors while males dominated the ranks of associate and full professors (National Academy of Sciences, 1979). Thus, policy-making in the late 1970s focused on discrimination in salary differences and promotional practices among males and females in the workplace. Educational strategies were also seen as paramount to advancing the roles of women in science. Results of tests administered by the National Assessment of Educational Progress (1978) and the SAT in 1980 revealed wide gaps, respectively, in terms of male and female science achievement and performance in mathematics. In response, research focused on *differences* between males and females, followed by recommendations for instructional strategies designed to help females overcome their insufficiences. For example, research studies correlating visual spatial skill and mathematical performance implicated females as lacking in their visual spatial ability; thus, instruction focused on remediation to develop these skills (Maccoby & Jackline, 1974). Emphasis was placed on providing positive classroom learning environments, screening texts for sexist characteristics, and monitoring classroom interactions to ensure equitable participation among teachers and students (Kahle, 1985). The following vignette illustrates how science teaching might be seen in respect to the science pipeline scenario:

> *Linda, a middle school science teacher, was concerned about an apparent decline of interest and participation among girls in her science classes. Over the past eight years, she had observed how girls in sixth grade initially expressed intentions to pursue science-related careers, yet became disinterested by the time they reached eighth grade. One the one hand, Linda was aware of reports predicting a future crisis due to shortages of workers needed to support society's increasing reliance on technology. More importantly, Linda was concerned that girls may be shortchanged in reaching personal goals; she could relate, as she had aspired to become a chemical engineer but somehow found herself teaching science. Linda decided she would take action to help girls maintain their interest in science and receive support in their studies. In her own classroom, Linda made sure there were posters depicting both men and women who had made important contributions to science. As students engaged in lab activities, she was careful to ensure that males and females had active roles using equipment and equal opportunities to contribute in discussions; girls were not merely regulated to secretarial roles. Linda also met with the school curriculum task force and counselors to outline courses of study that would optimally prepare females to perform well in advanced science and mathematics courses. She organized a monthly luncheon, where female students could meet women working in science-related professions. Linda hoped these interventions would have a positive impact on the retainment of female students in science studies.*

While Linda's efforts might have some positive impact with respect to encouraging females to participate in science, little was done to examine conditions that have historically resulted in the disenfranchisement of women and minorities from science. As Kahle and Meece (1994) pointed out: "Changes in the pipeline [after high school] are due to emigration from, not immigration to, the [talent] pool (p. 543)." The pipeline perspective is problematic in that questions that might lead to the critique of how science is practiced are avoided. The problem is not simply *who* is or is not practicing science; science educators must go further to question *how* and *why* science has been conceptualized and *how* this influences societal perceptions of science as a way of knowing. It is essential for the professional development leader in science education to nurture the type of learning environment that provides teachers with the freedom to ask questions that lead to the critique of science.

Assumption #3: Border-Crossing into School Science
Issues of cultural diversity are becoming more apparent in schools as many communities are becoming more ethnically diverse. Groups historically referred to as mi-

nority populations are quickly becoming the majority in many urban areas across the United States (National Center for Educational Statistics, 1994). Consistently, gaps have appeared between the performance and participation of Anglo-European and Asian students and minority groups in mathematics and science (National Education Goals Panel, 1995; NSF, 1996). In response, science educators have promoted the notion of multicultural science education as a means of facilitating the education of culturally diverse learners. Interpretations of what constitutes a *multicultural* science education, however, have become topics of tremendous debate. For some, the issue of multicultural science is a philosophically-oriented dilemma in which Western science is contrasted with other world views. Central to this debate is concern regarding whose views legitimately count as science. Representing science from a

> *Representing science from a Western worldview privileges a type of science portrayed as a masculine, objectivist, and value-free domain of thought.*

Western worldview privileges a history of science emergent from ancient Greek and white European cultures—a type of science portrayed as a masculine, objectivist, and value-free domain of thought. Promoting Western science can be alienating to learners whose lives reflect non-Western orientations. Accordingly, multiculturalists call for a more holistic account, in which science has a pluralistic heritage that can collectively refer to other worldviews. Multicultural science, in this sense, would include "Traditional Ecological Knowledge (Snively & Corsiglia, 1998)," which reflects how groups such as the Yupiaq of southwestern Alaska, aborigines of Australia, or Maoris of New Zealand have constructed ecological knowledge over hundreds of years of observation. Some science educators have passionately reacted to such a proposal, concerned that science would lose its unique description as a domain of knowledge qualified by its "technical precision, control, creative genius, and explanatory power"; additionally, they have expressed concern that indigenous knowledges would be "absorbed by the dominant discourse of science (Cobern & Loving, 1998, p. 10)."

Another perspective is concerned with the representation of science as a sociocultural practice in educational settings. Science is a social enterprise; however, school science rarely acknowledges the social dimensions of scientific practice. Advocates argue that teaching the sociology of science would facilitate teaching a more authentic, inclusive science education (Cunningham & Helms, 1998). Emphasis on science as a human practice would debunk a mythical view of science as the domain of the intellectually privileged or as value-free. Teaching the sociological nature of scientific endeavors would emphasize roles, such as social networking, peer review, and skeptical critique in science classrooms. While this pedagogical approach might encourage a more authentic representation of science, it must also address the diverse social and cultural backgrounds of students. Schools are social institutions that present students with various types of *borders* that may generally challenge their participation, specifically in subcultures associated with learning in subject areas such as science. As students move between their everyday "life-world" cultures to the subculture of the science classroom, they encounter borders as they negotiate shifts in language, beliefs, and conventions of practice (Aikenhead, 1996). The crossing of borders may appear as insurmountable obstacles to students or may force students to abandon traditional knowledge from home to assume a new scientifically educated way of knowing. The following vignette illustrates an example of border crossing in a middle school science classroom:

> *Ms. Kelley, an eighth grade teacher, was frustrated because many of her students had, once again, not completed their homework assignment. In the past, she might have experienced this problem with a few students, but it seemed that lately struggles with student participation had increased in conjunction with the recent influx of truck-driving families from Mexico. Janelle, a typical example, had recently moved with her family to El Paso, as her father wanted to take advantage of the growing trucking business. A new trade agreement established between the United States and Mexico had created huge demands for individuals who could drive semitrucks across the border. Janelle's mother had a third grade education, and her father had completed only the eighth grade. Local authorities insisted that Janelle attend school; this had presented problems at home, where Janelle was expected to help raise her younger siblings. Janelle had shown an interest in the homework assignments, but found it difficult to work at home. She shared a bedroom with four younger sisters and brothers and had nowhere to concentrate. In addition, when Janelle had questions and could go no further with assignments, there was no one at home to provide help. Ms. Kelley had given her a phone number for a "Homework Hotline," but as Janelle did not have a phone at the trailer nor one nearby, she had thrown away the number. She wanted to share with Ms. Kelley her reasons for not doing the homework, but she did not want to embarrass her family in doing so. Janelle felt it would all be for naught because she anticipated that she would not be attending school much longer anyway.*

While philosophical debates challenge science educators to reflect on deeply embedded beliefs that shape how science is represented in the classroom, there is a more immediate need. Professional development leaders must challenge teachers to consider the impact of border-crossings experienced in science classrooms that are becoming more culturally diverse. They must make a commitment to supporting teachers as learners and recognize that teachers can engage in sophisticated classroom research that can shed light on these border-crossings. Ultimately, professional development leaders and teachers must support each other in their efforts to push their knowledge of students, subject matter, the community, and pedagogy to new levels.

Assumption #4: The Promise of Scientific Literacy: Science for All

The rhetoric of modern day reform is replete with references to scientific literacy and descriptions of how it might be developed or obtained. An impressive number of science education researchers, reformers, and practitioners have joined in echoing the call for scientific literacy in today's schools. One need not look beyond the first sentence of the NSES, which stated, "in a world filled with the products of scientific inquiry, scientific literacy has become a necessity for everyone (National Research Council, 1996)."

At the heart of this Standards-based vision of scientific literacy is a belief that everyone can do science and, by extension, science must be relevant to all learners.

At the heart of this *Standards*-based vision of scientific literacy is a belief that everyone can do science and, by extension, science must be relevant to all learners. The "science for all" metaphor has become a banner that affirms the belief that school science is essential to maintaining and participating in a democratic society. The belief that everyone can do science is not a new idea. Even early in the 1900s, educators embraced the principle of "all children can learn." Yet cultural norms of that time supported concepts of intelligence based on individual and group differences, initially giving rise to programs that tracked students on the basis of ability. Some would argue that little has changed since that time and that our current treatment of the all-children-can-learn principle offers little more than superficial "window dressing" for old beliefs and practices (Oakes, 1995).

Traditionally, a Eurocentric or androcentric perspective has permeated school science. Science curricula and textbooks privileged the perspectives and histories of some groups, while excluding the contributions of many culturally diverse individuals and groups. As our society has become increasingly more diverse, there has been an explicit recognition of the need to include and value the knowlegdes, ways of knowing, and contributions of less dominant cultures in school science. Under the slogan of "science for all," a plethora of new curricula and programs have risen to the forefront. In the attempt to customize science to fit a variety of learners, we now have "girl-friendly," "antiracist," and "indigenous science" curricula and programs, to name a few. In their roles as professional development leaders, teachers may find themselves charged with the task of helping school colleagues find ways to make science culturally affirming for all students. But the attempt to customize science to fit every type of learner may simply lead to the creation of new stereotypic boxes. There is a real danger that in the process of creating boxes for every type of learner, we simply reinforce traditional stereotypes, as the following vignette illustrates:

My name is Elena. For the past five years I have been teaching at an elementary school nestled within a lower middle-class suburb. I have always loved science. At an early age, I was interested in animals and had hopes of one day becoming a veterinarian. I soon learned, however, that this was not considered to be a suitable career for girls. Although I love teaching, I can't help but wonder if I became a teacher by default. Even today I sometimes wistfully reflect on those early dreams. As an experienced teacher, I know that fifth grade is a pivotal year in the transition from elementary to middle school, childhood to adolescence. I also believe that it is a critical time for nurturing students' awareness of career possibilities. I hope that all students will leave my class believing that they can choose to participate in a variety of science-related careers. In particular, I have made it a goal to include and develop a learning environment that invites girls to participate in science. This year I was confronted with a dilemma in my efforts to create a gender-inclusive science curriculum. I learned that even the best intentions sometimes have unexpected outcomes.

As part of a unit on oceanography, I created an interest center that I hoped would entice the students in my classroom to consider a variety of marine science careers. At the center, I included a poster of women scientists, a book and cassette entitled "You Can Be a Woman Marine Biologist," biographies of women oceanographers, and similar materials. I was pleased to see students demonstrating an interest in the center throughout the week. Thus, the conversation between two of my students, Rusty and Kip, came as a surprise. We had just finished an experiment involving the density of ocean water. Students were cleaning up when I overheard Rusty's conversation with Kip: "I hope we're almost finished with this. Who cares about studying the ocean anyway? It's only for girls—they're the only ones who get jobs working in the ocean."

In this vignette, Elena was searching for ways to communicate the message that "You too can do science." Her efforts to make science accessible for female students communicated a message of exclusion for the male students in her class. Teachers must take care to include culturally diverse role models, both male and female, in curricula and other aspects of the learning environment. Professional development leaders can assist teachers in identifying appropriate resources for creating a mutually inclusive environment for learning science.

Theoretical and Practical Implications for Professional Development Leaders in Science Education

Professional development leaders cannot assume that teachers recognize the need for multicultural emphasis in the practice of science. Even when the awareness level among school personnel is high, professional development leaders need to help teachers see how multicultural issues are explicitly related to the content area of science.

The role of a professional development leader is essential to enhancing or defeating the potential of a culturally inclusive science curriculum. The leader must be able to model and value alternate ways of thinking that are culturally relevant to science. The leader must actively promote the need to build upon students' prior knowledge, affirm student and community "funds of knowledge," and develop coherence between home and school cultures.

It is important for leaders to recognize that equitable science teaching practice is not something that can be mandated. Teachers, students, administrators, university faculty, and other community members must have opportunities to learn from one another in order to draw inspiration from and build the science curricula and ways of knowing around individual differences.

Teachers must take care to include culturally diverse role models, both male and female, in curricula and other aspects of the learning environment.

Professional development leaders must work to bring about structural changes in schooling that are essential to changes in the culture of teachers. In so doing, they must reconceptualize opportunities for teachers to have time to reflect on and reconstruct culturally relevant and equitable practice. A wide array of reflective tools can be used to help develop and apply multicultural understandings to science teaching and learning. In this final section, we describe several of the reflective tools that the professional development leader can use to invite teachers to reflect on their own assumptions about multicultural science education. The tools are intended to support teachers as they construct their own practices and purposes of critique. We hope these tools will encourage teachers to move beyond *Standards*-based visions of multicultural practice. (For additional information about these tools, see Nichols, Tippins, & Wieseman, 1997).

Classroom Cases

Case-based pedagogies in science education are a useful tool for promoting reflective inquiry, engaging teachers in learning from experiences, and strengthening decision making and problem solving skills. A classroom case is a narrative description of a realistic classroom dilemma that provides context for analyzing and solving problems. Open cases involve unresolved dilemmas, whereas closed cases involve dilemmas with a resolution. We encourage teachers to write open or closed cases based on their personal experience with dilemmas of multicultural practice. Cases can be shared with colleagues who construct solutions to open cases and react to closed cases.

Video Cases

Video cases are a relatively new format of classroom cases that can serve as a backdrop for examining multicultural practice in science classrooms. The recently released *Harvard-Smithsonian Video Case Studies in Science Education* (Harvard-Smithsonian Center for Astrophysics, 1997) highlights a number of science teaching and learning dilemmas with implications for multicultural practice.

Cultural Maps

Cultural maps are a type of critical autobiography that enables teachers to reflect on their own culture or life history. Teachers are asked to draw or map their own culture without the linear constraints of written or spoken autobiographies. As teachers analyze their maps, they reflect on how science and science learning is (or is apparently missing) in their culture and life histories. The cultural map is an important beginning point for many teachers in the critique of multicultural practice; for many, the map is their first consideration of the experiences, relationships, beliefs, and events comprising their own culture.

Language has the potential to facilitate teacher change by providing alternative metaphors and images with which to conceptualize multicultural practice.

Decision Making Grids

The decision making grid serves as a tool to highlight common interests, feelings, and purposes with respect to multicultural practice. As shared decision making gains momentum in our schools, the professional development leader in science may find this tool particularly useful for helping teachers describe the nature of decisions to be made and for involving them directly in the decision making process. The tool consists of a 5" x 4" grid of 20 blocks. Categories of choice listed at the top of each column include: strongly agree, agree, neutral, disagree, and strongly disagree. Teachers place their choices into columns on the grid, depending on how they rank items from highest to lowest within a category. For example, in the textbook adoption process, teachers may use the grid to consider the extent to which curricula are culturally relevant.

Metaphors

Language has the potential to facilitate teacher change by providing alternative metaphors and images with which to conceptualize multicultural practice. Metaphors are tools useful for: conceptualizing teacher roles (e.g., Briscoe, 1991; Tobin, Tippins, & Hook, 1994); framing events, problems, and solutions (e.g., Gozzi, 1991); or serving as a vehicle to facilitate teacher change in beliefs with respect to multicultural practice (e.g., Tobin, Kahle, & Fraser, 1990). A metaphor role-play is a useful way of initially introducing this tool. A set of index cards is prepared, each with a science teaching and learning metaphor relevant to multicultural practice. Examples of metaphors that may be used include: teacher as gardener, teacher as interior designer, teacher as skydiver, teacher as soldier, teacher as nurse, teacher as sports trainer, and many others. Working in teams of two, teachers discuss the significance of their metaphor with respect to multicultural science practice. As each team pantomimes their metaphor, class discussion may center on understanding the nature of science, teaching, and learning through experiences that are grounded in personal and cultural beliefs.

Conclusion

In summary, as professional development leaders work with teachers to transform classroom science teaching and learning practices, it is important for them to be aware of assumptions underlying various views of multiculturalism and equity. Educators have framed issues associated with teaching diverse learners from a variety of perspectives. Models such as the *Iceberg View of Culture*, for example, while intended to celebrate cultural diversity may unintentionally encourage teachers to stereotype students and their families. The rhetoric of reform documents, such as the slogan "science for all," overlook conditions which have historically dissuaded some groups from participation in science learning and science or science-related careers. Recently, science educators have begun to frame diversity from the assumption that students perceive and negotiate complex social borders between home and school. Seeing multiculturalism as a complex negotiation of borders calls for science educators and students to explore each other's experiences and assumptions that shape their participation or nonparticipation in science classrooms.

Changing classroom teaching practices to involve all students in science learning can not be simply mandated through policy. Teachers and students need opportunities to share with each other their expectations and goals for participation in school science. There are many ways that professional development leaders can model teacher-student communication and help teachers analyze their views of science teaching and learning. A number of tools suggested in this chapter can be used to support this process, including: cases, cultural maps, decision making grids, and metaphors. Ultimately, the transformation of classrooms to equitably involve teachers and students in science learning must be a shared commitment to learn science.

References

Aikenhead, G. S. 1996. Science education: Border crossing into the subculture of science. *Studies in Science Education* 27:1–52.

American Association for the Advancement of Science (AAAS). 1989. *Science for all Americans.* Washington, DC: Author.

Briscoe, C. 1991. The dynamic interactions among beliefs, roles, metaphors, and teaching practices: A case study of teacher change. *Science Education* 75:186–199.

Campbell, J., K. Voelkl, and P. Donahue. 1998. Report in brief: NAEP 1996 trends in academic progress (NCES 97-986). Washington, DC: National Council for Educational Statistics.

Cobern, W. W., and C. C. Loving. 1998. Defining "science" in a multicultural world: Implications for science education. Paper presented at the annual meeting of the National Association for Research in Science Teaching, April. San Diego, CA.

Cunningham, C. M., and J. V. Helms. 1998. Sociology of science as a means to a more authentic, inclusive science education. *Journal of Research in Science Education* 35(5):483–500.

Gozzi, R., Jr. 1991. The metaphor of the mind as computer: Some considerations for teachers. Paper presented at the meeting of the Conference on College Composition and Communication, March. Boston, MA.

Harvard-Smithsonian Center for Astrophysics. 1997. *Harvard-Smithsonian video case studies in science education*. Burlington, VT: Harvard-Smithsonian Center for Astrophysics.

Kahle, J. B. 1985. Retention of girls in science: Case studies of secondary teachers. In *Women in science: A report from the field*, ed. J. B. Kahle, 49–76. Philadelphia: Falmer Press.

Kahle, J. B., and J. Meece. 1994. Research on gender issues in the classroom. In *Handbook of research on science teaching and learning*, ed. D. Gabel, 542–557. New York: Macmillan.

Maccoby, E. M., and C. N. Jackline. 1974. *The psychology of sex differences*. Stanford, CA: Stanford University Press.

National Academy of Sciences. 1979. *Climbing the academic Ladder: Doctoral women scientists in academe*. Washington, DC: National Academy of Sciences.

National Assessment of Educational Progress. 1978. *Science achievement in the schools*. Science Report No. 08-S-01. Denver, CO: Education Commission of the States.

National Center for Educational Statistics. 1994. *Digest of educational statistics*. Washington, DC: U.S. Department of Health, Education and Welfare.

National Education Goals Panel 1995. *The national education goals report: Building a nation of learners*. Washington, DC: National Education Goals Panel.

National Research Council. 1996. *National science education standards*. Washington, DC: National Academy Press.

National Science Foundation. 1987. *The science and engineering pipeline*. PRA Report, 67-2. Washington, DC: NSF.

———. 1996. *Indicators of science and mathematics education 1995*. Arlington: NSF.

Nichols, S., D. Tippins, and K. Wieseman. 1997. A toolkit for developing critically reflective science teachers. *Journal of Science Teacher Education* 8(2):77–106.

Oakes, J. 1995. Normative, technical and political dimensions of creating new educational communities. In *Creating new educational communities: Ninety-fourth yearbook of the national society for the study of education*, ed. J. Oakes & K. Quartz, 1–15. Chicago: University of Chicago Press.

Rodriguez, A. 1996. The dangerous discourse of invisibility: A critique of the National Research Council's national science education standards. *Journal of Research in Science Teaching* 34(1):19–38.

Snyder, T., and J. Wirt. 1998. *The condition of education 1998* (NCES 98-013). Washington, DC: National Center for Educational Statistics.

Snively, G. and J. Corsiglia. 1998. *Rediscovering Indigenous Science: Implications for Science Education*. Paper presented at the Annual Meeting of the National Association for Research in Science Teaching.

Tobin, K., J. Kahle, and B. Fraser. 1990. *Windows into science classrooms: Problems associated with high level cognitive learning in science*. London, England: Falmer Press.

Tobin, K., D. Tippins, and L. Hook. 1994. Referents for changing a science curriculum: A case study of one teacher's change in beliefs. *Science and Education* 3(3):245–264.

Knowing Others and Other Ways of Knowing: Cultural Issues in the Teaching of Science

M. Elaine Davis
Crow Canyon Archaeological Center, Cortez, Colorado

M. Elaine Davis is director of education at Crow Canyon Archaeological Center in Cortez, Colorado, where she develops and supervises programs in archaeological research for precollege students and other members of the lay public. Previously, Dr. Davis was an education specialist with the Center for Mathematics Education at the University of North Carolina at Chapel Hill. She worked in public education for 14 years, serving as a classroom teacher and as a gifted education specialist in the Chapel Hill-Carrboro City Schools. Davis' research focuses on the way learners construct their knowledge of the human past.

Learning does not come from one source, nor is it best learned from be-hind a desk, hands folded, feet flat on the floor, and eyes front. Before the child entered school, he learned language actively, by interacting with his environment. He used language purposefully to get things done. As educators, we must merge our traditional sense of schooling with the real world. What we do in school must not insult the child's past but must build on his past and encourage future learning (Boloz, 1985).

One of the greatest challenges faced in the classroom, perhaps in life, is knowing and appreciating others. "Others" are defined by their relationship to the dominant group, they are not mainstream; they come from marginalized communities—they are the people not like "us." The term, "other" is obviously a subjective one; it places self at the center and identifies those unlike self as the "other." As teachers, the students we face daily are, to varying degrees, the other. We are connected to them and separated from them by gender, age, class, religion, race, ethnicity, values, and countless other criteria that can be used to distinguish one group of people from another. It is probably safe to assume that the greater the diversity within a community of learners, the more challenging it becomes to meet their needs instructionally. This is particularly true in science, which is not just a body of knowledge but a way of knowing. "Science distinguishes itself from other ways of knowing and from other bodies of knowledge through the use of empirical standards, logical arguments, and skepticism, as scientists strive for the best possible explanations about the natural world (National Research Council

[NRC], 1996, p. 201).” A way of knowing and understanding the world is the foundation upon which a group builds cultural identity: Sometimes, that way of knowing runs

A way of knowing and understanding the world is the foundation upon which a group builds cultural identity.

counter to the process of scientific inquiry. In other cases, the
methods of science may parallel traditional approaches to explanation, but the content itself may offend or contradict sa-
cred knowledge. In still other instances, it is not the logic of
science nor its content that presents difficulties, but an im-
bedded image of who scientists are and who can be a scientist.

Given such constraints, how do educators develop a scientifically literate nation and, as Boloz calls for (1985), not
insult the child's past but instead build upon it and encourage future learning? This chapter addresses some of the fundamental issues that we, as professional educators, must concern ourselves with in
order to teach science in a way that is both academically sound and socially responsible.

Defining Culture

In order to grasp the complexities of multicultural education, it is first necessary to
have an understanding of the concept of culture. A common and simple definition for
culture typically reads something like *the totality of ideas, beliefs, values, and knowledge held by a group of individuals who share a common history*. A more detailed
version might go on to say that artifacts and patterns of behavior are reflections of
culture. Anthropologists have emphasized the communicative nature of culture and
its function as an adaptive mechanism.

An understanding of culture at the conceptual level is essential for education and
other social disciplines. However, at the level of application and practice, culture can
be a problematic construct. Within anthropology, debates exist over whether cultures
are discrete entities with recognizable borders or whether they exist in a layered and
overlapping fashion with variations, such as subcultures, countercultures, and alternative cultures. For example, in communities that have remained intact for generations,
there are generally those factions that adhere to the more traditional ways of their
ancestors and those who believe that the prosperity of the people depends on their
ability to integrate more modern approaches to living. Does this merging of new and
old practices result in a new culture or in a variation of the old? Are the traditionalists
and the moderns still members of the same cultural group?

Elementary and secondary educators frequently use culture as an organizational
scheme for the study of human groups. Unfortunately, rather than increase student
understanding of human diversity, this can be a reductive approach that results in a
simplistic and impoverished understanding of a group of people or, worse, the creation and perpetuation of stereotypical images. For example, Native American peoples
have, in some classrooms, become a homogenized, singular group characterized by

corn, beans, and squash or tepees and moccasins. In many cases, cultural studies at the K–12 level is little more than an ethnic food-fair, and students come to think of people in terms of the objects that are part of their lifestyle rather than the totality of their ideas, beliefs, knowledge, and shared history.

Given the ambiguity of meaning and the difficulty in applying the concept of culture in classroom studies, how can educators work toward a culturally sensitive or multicultural pedagogy? Atwater, Crockett, and Kilpatrick stated that: "A successful multicultural science curriculum includes both the integration of culture and the use of various teaching strategies to accommodate different ways of knowing (1996, p. 171)." The last portion of this statement is particularly important; in order to teach science in an equitable way, it is essential to accommodate different ways of knowing. Less clear is how culture can be integrated into the teaching of science when culture is such a complex concept.

In many cases, cultural studies at the K–12 level is little more than an ethnic food-fair— students come to think of people in terms of the objects that are part of their lifestyle rather than the totality of their ideas, beliefs, knowledge, and shared history.

Differences That Make a Difference

Difference is used in some educational circles to avoid the difficulties of interpreting and applying the concept of culture. However, the term difference also presents problems at the level of application and practice because it is a term that calls for comparisons. The inclination is to place the dominant group at center and anyone else, in comparison, is different. The term *diversity*, which simply indicates variation and does not departmentalize groups in the way that the term *culture* does, is perhaps more useful for the development of inclusive science programs. Diversity is, after all, an important concept in science and a critical one to understand as it relates to systems, whether they be biological, economic, or social.

Student populations in American schools are becoming increasingly diverse; however, not all differences carry the same weight in terms of educational equity, particularly for equal opportunities in science. Within science education, *the differences that make a difference* tend to be constructed around race, class, gender, worldview, and local knowledge. Because these factors tend to exist in various combinations, rather than as easily observed isolates, it may be impossible to say that inequity is more closely associated with one than another. In Kozol's *Savage Inequalities,* the convoluted nature of inequity was brought forth in the words of a high school student in East St. Louis:

> *"If you don't live up there in the hills, or further back, you can't attend their schools. That, at least, is what they told my mother."*
> *"Is that a matter of race?" I ask. "Or money?"*

"Well," she says, choosing her words with care, "the two things, race and money, go so close together—what's the difference (1991, p. 31)?"

Regardless of the reasons for inequality in education, practices of exclusion occur at many different levels; some of these are overt, whereas others are embedded practices that may have reached a taken-for-granted status. This latter group is far more difficult to address because the problem of exclusion goes unrecognized. Worldview and informal or local knowledge are powerful factors that come to play in an individual's ability to enter into the world of science. These often go unnoticed because it is very difficult for many educators to recognize their own worldview or to remain conscious of the fact that science is a way of knowing rather than ultimate truth. Because of this blind spot, teachers may view the traditional or religious knowledge that some students bring to school with them as superstitious or ignorant if it conflicts with scientific explanation.

Science and Power: Answering the "So What?" Question

Does everyone need science? How does the study of science or the exclusion from it make a difference in an individual's life? The *National Science Education Standards* were based on the conviction that, "…all students deserve and must have the opportunity to become scientifically literate (NRC, 1996, p. 1)." Science educators who are truly committed to an inclusive science program must understand the implications of leaving students or groups of students out of science instruction. According to the *Standards*, there are four primary reasons that all students need to become scientifically literate: (a) an understanding of science offers personal fulfillment, (b) scientific information and ways of thinking allow people to make better decisions regarding the social and physical world in which they live, (c) scientific knowledge and skills will allow students to hold meaningful and productive jobs, and (d) a scientifically literate nation will allow the country to remain globally competitive. Some of these reasons focus on the importance of science at the societal level, whereas others more directly address the needs and welfare of the individual. With each statement of what science education can provide is also an implied message regarding the consequences that may come about if individuals or groups of people are denied access to quality science instruction.

Science is a way of knowing, but not all kinds of knowledge are equally valued within a society.

The implied messages conveyed through each of these statements do not, however, carry equal weight nor are they equally logical. For example, although scientific understanding can provide greater personal fulfillment, probably no one would argue that it is impossible to lead a fulfilling life without a strong scientific foundation. The implications carried in some of the other implied messages are more serious. The ability to make informed judgments about the natural world or to evaluate the kinds of health care available are critical to the quality of life in the present and perhaps for generations to come. When this type of knowledge is not available to individuals or to whole communities, they are at risk of being taken advantage of by unethical land developers, powerful corporations, and even by government agencies. They do not have the knowledge or skills to think critically about important issues or to act as advocates on their own behalf.

Science is a way of knowing, but not all kinds of knowledge are equally valued within a society. Within Western culture, the thinking and technical skills learned through science instruction are those that have become most valued in the workplace. Scientific knowledge may be viewed as a kind of capital, not just in the monetary sense that it allows access to higher paying professions but because it also allows greater access to power. It is undeniable that the groups who are underrepresented in science and mathematics classes are the same groups who are underrepresented in positions of power and authority. Returning to the "So what?" question, not everyone will become a scientist and not everyone will engage in scientific discourse at the same level, but educators must understand the link between scientific literacy and social/economic empowerment.

Toward an Inclusive Science: Recognizing Appropriate Practice

Goals and objectives like those identified in the *National Science Education Standards* must necessarily precede changes in professional practice and behavior, but they in no way guarantee that changes will come to pass, nor do they present a pathway to those changes. What the *Standards* do provide is a change in tone and emphasis for professional development. Of the new standards for professional development, the call to integrate theory and practice in school settings and a change in teacher identity from technician to intellectual and reflective practitioner are the most important to developing inclusive science programs.

It is undeniable that the groups who are underrepresented in science and mathematics classes are the same groups who are underrepresented in positions of power and authority.

Some educators may find it difficult to read these new standards for professional practice without a degree of skepticism. There should be no doubt that these attitudes are critical to "new science" instruction but there are changes—and there are changes. Changes in fundamental attitudes and deeply embedded, habituated behaviors are the most difficult to achieve. Research in the area of prejudice reduction and diversity education indicates that a brief course or workshop raises an individual's level of awareness regarding issues of culture but that these interventions have not proven to be very effective in terms of behavioral change (Brooks, Gersh, Currey, & Davis, 1996). How, then, does one provide the kind of professional development that makes a difference? To address this, it is helpful to examine situations where teachers already exhibit appropriate practice. The following cases provide a window for observing inclusive science in practice.

Teaching Science in a Hopi Classroom

In his book, *Enduring Seeds,* Gary Nabhan, ethnobotanist and cofounder of Native Seeds/SEARCH, tells a story of being invited to a Hopi community school to teach the students about plants. He stresses the fact that he and his colleagues were not expected to teach about plants in the same way that the elders would but that they had been encouraged to "link what was already familiar to that formidable phantom named *science* (1989, p. 67)." To make the connection between the familiar and science, they chose to teach the students about adaptations to wind, sand, and drought using the plants that the children knew best, Hopi crops. For the first lesson, they came prepared with teaching tools: sand, seeds, posters, and other equipment for conducting experiments. The posters showed diagrams of corn and bean seedlings and their different parts. As they were assembling these materials for instruction, a Hopi teacher walked past the classroom and asked, "What are you planning to do with that drawing of bean sprouts?" Nabhan explained that they would teach the kids about seedling shapes and parts. She then asked, "How about that box full of sand?" Nabhan's colleague informed the teacher that they would have students measure the growth of corn roots and shoots as they expanded in the sand. Considering his reply, the teacher responded;

> *Hmmm...The box and growing plants in the sand seem just fine. But the bean sprouts on the poster...Unh-uh. See, the children here are presented with bean sprouts, but at a special time. The Katsina dancers hand them bundles of sprouts early one morning, as part of the nine-day Bean Dance sequence. The children take these gifts back to their families, and a traditional food is fixed from them. That's when Hopi kids are supposed to see sprouts out in the open. I don't know if it can be anytime at all. It's because they are part of something sacred, we have our own way of teaching the children about them. Would there be any way that you could teach the students what you want to without showing them the bean sprout poster?* (Nabhan, 1989, p. 68.)

Nabhan and his colleagues agreed that they could use the poster of the corn to relate the seeds to the seedlings and the seedlings to whole plants. They also decided that they could talk about the differences between corn and beans, which was apparent even at the seed stage. The teacher approved of this modification, and the students were able to learn about plant growth. They worked with Nabhan and the others to compare the seeds of different varieties of Hopi corn and beans. They processed and ate them, learned about adaptations, compared the growth rate for two types of corn, and had an opportunity to participate in the planting of some rare native crops. Nabhan summed up this experience saying,

> *The children had their hands and minds working with crops that some of them might cultivate, cook, and consume for much of their lives. As three outsiders,*

we had learned how to place science in a particular cultural context, a lesson more valuable than the display of one bean diagram (1989, p. 68).

Teaching Science at Crow Canyon Archaeological Center

Crow Canyon Archaeological Center is a not-for-profit research and education facility located in southwestern Colorado. The area, part of a larger region known as the Four Corners, is rich with the material remains of past cultures. The artifacts and ancient architecture that riddle this arid land are the focus of researchers at the Center, who attempt to reconstruct the story of the ancestral Pueblo people who occupied the area until around 1300 A.D.

In addition to archaeological research, the Center conducts education programs with members of the lay public, the youngest being fourth graders and the oldest being senior citizens. The Center is unique in that participants are taught through involvement in the research process. For adults and older children, this experience includes excavation on an archaeological site and laboratory analysis. Educators at the Center introduce younger students to the archaeological process through site visits, inquiry lessons with artifacts, and simulated research components. Approximately 3,500 students come to Crow Canyon's campus each year to participate in the science of archaeology; roughly 75 percent of them are visiting the Center with a school group.

Although schools from as far away as Pennsylvania and Florida travel to Crow Canyon, a large percentage of them are also local, coming from Colorado and surrounding states. Because of these varied backgrounds, Crow Canyon's student population is diversified in a number of ways, including age, race, and ethnicity, meaning that the educators have many variables to consider in designing lessons and programs. One of these challenges has been adapting activities for the more than 300 Navajo sixth graders who come to the Center each spring from eastern Arizona.

Teaching the science of archaeology to these students presents several problems. Historically speaking, the relationship between archaeologists and Native Americans has not been a warm one. Although much of the archaeological research conducted in America is concerned with the Native American past, the profession has not, until more recently, considered the perspectives of Native peoples nor has it conducted research in consultation with them.

I watched archaeologists discount most of what they heard from Indians as political rhetoric, repeatedly reassuring themselves that if they could just educate the Indians, then, after an epiphany, the Indians would leave them alone to continue sciencing. The Native Americans, for their part, simply could not believe that scientific curiosity was sufficient justification for the desecration of the graves of their ancestors. Nor could they believe that anyone, let alone archaeologists— who after all, traced their intellectual lineage to the founders of American anthropology—could be so insensitive to the beliefs of Native Americans. Finally, they could not believe that archaeologists as anthropologists, practitioners of the "most human" of the social sciences, could so thoroughly dehumanize and objectify the people they studied (Downer, 1997, p. 23).

Although the relationship between archaeologists and Native peoples is changing, and part of Crow Canyon's mission is to conduct research in partnership with Native Americans, these sixth graders must find it a bit awkward to be studying at an archaeological center. They have doubtlessly heard from older members of their family that "archaeologists dig up pots" and that "they rob the graves of our ancestors." The situation is additionally problematic for these youngsters because they are Navajo, and for Navajos who live in a more traditional way, those objects that belonged to people now dead are considered taboo.

Educators at Crow Canyon had to assume that the parents were open to finding out more about archaeology—or at least not so opposed as to forbid any consideration of it—or they would not be allowing their children to participate in the program. Addressing the issue of the Navajo students coming into contact with artifacts was more complex. Realistically speaking, it would be difficult to conduct archaeological research without coming face to face with the artifacts of past cultures. However, the primary objective for this group was not to have them excavate or conduct actual lab analysis, but to teach the process and thinking skills archaeologists use to learn about the past. To accomplish this, the staff replaced all cultural materials from the teaching kits and simulations with replicated artifacts. In addition, they covered display cases that contained artifacts and assured teachers that the students would not visit any archaeological sites. When the Navajo students asked if the pottery shards or projectile points were "real," the educators were able to say, "No, they are modern; we made them here at Crow Canyon." Removing the kinds of barriers that would have prevented these students from engaging in archaeology permitted them to learn more about this particular area of scientific research and did so in a way that did not insult their own past.

Having Wonderful Ideas: The Science Lab Model

According to Duckworth (1987), the essence of intellectual development is the ability to have wonderful ideas or to set tasks for one's self. Some students come to school with a greater facility for doing this than others; innate ability and social influences are involved to some degree, but the stimulation a child receives from her or his environment also plays a critical role in the development of curious behavior.

Deanna Tebockhorst has been science coordinator at Frank Porter Graham Elementary in Chapel Hill, North Carolina, for 15 years. In that period of time, she has developed a school science lab that has grown from a few shelves filled with equipment to a large interactive room filled with an ever-changing array of rabbits, reptiles, guinea pigs, birds, bones, shells, computers, leaves, animal footprints, etc. As coordinator, Tebockhorst has used this room and its resources to instruct whole classes, individual students, teachers, parents, and anyone else who walks in and says, "Wow!" It is a place designed to inspire "the having of wonderful ideas." Tebockhorst sometimes bases lessons on curriculum needs for a particular class, but they also grow from the questions generated by students while "investigating stuff" in the lab. It would be a fallacy to say that the environment does all the teaching; Tebockhorst is highly skilled at identifying curious behavior in students and in guiding them through systematic investigation. Students beg their parents and "Ms. T." (as Tebockhorst is fondly referred to) for the opportunity to stay after school and visit the science lab. These students are not just from the middle-class, academic neighborhoods surrounding Chapel Hill, but also from nearby trailer courts, as well as some of the more elite neighborhoods. They are ESL students, gifted students, learning disabled students; they are Anglo, Hispanic, African American, male, and female—they are as diverse as the room itself. Through this science lab, Tebockhorst has helped transform countless students, teachers, parents, and even administrators into scientifically literate individuals, and she has helped others replicate the model throughout the country.

Common Themes

Several important points can be drawn from an examination of these three cases. First, the instructors in each case were open to a consideration of alternative paradigms. In the first two, at the Hopi school and at Crow Canyon, the educators acted on suggestions based on different paradigms for perceiving the world and constructing knowledge about it, and they found ways to modify lessons accordingly. It is also important to note that the ways in which they altered their plans did not require sacrificing important learning objectives. In the third case, Tebockhorst thought outside the paradigm of traditional elementary school science; she relied little on textbooks and, instead, privileged authentic inquiry.

The second point of intersection is that each of the instructors in these cases demonstrated respect for the various communities their students came from through collaboration with members of those communities. In the first two cases, the collaboration was with teachers; the third was with various community members, including teachers, parents, and students.

A third commonality among these cases was that all recognized the importance of inquiry and of structuring science classes in a way that will stimulate inquiry. Nabhan and his colleagues, as well as the teachers at Crow Canyon, did not change the kind of thinking that their students would be engaged in; they simply changed some of the materials they taught with in order to honor traditional beliefs held by families in the community. Tebockhorst created a diverse environment that promoted interaction and inquisitive thought, a place where anyone could walk in and find something they wanted to know more about.

Knowing and Teaching Others: A Complex Act

An analysis of these three cases provides insight into what inclusive science teaching looks like and the kinds of decisions inclusive science teachers make, but the challenge of moving teachers toward inclusive practice remains. The act of teaching does not easily translate into neat packages that others can interpret and replicate. If one accepts that the social world is complex and that teaching is a social act, then it follows that reform efforts will be of a similar nature. This is particularly so when considering issues of culture. As was brought forward earlier in this chapter and exemplified in the three cases, the development of inclusive science programs is not so much a method as it is an attitude and disposition held by teachers, along with an environment that nurtures and stimulates inquiry.

The learning environment is easier to shape or modify than the individual, but the setting itself does not guarantee inclusion or equity; in the end, teachers and the decisions they make are the defining difference.

The learning environment is easier to shape or modify than the individual, but the setting itself does not guarantee inclusion or equity; in the end, teachers and the decisions they make are the defining difference. The science lab that Tebockhorst developed grew out of an attitude that said curiosity is central to scientific inquiry and everyone has it; teachers can help students tap into their own curiosity by developing a stimulating environment and guiding them through systematic inquiry. Teachers could create a science lab identical to Tebockhorst's, but it would not transform them into a "Ms. T." They could study Hopi culture, but they would not become a Gary Nabhan. Professional development that addresses cultural issues in the teaching of science must first and foremost nurture the spirit of inclusion and respect demonstrated by these teachers.

Characteristics of Inclusive Science Teachers

Although it is not easy to transmit the spirit of inclusion, it is possible to recognize some of the traits associated with this attitude of mind and identify possibilities for the type of professional development that will lead to growth. Following are four characteristics that seem to be essential to fostering the spirit of inclusion.

1. Inclusive science teachers know their students and the communities they come from. In anthropology, the most common method for getting to know others is to go into their community and spend time with them. For professional anthropologists, this usually means living in that community for an extended period. It is unrealistic to expect this same commitment from teachers, especially considering the diverse communities that are represented in most classrooms. It is not unrealistic, however, to expect teachers to visit the communities their students come from. Imagine, for example, a professional development program where teachers earn credit for attending church in a community where some of their students live or for shopping in their local supermarket or attending a community event. Another way that teachers can develop a better understanding of the cultures represented in their classrooms, is through reading good ethnographies and first-person accounts.

Chicana writer Gloria Anzaldua referred to the common territory occupied by people who are different from one another as the *borderlands*. Anzaldua said that borderlands exist anytime the space between two people shrinks with intimacy. The intimacy created when one person learns the personal stories of another helps shrink the space between the two individuals (Anzaldua, 1987). Teachers can shrink the space between themselves and their students by visiting the communities their students live in and, in doing so, move toward developing the kind of intimacy Anzaldua wrote of.

2. Inclusive science teachers know themselves. There is a great deal of truth in the oft-quoted phrase, "To know others you must first know yourself." Those who cannot recognize the different lenses through which they view the world are inclined to interpret their own perspective as "the right" perspective. However, when perception is viewed within the context of self, the community, and local knowledge, one becomes less inclined to view life as contrasts in black and white. Additionally, as one comes to recognize the dynamics at work in the construction of personal perceptions, they are granted the vision for better understanding the perceptions of others. The struggle has always been inner and is played out in the outer terrains. Awareness of our situation must come before inner changes, which in turn come before changes in society. Nothing happens in the real world unless it first happens in the images in our heads (Anzaldua, 1987, p. 87).

The path to a true understanding of self is probably a lifelong journey, but there are some ways to facilitate that process. One method is through training programs designed specifically for the purpose of raising self-awareness regarding prejudice and bias. As was mentioned earlier in this chapter, these programs are not generally effective in regard to behavioral change, but they can help participants recognize aspects of self that limit their understanding and acceptance of others. Another approach is through efforts that promote self-reflective practice, such as action research.

3. Inclusive science teachers understand the concept of culture. This chapter began with an emphasis on culture and the importance of developing an understanding of culture at the conceptual level. Unfortunately, the depth of understanding required to impact instructional practice does not come naturally to most people and requires some form of focused, disciplined study. For this reason, the development of cultural understanding should be integrated into every undergraduate teacher-education program in the form of required courses in anthropology. Specifically, everyone aimed at a career in education should be required to take, at the very least, one course in general anthropology and one in educational anthropology. This is not to imply that anthropology is the path to enlightenment, but it is the discipline that most focuses on the study and understanding of culture.

Teachers of science must be able to recognize their discipline as a way of knowing rather than as merely the content that students should come to know.

4. Inclusive science teachers understand the nature of science. Teachers of science must be able to recognize their discipline as a way of knowing rather than as merely the content that students should come to know. Unfortunately, many teachers themselves have never known the excitement of scientific investigation. Until educators come to experience the scientific process firsthand, they cannot truly know the nature of science and they will defer to authorities—the writers of textbook "facts." Professional development for science teachers must provide, among other things, the opportunity for teachers to work with professional researchers and experience science learning for themselves.

Conclusion

This chapter is by no means a comprehensive treatment of cultural issues in the teaching of science. It does, however, present some foundational understandings that are essential for the development of inclusive science programs for a diverse society. Inclusive science teachers are flexible thinkers and capable of considering alternative paradigms, they show respect for other communities by working with members of those communities in collaborative ways, and they recognize the need for creating stimulating learning environments where all students can become engaged in scientific inquiry. Professional development opportunities must focus on experiences that increase the individual teacher's knowledge of community and of self. They must also develop a stronger understanding of the concept of culture and of the nature of science. Inclusive science educators must know the "others" in their classrooms and not condemn other ways of knowing. In this way, they can "build on a child's past and encourage future learning (Boloz, 1985)."

References

Anzaldua, G. 1987. *Borderlands, La Frontera.* San Francisco: Aunt Lute Books.

Atwater, M. M., D. Crockett, and W. J. Kilpatrick. 1996. Constructing multicultural science classrooms: Quality science for all students. In *Issues in science education*, ed. J. Rhoton, & P. Bowers, 167–176). Arlington, VA: National Science Teachers Association.

Boloz, S. 1985. [Poster] Cortez, CO: Mesa Verde Press.

Brooks, L., T. Gersh, D. Currey, and M. E. Davis. 1996. *Diversity training evaluation.* Chapel Hill, NC: University of North Carolina.

Downer, A. S. 1997. Archaeologists—Native American Rights. In *Native Americans and archaeologists: Stepping stones to common ground*, ed. N. Swidler, K. E. Dongoske, R. Anyon, & A. S. Downer, 23–33. Walnut Creek, CA: AltaMira Press.

Kozol, J. 1991. *Savage inequalities.* New York: Harper Collins.

Nabhan, G. P. 1989. *Enduring Seeds.* San Francisco: North Point Press.

National Research Council. 1996. *National science education standards.* Washington, DC: National Academy Press.

Reform and Museums:
Enhancing Science Education in
Formal and Informal Settings

Judith K. Sweeney
Museum of Natural History and Planetarium, Roger Williams Park
Providence, Rhode Island
Susan E. Lynds
Hatfield Marine Science Center, Oregon State University

Judith K. Sweeney is curator of education at the Museum of Natural History and Planetarium, Roger Williams Park, in Providence, Rhode Island. As an adjunct professor at the University of Rhode Island and Providence College, she teaches preservice and inservice courses in science education. She is the founder and chair of the standing committee on informal science education of the Association for Education of Teachers in Science.

Susan E. Lynds is a program associate with Oregon Sea Grant at Oregon State University. Her specialty is science education program evaluation, with an emphasis on authentic assessment of exhibits and programs at informal science learning facilities.

Education standards and reform initiatives are building momentum around the country. Most of the activity focuses on developing standards-based curriculum and evaluation materials as well as new pedagogy for classroom settings. There are also recommendations in the reform documents that specifically address the roles of informal science learning centers (ISLC). Providing equitable access to science learning, enhancing professional development for classroom teachers, promoting a science-literate society, and expanding classroom experience are four areas in which informal education excels. Science education efforts in formal (classroom-based) and informal (e.g., museums, science centers, zoos) learning environments benefit from having common curriculum goals in place. The national and state goals provide an effective meeting ground for all science educators as they develop and evaluate their programs.

Promoting a Science-Literate Society

ISLCs are science education facilities, such as museums and science centers, that are located outside the formal classroom. They provide the members of a community with various ways to learn about the sciences. Through collections, exhibitions, unique environments, and staff expertise, these institutions create powerful firsthand learning experiences that honor multiple learning styles and backgrounds. Parents can explore exhibits with their children, researchers have the opportunity to share their investigations with the community, and students of all ages can experiment with science and technology in a hands-on environment. The general public, as well as educators, can come to understand and support the new educational standards within the context of a science center.

Opportunities for the general public to learn science by inquiry are rare.

Reform documents repeatedly encourage widespread participation in science education. In *Benchmarks for Science Literacy*, teachers were encouraged to "exploit the rich resources of the larger community" (American Association for the Advancement of Science [AAAS], 1989, p. 206) as they involve parents and other adults. The *National Science Education Standards* called for more emphasis on "access to the world beyond the classroom" (National Research Council, 1996, p. 220) for field trips and other programs.

Opportunities for the general public to learn science by inquiry are rare. Passive learning opportunities are readily available. Science-related documentaries are common on cable television, computer-based science materials are widespread on the Internet, and scientific computer packages are becoming more popular. Even when this information is of high quality, it often does not have the impact and multidimensionality of tangible objects, multisensory experiences, and reality-based learning situations offered in a museum, science center, or other ISLCs.

Americans visit a science museum an average of twice a year (Miller & Pifer, 1995). ISLCs offer adults the opportunity to learn about the latest trends in science, technology, and science education reforms. Many institutions are explicitly describing how their exhibits reflect the visions of national reform documents via text panels and supplementary programs. Increasing citizens' comfort level with scientific principles through hands-on experience and awareness of real-world applications may enhance their understanding of current issues in the news and on the ballot.

Equitable Access to Science Learning

Equity requires the availability of quality educational facilities to all students, classroom teachers, and schools. The hands-on exhibits and programs at an ISLC provide opportunities to all schools in the service area. If the ISLC is used as an adjunct laboratory to the classroom, school systems can more easily achieve high educational standards. Teachers can introduce, reinforce and enhance, and/or assess their students' learning by creatively using the novel, rich resources in exhibits and programs. Instead of being treated as a "day off" for students and classroom teachers, the field trip experience can be a highly-charged educational experience that is fully integrated into the curriculum. Informing teachers about the standards-based learning opportunities available at the ISLC is crucial.

Another aspect of equity is developing educational opportunities for a wide variety of learners. Many informal science education settings effectively address accessibility issues and different learning styles. Diverse presentation methods (multisensory, participatory, and interactive exhibits, for example) are often part of exhibit development priorities at ISLCs. In addition, these facilities offer students a place to "go beyond the core [curriculum] in response to their individual interests, talent, and plans for the future (AAAS, 1993, p. 385)."

Even if teachers have a general understanding of education resources in their community, they may not be aware of specific opportunities available at nearby ISLCs.

Professional Development of Educators

Many ISLCs offer excellent facilities for teacher education and enrichment (Leroux, 1989). Teacher education programs at some ISLCs provide inservice and preservice teachers with standards-based curriculum materials, a chance to find out more about field trip programs, and opportunities to network with other educators.

Many museums and science centers offer curriculum libraries to classroom teachers as part of their educational mission. Some of these libraries are now online; they are examples of another growing field for ISLCs—electronic outreach via distance learning and Internet-based resources. Gearing inservice and preservice events, as well as the resource collection, toward the common goals and standards used in the region greatly enhances the effectiveness of these services. In addition, educators at ISLCs are being recognized as a significant component of the science education community. In many states, informal educators are actively participating in education conferences, action teams, curriculum and evaluation committees, and other efforts to implement standards. Professional science education organizations have also recognized the role of informal education. Both the National Science Teachers Association and the Association for the Education of Teachers in Science have standing committees on informal science education.

Enhancing the Classroom Experience

Classroom teachers will find it easier to integrate informal education opportunities into their curriculum design if ISLCs provide schools with detailed information on the curriculum goals that their programs meet. In addition, ISLCs can increase their visibility, effectiveness, and funding opportunities through specifically identifying their participation in the education reform process. Even if teachers have a general understanding of education resources in their community, they may not be aware of specific opportunities available at nearby ISLCs. It is important that state- and district-level administrators increase teachers' awareness of ISLC programs that enhance classroom science teaching and learning.

The AAAS (1995) acknowledged two facilities, Mid-West Public Garden Collaborative and the Cranbrook Institute of Science, for taking the lead in supporting the classroom environment. Since then, there have been similar efforts at other institutions. Unfortunately, much of this development has gone unnoticed by classroom teachers as they focus on incorporating the reforms into their curricula.

In supporting the classroom environment, the ISLC's role is twofold. First, it is essential that ISLCs incorporate education standards and reform goals into their programs. Second, they must inform their audience of the resources they offer in this area. Nielsen (1997) lists several case studies as examples of this effort; she also outlines several approaches that ISLCs may use to begin a standards-based program focus. Two additional institutions currently using national and state standards in education programs are the Museum of Natural History and Planetarium in Providence, Rhode Island, and the Hatfield Marine Science Center (HMSC) in Newport, Oregon.

Two Case Studies

The Museum of Natural History and Planetarium was built in 1896 and has a long history of serving as an informal learning resource for the community. When it first opened 102 years ago, it was fondly referred to as the "People's University." Through the years, the museum evolved, transforming from an almost exclusive role as a repository of knowledge to a role that put the communication of knowledge on an equal plane of importance. Through professional development programs, teachers are once again considering the museum a university of the people, offering unique learning opportunities for themselves and their students.

Teachers are once again considering the museum a university of the people, offering unique learning opportunities for themselves and their students.

Joint Ventures, an exhibit of vertebrate skeletons from around the world, has provided the Museum of Natural History and Planetarium with a laboratory for new professional development opportunities for classroom teachers. This exhibit showcases 35 real skeletons arranged in five different global settings: the South American rain forest; the Australian Outback; the African savanna; the American West; and a typical home setting, which features domestic animals. All of the skeletons are of animals that presently exist on earth.

The brightly illuminated skeletons are in realistic poses within each diorama with minimal environmental props (e.g., plants, murals, habitat cues). The visitor's guide on this global tour is "Bone Phillips," a human skeleton, who can be found positioned differently in each habitat. As contrast, the floor, ceiling, and walls are all black. It is left to the visitor's imagination and prior knowledge to fill in the missing elements of this "bare bones" exhibit. A classroom area within the exhibit encourages teachers to conduct discussions.

National science reform documents were considered during the planning of the Joint Ventures exhibit. The unifying concepts in the *National Science Education Standards* were used as organizers for each setting and served as a framework for future programs for the general public, as well as teachers. In this way, the museum helps all members of the community to be aware of the reforms, illustrates their applications within the exhibit, and models how they can be taught through participation in workshops and programs.

Similarly, the tenets of the national reforms have guided the professional development programs designed in conjunction with this exhibit. A series of workshops was offered that showed how to use the exhibit in teaching unifying concepts and common themes. Form and function, for example, is clearly reflected in the collection of skeletons. Most visitors, adults and children, had seen only reconstructed dinosaur skeletons displayed in museums, animals of which they have had no firsthand knowledge. However, they did have some familiarity with the animals whose skeletons were on display in Joint Ventures and could easily find out more about each from videos, television, books, zoos, wildlife centers, or even pet stores. Teachers learned how to make appropriate connections between a skeleton and behavior patterns, as well as inquiry-based methods to help teach these concepts to their students.

Another series of professional development involved bringing together middle- and secondary-level teachers from different academic disciplines to identify common themes across content areas. Teachers worked in cross-disciplinary teams to develop curriculum modules to use in their classrooms. In this way, the museum exhibit was meaningfully integrated into the local curricula of the respective teachers. Instead of the typical model of professional development, this was a give-and-take collaboration that enhanced the quality of the curricula.

In 1997, HMSC opened a new visitor center to showcase its scientists' research activities. The HMSC visitor center is a state-of-the-art science museum designed to give the visitor the experience of joining with scientists in their investigations. Multisensory exhibits, interactive computer displays, video terminals, and natural history exhibits offer many types of science information. In designing a new set of school (and group) programs to complement the visitor center, the Education Department pinpointed specific state and national curriculum goals and standards to address in each of the programs. Group leaders receive previsit materials in printed form or through the World Wide Web (e.g., Sea Grant Marine Education Program, 1997). Each previsit packet begins with a list of goals, objectives, and standards covered by the program (Table 1). The initial feedback from this presentation has been quite positive. HMSC educators plan to continue including standards and reform applications as they develop future materials and programs.

Evaluation of ISLC Exhibits and Programs

The standards and reform goals provide powerful tools to use in both formative and summative evaluations of exhibits and programs at ISLCs. Evaluation is an essential element in assessing the effectiveness of science learning opportunities in informal settings. Formative evaluation is a progressive tool, as developers plan, evaluate, modify, and then reevaluate exhibits in an ongoing cycle. Exhibit designers can target reform goals starting with the conceptual stage and continuing throughout the

Table 1: Sample First Page from HMSC School Program Previsit Materials

Endangered Species Laboratory
This lab experience will offer students the opportunity to learn about endangered species in Oregon. A review of species that are listed and the causes of their decline will be presented. A hands-on activity to demonstrate genetic diversity and extraction of DNA in the lab will be conducted.

Oregon Education Common Curriculum Goals and Benchmarks

Curriculum Goal:	Students will understand the transmission of traits in living things.
Grade 8 Benchmark	Students will be able to describe how the traits of an organism are passed from generation to generation.
Grade 10 Benchmark	Students will be able to analyze the structure and function of DNA and its role in information transfer from one generation to the next, including laws of heredity.
Curriculum Goal:	Students will understand the relationships between living things and their environments.
Grade 8 Benchmark	Students will identify and describe the factors that influence or change the balance of populations in their environment.

project. Publications like the *National Science Education Standards* and *Benchmarks for Science Literacy* are valuable content resource summaries that can be used in designing both public and education programs.

A summative evaluation (assessment of an existing facility's exhibits) will provide a set of features and programs that meet educational goals of the school audience. This information can then be actively disseminated to classroom teachers and administrators in the local field trip region. Similar information can be communicated to the general public and parents and may be distributed to classroom teachers during inservice and preservice events.

Conclusion

The development of national and state educational goals has given ISLCs an unprecedented opportunity to become active, valuable partners with formal education in achieving widespread scientific literacy in this country. Working toward these goals both in conjunction with schools and independently as lifelong learning resources, ISLCs have exciting challenges to face between now and the year 2061. Both informal and formal science educators will benefit from working within the overlapping frameworks of curriculum, assessment, and pedagogy provided by the reform documents.

References

American Association for the Advancement of Science (AAAS). 1989. *Science for all Americans.* New York: Oxford University Press.

———. 1993. *Benchmarks for science literacy.* New York: Oxford University Press.

———. 1995. *Project 2061: Science literacy for a changing future, a decade of reform.* Washington, DC: AAAS.

Leroux, J. A. 1989. Teacher training in a science museum. *Curator 32*: 70–80.

Miller, J. D., and L. K. Pifer. 1995. *Public attitudes toward science and technology, 1979–1995, integrated codebook.* Chicago: International Center for the Advancement of Scientific Literacy, Chicago Academy of Sciences.

National Research Council. 1996. *National science education standards.* Washington, DC: National Academy Press.

Nielsen, N. 1997. Project 2061: Science literacy in museums. *ASTC Newsletter* 25:1, 5–8.

Sea Grant Marine Education Program. 1997. *Endangered species laboratory.* Oregon State University: Hatfield Marine Science Center. http://www.hmsc.orst.edu/education/programs/endsp.html.

Access to Technology: The Equity Dilemma for Science Educators

Rebecca P. Butler
Instructional Technology/Leadership and Educational Policy Studies
Northern Illinois University

Rebecca P. Butler is an assistant professor of educational technology, and school library media certification and endorsement advisor, at Northern Illinois University. Her research interests and writing focus on ethical issues in instructional technology and school library media.

Inequity of access to today's new tools becomes tomorrow's enduring societal loss.

—Gaines, Johnson, and King, 1996

The purpose of this chapter is to address the issue of technology equity in the world of science educators, with an emphasis on professional development. This subject becomes staggering when one begins to realize that technology in education can cover such diverse software areas as videos to CD-ROMs to audio tapes and an equally varied hardware contingency, ranging from VCRs to computer hardware to laser-disk and audiotape players. In addition, the overwhelming discussion area within equity is often given as access to this technology. Herein lies another overwhelming topic, in that the number of ways to address the acquirement or obstruction of technological access varies greatly. With these two related areas in mind, definitions of importance, as well as which access issues are covered in this chapter will be addressed first. Next, a sampling of some of the literature available on this topic will be covered. Lastly, this chapter will discuss how concerned educators can deal with the equity issue, as well as create change to help and encourage students to survive intact in an ever-evolving technological world.

Definitions

For the purposes of this chapter, all definitions will focus on the access to technology in education, in general, and science education, in particular. This will include special emphasis on the professional development of said science educators.

Access: Access is defined as "The right to …make use of." It is also used in the following manner: to obtain "…access to (goods or information), usually by technological means" (*American Heritage Dictionary*, 1993). For the purposes of this chapter, access is seen as the means by which students are able to obtain needed current technologies in order to learn science skills, concepts, etc.

Equity: "Equity is qualitative and concerns issues of justice; equity may demand inequality, i.e., being evenhanded may not always be the answer. For some groups to have an even chance may require special efforts" (Sutton, 1991). This is in contrast to equality, which can be defined as "Having the same quantity…" and "…being the same for all members of a group (*American Heritage Dictionary*, 1993)."

Technology: Technology, as used in education, is an umbrella term combining old technologies, including filmstrips and 8mm films, with new technologies, such as CD-ROMs and videodiscs. To most educators today, technology means only the new technologies, with an emphasis on computer hardware and software. For the purposes of this chapter, focus is on these new technologies.

Selected Technology Access/Equity Issues

"Schools lag behind workplaces, leisure places, and other realms of life in their access to new information technologies. Moreover, current technologies are not equitably distributed among different kinds of schools, special groups of students, or households (Secretary's conference on educational technology, 1995)." A number of access issues are currently being debated in today's educational environments. Among these is equity in terms of diverse populations. Such diverse groups include race, culture, religion, economic status, education level, region, sex/gender, age, special needs, and population strata (rural/suburban/urban). The finance question—given the funding received by or awarded to a particular school system, educational department, or teacher for a specific area of study (in this case, science)—is also important. In fact, funding is related to all of the other areas mentioned in this chapter. Such discussion areas, with interrelated subjects, are still by no means comprehensive. Surfing the Internet and searching print reference tools, as well as many other means of information gathering, may produce any number of other ways to look at technological equity in American schools, and each of these areas deserves attention. Because it is impossible to cover all here, chapter focus is on a few of the more commonly debated equity/access issues found in the educational environment today: funding; diverse communities, including economic and geographical population areas; racial and ethnic groups; special needs populations; and sex/gender.

Funding

The idea of equal educational opportunities has been a part of the American environ from the mid-1800s, when early political figures, such as New York Governor DeWitt Clinton, as well as other concerned citizens, looked to provide access to materials in the schools, including setting special funds for materials' provision (Bowie, 1986).

Many years later, the amounts and formats of materials available in schools—especially in the areas of science, math, foreign languages, counseling, and nonprint media—grew with the establishment of the National Defense Education Act of 1958.[1]

The NDEA provided federal monies that educators were to apply to the above-specified areas (Butler, 1995). Awareness of technology in education continued. In 1987, Cole and Griffin pointed out that in order for a program to function as an essential component of an exemplary pedagogy, it was essential to assure that all students have equitable access to technology. Now, as the new millennium approaches, the Clinton Administration is championing " ... ongoing federal investments in key activities such as distance learning, use of technology in math and science education, and research and development of new, effective educational technology (United States Department of Education, 1996)."

Science educators, as well as others in American schools, find themselves needing more financial support than ever before. As the costs of educational technologies expand, keeping current becomes a never-ending task. Educators and students alike may find themselves questioning whether there is something more hi-tech or newly created—perhaps existing in cyberspace or being cut into a CD-ROM—which they need to add to the science classroom. Therefore, obtaining the funding necessary to remain current is an umbrella equity concern in the ever-expanding technological environment. For the purposes of this chapter, socioeconomic, multicultural, and special needs populations are thus included under this umbrella.

Populations (Socioeconomic)

Many schools do not have the necessary finances available to provide the adequate hardware and software needed (Gaines, Johnson, & King, 1996).[2] This may be the result of disproportionate funding (Sayers, 1995). Such funding differences, which between rich and poor districts can be substantial, often result in less access to technology for students of low-income and minority backgrounds (Northwest Educational Technology Consortium, 1997). Indeed, it has been found that "Leading edge technology districts are more likely to be located in affluent suburban communities (United States Department of Education, 1996)."

Disproportionate funding can also occur within schools or between schools in a district. This could be the result of an internal budget structure within the organization which allocates monies to one area or group over that of another or of preferred-user status. Thus, computer hardware support might be allocated in one subject area but little earmarked for software purchase. For example, recently in one Chicago public school, a computer lab was found to be outfitted with new Windows machines and NO software (A. Torok, personal communication, September 27, 1998).

In addition, those students in higher socioeconomic areas are more likely to have personal computers in the household (Milone & Salpeter, 1996; Mosle, 1995). While a few poorer districts may be able to place computers and software in students' homes through grant monies or programs that provide older hardware

While a few poorer districts may be able to place computers and software in students' homes through grant monies or programs that provide older hardware from area business, this is not a common occurrence.

from area business, etc., this is not a common occurrence. Thus, those who may most need computer support at home—because they are unable to obtain it in the schools—are also those least likely to secure such support (Milone & Salpeter, 1996). According to Robert Hennely (1996) in an article for *Education Digest*, those children least likely to have computers in the home are those in inner cities or rural areas—traditionally lower-income locales.[3] However, both urban and rural disadvantaged, when given access to technology, are zealous users (United States Department of Commerce, 1995). Thus, the Information Age exacerbates disparities between these groups and the wealthy and middle class (Hancock & Wingert, 1995; Hennely, 1996). As a result, Internet use is also most likely to occur with children on a higher socioeconomic plane, given that lower-income families may not even be able to afford a phone (Katz & Aspden, 1996).

Schmid (1996) finds that suburban schools are more apt to be on-line than are urban, and Berenfeld (1997) concludes, given the same online resources, that all students have an equal ability to obtain information. Indeed, in a decade when it is said that "the use of technology in the classroom improves students' motivation and attitudes about themselves and about learning (U.S. Department of Education, 1996)," the ability to access at all or in part, such important technological information sources as the Internet or various software reference tools like "Encarta" (1998) or "Encyclopedia Americana on CD-ROM" (1996), has a strong influence on American education. As such, inequities in technology between those who have none or little and those who have much more can and could create a division in U.S. schools, thus stratifying American society intellectually. Additionally, at a time when computer literacy is becoming a "must" in terms of employment, the broadening disparity in technology access is subduing any financial aid increases (Hennely, 1996).

Related to the funding/access quagmire is format-dependent access. According to a number of student teachers polled in a math and science methods class, use of technology in their science classrooms depended on, among other things, the availability of the proper hardware and/or software needed in order to present the material (Cummings & Oppewal, 1997). In addition, Butler and Cunningham (1996) found, when comparing Internet versus CD-ROM access in both K–12 schools and higher academia, that "...the availability of funds, equipment, software, and training" affected equity/access. This is true for both the Internet and CD-ROMs. Of the four criteria, three (equipment, software, and training) are directly dependent on the fourth (funding). Indeed, financial considerations are of importance in educational technology equity for all educators.

Populations (Multicultural)

In her piece, "Technology and Equity," Neuman (1991) points out that the two terms in her title have not always been allies. Development of such a partnership has been hampered, especially in view of computers and software, by distribution inequities within the schools (see funding discussion above). Nowhere is this more evident than with minority students. Becker (1983, 1985) found that a disproportionate number of African American and Hispanic students were using drill-and-practice software as compared to their white counterparts, who were more likely to be learning programming. According to Roblyer, Dozier-Henry, & Burnette (1996): "...when economically disadvantaged students do get to use computers, they are used primarily for remediation and basic skills." In light of this statement, Yeaman (1991) considers computer use as a method of social stratification. However, Roblyer, et al., (1996) and Cummins & Sayers (1996) both find technology as worthy of being in the schools. Technology allows students to learn about and communicate with others and can introduce students to very different cultures.[4]

While divergent cultures may support varying learning styles, Schwartz (1995) sees children not only learning English through computer use, but their native language as well. Indeed, because "language can ... emerge ...as a way of defining 'us' in comparison to 'them'" (Valdes, 1998), the computer becomes a tool to join students of diverse cultures into one linguistic group within a classroom.[5] Schwartz (1995) also perceives computer use for all students as a critical thinking tool and as a host for practical reasoning skills. These ideas can be applied to Lee and Fradd's article, "Science for All, Including Students From Non-English-Language Backgrounds." In this article, the two authors point out that students from diverse cultural and language backgrounds have varying communication patterns that influence their learning styles. As such, they "...propose the notion of *instructional congruence* to indicate the process of mediating the nature of academic content with students' language and cultural experiences to make such content (e.g., science) accessible, meaningful, and relevant for diverse students... (Lee & Fradd, 1998)." Because science instruction in the 1990s means working with CD-ROMs, computer programs, and videos, as well as with direct observation and experimentation (Cummings & Oppewal, 1997), the position of instructional congruence, additionally, might be applied to instruction via technological means. Thus, "...technology can fundamentally assist by opening up avenues for communication (Roblyer, Dozier-Henry, & Burnette, 1996)."

Populations (Special Needs)

Technology access for special needs students falls into two categories of disabilities: physical and learning. Because a number of federal and state laws look to provide disabled children the same rights to education as that of all other children (Parette & VanBiervliet 1990; Milone, 1997), it is often necessary to find technologies that will support meeting these educational goals. A variety of manufacturers have developed assistive technologies[6] to help both the physically and learning disabled overcome a myriad of barriers (Coombs & Cartwright, 1994). While assistive technologies normally are assumed to include modified software and hardware choices for those with physical disabilities (including visual and audio barriers), they may also help those to whom content or barriers to understanding are obstacles ("Products which enhance access to the WWW: Understanding," n.d.).

Technology access for special needs students falls into two categories of disabilities: physical and learning.

Solutions for physically disabled students involve providing specialized hardware. For example, consider the variety of tools available should a mouse be a barrier for computer access. Among such hardware are joysticks, electronic pointing devices worn on the head, sip and puff straws, alternative keyboards, track balls, and touch screens ("Products which enhance access to the WWW: Mouse emulators," n.d.). Solutions may also involve software, including that which allows keys on the numeric keyboard to take the place of mouse movements and cursor voice recognition software. Programs are also available which can synthesize speech and text translators/closed captioning (Coombs & Cartwright, 1994; United States Department of Education, 1996; Harkins, Loeterman, Lan, & Korres, 1996; "Products which enhance access to the WWW: Understanding," n.d.). Additionally, it is now possible for many physically disabled individuals to access the web. For example, WGBH Online provides navigational aids for the blind, audio services for the deaf, etc. (WGBH, 1997). Other useful items that students with visual disabilities might access include: screen magnification software, screen-reading software, "talking" browsers, digitized sound clips, and so on. Those who are hearing disabled might benefit from text captions of video images ("Products which enhance access to the WWW," n.d.; "Products which enhance access to the WWW: Vision," n.d.).

Learning disabled students can also take advantage of a variety of software programs. These programs—with simple, explicit directions—may provide such students with the ability to word process, find and remember information, and develop proficiency in problem solving (United Stated Department of Education, 1996). While most web page access for the disabled student appears to veer on the side of the physically disabled, inclusion of those with cognitive or learning disabilities has also been addressed. Such students will benefit from web pages designed to cater to their strengths. Some may find graphics informative or need graphic bookmarks instead of text-based ones. Others may need to make use of screen-reading software, should text prove a barrier to their understanding of web page information ("Designing access to WWW pages," n.d.).

Many states, organizations, and private individuals are concerned with issues of access for those with disabilities (Alliance for Technology Access, 1996; Parette & VanBiervliet, 1990; Center on Information Technology, 1997; Wakefield, n.d.; WGBH,

1997). The state of Arkansas, for example, stresses that technology can help the disabled obtain an appropriate education and create a less restrictive school setting. It also emphasizes that schools within its borders need to evaluate disabled students, identify and provide them with the most current technology available for their needs, and use an individualized education program[7] to best help each student in his or her learning (Parette & VanBiervliet, 1990). In addition, working with specific hardware and software for the disabled can also help teachers of such students avoid "individualization burnout" which "...occurs when teachers are buried by the tasks of aligning materials with the curriculum, pretesting, making prescriptions, tutoring and post-testing individually every student in the class" (Foshay, n.d.). This in itself may encourage equity in the classroom, especially for mainstreamed students who might otherwise be lost in the shuffle of the class as a whole. On a more somber note, given this discussion into specialized hardware and software, the issue of financial support once again arises. For more on this, see the section on funding above.

Sex/Gender

"No person in the United States shall, on the basis of sex, be excluded from participation in, be denied the benefits of, or be subjected to discrimination under any education program or activity receiving Federal financial assistance" (Title IX, 1972). While this may seem a given in today's society, the concern over sex and gender equality in educational technology has waxed and waned in the United States for decades.

Originally, access to technology and related technological issues in education was not a battle of the sexes. The first textbook author to cover aspects of technology in education (then called audiovisual education) was a woman, Anna Verona Dorris, who published her book in 1923. Later educators, dealing with such aspects of technology as educational radio, sound recordings, films, and much more, were equitable—whoever was skilled and knowledgeable was the expert, sex notwithstanding. It was not until World War II that the technology/education focus became almost predominantly male. This was a direct result of the civilian war effort and the military, both male-dominated, and proactive in educational films and other training materials. Additionally, the presence of males in a majority of administrative posts within K–12 educational institutions and higher academia at this time encouraged a more masculine view of the world (Butler, 1995). However, times changed. Some 30 years later, an interest in gender equity via science and technology resulted in the 1979 establishment of an international conference entitled "Girls and Science and Technology (Daniels & Butler, 1987)." By the early 1980s, Pamela M. D'Onofrio-Flores held (in a United Nations report) that "...technology ...reinforces the division of labour between nations, classes, and the sexes (1982)." Related to this is the work of Reinen and Plomp (1994), which found that females were less likely than males to use and understand technology and more likely than males to see software as problematic. Presently, the focus in nonprint education continues to be male-dominated

(Geisert & Futrell, 1995; Gipson, 1997; Knupfer, 1997; Mark & Hanson, 1992). Nevertheless, in the 1990s, we are beginning to see a concerted effort to again make this a more equitable area.

Nonetheless, access to technology in education, in terms of sex and gender issues, presents us with unique circumstances and varying points of view. According to Milone and Salpeter (1996), both males and females in schools today enjoy approximately the same amount and types of access, as well as similar responses to instructional/educational technology. However, their attitudes toward technology may differ, perhaps because girls are less likely to participate in after-class or optional in-class computer activities. Milone and Salpeter appear to hold a minority position, however, as is evidenced by the following authors. Knupfer feels that women have been partially excluded from technology, for example in planning, development, and implementation. She also observes that there is a male influence in computer software and on web pages—especially in areas of clip art and children's art (Knupfer, 1997). McInerney and Park (1986) suggest that sex-role stereotyping and few role models steer adolescent girls away from technology participation. Two other authors, Geisert and Futrell (1995), feel that software, especially computer games, is also inequitable—focusing on males and subjects of interest to them, such as battles and a myriad of action. Joe Urschel (1996) also states that computer games cater to males, thus "…further distancing the computer from girls (Urschel, 1996)."

Gunn (1994) writes that elementary-aged girls are shortchanged in education in areas of math, science, and technology. This observation is echoed by Fear-Fenn and Kapostasy (1992), who have found that high school girls are less likely to have taken courses in the sciences, math, and computer technology than are their male counterparts. Gunn's (1994) perceptions are that our society has different expectations for the two sexes, which contribute to gender differences in our classrooms and in computer use. These comments are sustained by Merri Rosenberg, who states: "Girls see computers as a means to an end. Girls have been socialized to believe that it's not quite an appropriate thing for them (Rosenberg, 1998)." Gipson (1997) observes that teachers are more likely to instruct boys on how to complete a project, while either showing girls exactly how to do something or doing it for them.

Access to technology in education, in terms of sex and gender issues, presents us with unique circumstances and varying points of view.

(The implication here is that such varied reactions to students, based on their sex, influences how these students perceive themselves in the technological world and how they then react to this world.) Mangione (1995) cites research showing that because much computer use has been developed in the traditionally male fields of math and science that the consequence is a bias toward masculine lines of reasoning. In addition, Kevin Maney, in an article for *USA Today*, maintains that high-tech jobs are more likely to be held by men than women, an "industrywide" problem which

"...begins in math class and ultimately ends with women closed out of one of the fastest-growing and most important job markets of the future (Maney, 1996)." Maney's assumption appears to be that K–12 education has a strong influence in later career development across the sexes.

How can gender equity be achieved so that all may have equal access to instructional/educational technology? Thompson, Simonson, & Hargrave (1992) suggest that educators encourage females to use technology and propose that inservice training in the area of equity may augment cognizance toward attaining educational equality. In at least one state, Iowa, concern over gender equity has resulted in a law which requires public and privately-accredited K–12 schools to teach all curriculum from both a multicultural and non-gender-biased point of view ("Sexism in education: Is there gender equity in your community school district?" 1993).

Please note the close inter-relationships in most of these areas of discussion above. The list of issues in terms of equity/access and technology in education is endless. Next is addressed how some of these issues can be handled in current teaching environments.

"All, regardless of race or class or economic status, are entitled to a fair chance and to the tools for developing their individual powers of mind and spirit to the utmost (National Commission on Excellence in Education, 1983)."

How This Relates to Science Educators and Professional Development

"All, regardless of race or class or economic status, are entitled to a fair chance and to the tools for developing their individual powers of mind and spirit to the utmost (National Commission on Excellence in Education, 1983). The above quotation relates to this chapter, because access remains an equity quagmire in a variety of educational arenas. In order to work toward achieving technological equality in science education, there are a number of things that can be done. Educators can become aware of the various types of access concerns, including those involving socioeconomic, ethnic and racial, disabled, and other special populations. Next, educators must plan for accountability, which is relevant to equity in that, given scarce resources, it is necessary to know if said resources are achieving their specified aim (Gaines, et al., 1996). It is also possible to address the primary access issue: funding. While educators may not be able to control local, regional, state, or federal school finances, they can learn to: lobby for more funds; write grants; arrange with companies and/or individuals for financial, equipment, or supplies' donations; obtain technology leasing capabilities; and take advantage of local college and university programs of interest in the financial arena. Educators may also be able to warrant more funds by concentrating on developing a program in one area (for example, of science), and when its student benefits are documented, use that as justification for additional funding in other areas (Van Orden, 1995). Through inservices, continuing education, college classes, the Internet, research, and other informational and educational resources, it is possible to obtain information and knowledge to support the search for equity excellence. Additionally, future teachers should also receive training in equity issues. Indeed, Miller, Metheny, and Davison (1997), in "Issues in Integrating Mathematics and Science," feel that "those of us involved in the education of science and mathematics teachers can perhaps suggest that preservice teacher education may be the key to restructuring efforts (Miller, Metheny, & Davison, 1997)." While Miller and his fellow authors are looking to restructuring traditional educational procedures, such thoughts can be applied to the technological access dilemma, as well. Another area of importance is in materials' provision, also affected by funding. Because much provision of this sort is a function of the school's media center, it is interesting to note that Barbara Stripling (1992), the author of "Libraries for the National Education Goals," specifically addresses "equitable access to technology for students regardless of economic status, intellectual ability, or sex." Teachers' achievements in the area of educational technology equity will mean that the various students taught—whether different because of economics, race, skill levels, or gender—will have equal access to all the learning technologies that can be made available.

Given socioeconomic and multicultural diversities, teachers can additionally look to themselves and acknowledge how they perceive and react to their various student populations. They can—whether through formal diversity training or their own introspection—work toward treating all groups in an equitable manner. Because educational technology itself can be seen as a social construction (Muffoletto, 1993),

Given socioeconomic and multicultural diversities, teachers can additionally look to themselves and acknowledge how they perceive and react to their various student populations.

educators must recognize—when some groups have less technological access—that even access may actually mean providing more technology for underprivileged and under-recognized groups, i.e., equity not equality (see definitions). (Extra access could be in the form of providing after school computer lab time, loaners, and local partnerships with area business people, etc.) Then, once all groups are at the same level, all students can be treated in an equitable manner. Additionally for multicultural/minority students, the equity issue may apply to more than access via financial support. Equity may also apply to access to the same software programs as their more privileged counterparts. Thus, the underprivileged should be afforded the opportunity to use software beyond tutorials and drill-and-practice. If, because of lower knowledge and skill levels, it takes them longer to achieve an advanced stage, then the concept of equity versus equality should furthermore apply.

Educational technology equity for physically and mentally disabled students also appears to be dependent on funding. Once funding is in place, educators will be better able to work with these groups. In addition, it is important that teachers develop areas in which disabled students can feel comfortable and work to their ability levels. This can be achieved through choosing less difficult software or supplying the necessary hardware to make the technology more accessible. Graf (1995) speaks to the fact that she uses both physically and mentally challenged students to perform in "real-life job situations" within her school library media center. Some of these chores involve inputting data on a computer. There is reason to expect that, given the proper training, such students might be employed in similar manners within other areas of the school, including, possibly, the science classroom.

When considering gender equity and educational technology access, there is a divergence in what various authors believe. Some afford the notion that there is little, if any, difference in how boys and girls use hardware and software. However, the majority feel that an equity issue, based, in part, on societal perceptions, does reflect how the two sexes use and react to technology in education. Of importance is that educators become sensitive to differences which may exist consciously or unconsciously within their classrooms concerning how they respond to their students. Once educators are aware of their responses, they can work toward reacting to both males and females in their classrooms in a similar manner. This may involve designing specific curriculum that is free of gender (McInerney & Park, 1986); providing role models and equal opportunities for technology use for girls (Gunn, 1994); or starting a computer club for girls, if the original club is male-dominated (Urschel, 1996). By having similar expectations for both sexes, working with software of interest to both groups, encouraging everyone to participate evenly in educational technology usage, and making technology activities available to all students, educators can hopefully provide equity in their classrooms in terms of technology and science education. Educators can also avoid biased instructional materials (in this case, software) and make a concerted effort to assign tasks involving technological usage (such as copying disks, adding software, or searching the Internet) to both boys and girls. Again, workshops, continuing education courses, partnerships between schools (Tucker, Seluke, & Tucker, 1997), and introspection may help in achieving these goals.

Conclusion

Technology can enhance science education by making instruction understandable and accessible to all. In order to do so, however, technology as an equalizer must be open to the entire student population in an equitable manner. This includes choices by science educators involving the communities of students they serve, the financial environments in which they teach, and the professional development they undertake.

Notes

[1]   This act was a direct result of the launching of Sputnik. Congressional concern that our education system was lagging behind that of the Soviet Union caused members of the U.S. Congress to pass the NDEA. This act provided increased funding for the nation's public schools (Hopkins and Butler, 1991; Butler, 1995).

[2]   It is important to remember here that the terms "hardware" and "software" address more than computers and the attending computer software (Gaines, et al., 1996). Other examples of hardware

include camcorders, laser disk players, and so on. Software concerns can include videos, laser disks, audiotapes, and others, in addition to that software used with computers.

[3] Rural people are less likely to be empowered in terms of education (Carter, 1997; Howley and Howley, 1995). (This fact also holds true for urban, minority populations.)

[4] It is important to note here that there is bias is some children's software (DeVaney, 1993). Often, such bias is in the form of presenting lighter-skinned peoples as having higher intelligence, being more positive role models, etc.

[5] Currently, technology is used in multicultural education in any number of ways. Among these are (1) use in telecommunications activities, such as partnering a school in the United States with one in the former Soviet Union; (2) using technology to teach students English; and (3) using multimedia to promote both cultural diversity and awareness of cultural similarities (Roblyer, et al, 1996).

[6] "...assistive technology means any device or service which can improve the quality of life for people. Assistive technology covers the entire range of human inventions from simple spoons for feeding to wheelchairs, to complex computer systems... (Parette & VanBiervliet, 1990)."

[7] The individualized education program (IEP) is "...a written plan between the school and the student and his or her parents. ... An IEP can call for use of a particular technology if it is needed for the student's education. IEPs also state *in detail how* often and how long the student must receive educational services... (Parette & VanBiervliet, 1990)."

References

Alliance for technology access impact 1996. 1996. [Online]. Available Web page: http://www.ataccess.org/Newsletter/Impact96T.html

The American heritage dictionary [Computer software]. 1993. U.S.A.: ClarisWorks.

Becker, H. J. 1995. Baseline survey of testbed-participating schools. National School Network Testbed—Phase 2. Wave One—Schools Included as of April 1995. (ERIC Document Reproduction Service ED397089.)

————. 1983. Schools uses of microcomputers: REport #1 from a national survey. *Journal of Computers in Mathematics and Science Teaching*, 3(1):29–33.

Berenfeld, B. 1997. *Telecommunications in our classrooms: Boondoggle or a power teaching tool?* [Online]. Available E-mail: boris_berenfeld@terc.edu

Bowie, M. H. 1986. Public libraries in the United States of America: Their history, condition, and management. *Historic documents of school libraries*, pp. 8–31. Littleton, CO: Hi Willow Research & Publishing.

Butler, R. P. 1995. Women in audiovisual education, 1920–1957: A Discourse analysis (Doctoral dissertation, University of Wisconsin-Madison, 1995). *UMI Dissertation Abstracts*, 9508907.

Butler, R. P. and C. Cunningham. 1996. The Tortoise and the hare or CD-ROMs vs. the Internet. *The Proceedings of the Consortium of College and University Media Centers*, 5–20.

Carter, C. S. 1997. *The Stuff that dreams are made of: Culture, ethnicity, class, place, and adolescent Appalachian girls' sense of self.* [Online]. Available Web page: http://www.ael.org/nsf/voices/rpdreams.htm

Center on Information Technology Accommodation. 1997. *What is CITA?* [Online]. Available Web page: http://www.itpolicy.gas.gov/coca/index.htm

Cole, M. and P. Griffin. 1987. *Contextual factors in education: Improving science and mathematics education for minorities and women.* Madison: Wisconsin Center for Education Research. In Burnett, G. *Technology as a tool for urban classrooms. ERIC Digest* [Online]. Available Web page: http://eric-web.tc.columbia.edu/digests/dig95.html

Coombs, N. and G. P. Cartwright. 1994. Project EASI: Equal access to software and information.

Coombs, N. and G. P. Cartwright. 1994. Project EASI: Equal access to software and information. *Change,* March/April, 42-44.

Cummings, X. and Y. Oppewal. 1997. How are teachers using technology in science class? Math and Science Undergraduate Class. Johnson City, TN: East Tennessee State University.

Cummins, J. and D. Sayers. 1996. Multicultural education and technology: Promise and pitfalls. In *Multicultural education 98/99.* 5th ed., ed. F. Schultz, 212–217). Guilford, CT: Dushkin/McGraw-Hill.

Daniels, J. Z., and J. B. Kahle, eds. 1987. *Girls and Science and Technology.* Washington, D.C.: National Science Foundation. (ERIC Document Reproduction Service No. ED 384 486)

Designing access to WWW pages. (n.d.). [Online]. Available Web page: http://www.ataccess.org/design.html

DeVaney, A. 1993. Reading educational computer programs. In *Computers in education: Social, political, and historical perspectives*, ed. R. Muffoletto & N. Nelson Knupfer, 181–196. New Jersey: Hampton Press Inc.

D'Onofrio-Flores, P. M. 1982. *Scientific-technological change and the role of women in development.* Boulder, CO: Westview Press.

Encarta [Computer software]. 1998. U.S.A.: Microsoft.

Encyclopedia Americana on CD-ROM [Computer software]. 1996. Danbury, CT: Grolier Educational Corporation.

Fear-Fenn, M. and K. K. Kapostasy. 1992. *Math + science + technology = vocational preparation for girls: A difficult equation to balance.* Columbus, OH: Ohio State University. (ERIC Document Reproduction Service No. ED 341 853)

Flowers, J. C. 1996. *Female educators and students assess gender equity in technology education. A Survey of women involved in technology education.* Richmond: Virginia State Department of Education. (ERIC Document Reproduction Service No. ED 405 507)

Foshay, R., (n.d.) Deciding what computer-assisted instruction can do for you: A guide for teachers and parents.

Gaines, C. L., W. Johnson, and D. T. King. 1996. Achieving technological equity and equal access to the learning tools of the 21st century. *T.H.E. Journal,* June, 74–78.

Geisert, P. G. and M. K. Futrell. 1995. *Teachers, computers, and curriculum: Microcomputers in the classroom.* Boston: Allyn and Bacon.

Gipson, J. 1997. Girls and computer technology: Barrier or Key? *Educational Technology,* 37(2):41–43.

Graf, N. 1995. How the library media center can serve special needs students-and how they can serve the library. *Technology Connection*, November, 11–12.

Gunn, C. 1994. *Development of gender roles: Technology as an equity strategy.* Boston: National Educational Computing Conference. (ERIC Document Reproduction Service No. ED 396 687)

Hancock, L. N. and P. Wingert. 1995. The haves and the have-nots. *Newsweek,* February 27, 50–53.

Harkins, J. E., Loeterman, M., Lam, K., and E. Korres. 1996. Instructional technology in schools educating deal and hard of hearing children: A national survey. *American Annals of the Deaf,* 141(2):59–65.

Hennelly, R. 1996. Forget computers: Kids without phones. *Education Digest* 61(5):40-43.

Hopkins, D. M. and R. P. Butler. 1991. *The Federal roles in support of school library media centers.* Chicago: American Library Association.

Howley, C. B. and A. Howley. 1995. The Power of babble: Technology and rural education. *Phi Delta Kappan,* October, 126–131.

Katz, J. and P. Aspden. 1996. *Motivations for and barriers to internet usage: Results of a national public opinion survey.* Paper presented at the 24th Annual Telecommunications Policy Research Conference, MD.

Knupfer, N. N. 1997. Gendered by design. *Educational Technology* 37(2):31–36.

Kolenda, P. 1988. *Cultural constructions of 'woman.'* Salem, WI: Sheffield Publishing Company.

Lee, O. and S. H. Fradd. 1998. Science for all including students from non-English-language backgrounds. *Educational Researcher* 27(4):12–21.

MacAdoo, M. 1994. Equity: Has technology bridged the gap? *Electronic Learning,* April.

McInerney, C. and R. Park. 1986. *Educational equity in the third wave: Technology education for women and minorities.* St. Paul: Minnesota State Department of Education. (ERIC Document Reproduction Service No. ED 339 667.)

Maney, K. 1996. Women missing good jobs in a key growth industry. *USA Today,* June 26, A1–A3.

Mangione, M. 1995. *Understanding the critics of educational technology: Gender inequities and computers 1983–1993.* Anaheim, CA: Association for Educational Communications and Technology. (ERIC Document Reproduction Service No. ED 383 311.)

Mark, J. and K. Hanson. 1992. *Beyond equal access: Gender equity in learning with computers.* Newton, MA: Education Development Center, Inc. (ERIC Document Reproduction Service No. ED 370 879.)

Miller, K., D. Metheny, and D. Davison. 1997. Issues in integrating mathematics and science. *Science Educator* 6(1):16–21.

Milone, M. N. 1997. Technology for everyone: Assistive devices for students with special needs. *Technology and Learning Abstract* 17(5):44.

Milone, M. N., Jr., and J. Salpeter. 1996. Technology and equity issues. *Technology & Learning,* January, 38–47.

Mosle, S. 1995. The Wrong box: Why public-school students are falling through the net. *The New Yorker* 71(17):6–7.

Muffoletto, R. 1993. *Schools and technology in a democratic society: Equity and social justice.* Delphi, Greece: International Visual Literacy Association. (ERIC Document Reproduction Service No. ED 393 418.)

National Commission on Excellence in Education. 1983. *A Nation at risk: The Imperative for educational reform.*

Neuman, D. 1991. *Technology and equity* (Report No. EDO-IR-91-8). Syracuse, NY: ERIC Clearinghouse on Information Resources. (ERIC Document Reproduction Service No. ED 339 400.)

Northwest Educational Technology Consortium. 1997. Issues: Access. *Equity in Educational Technology* [Online]. Available Web page: http://www.netc.org/equity/access.html

Overview of technology and education reform. (n.d.). [Online]. Available Web page: http://www.ed.gov/pubs/EdReformStudies/EdTech/overview.html

Parette, H.P. and A. VanBiervliet. 1990. *Assistive technology and disabilities: A guide for parents and students.* Little Rock: University of Arkansas.

Products which enhance access to the WWW. (n.d.). [Online]. Available Web page: http://www.ataccess.org/access.html

Products which enhance access to the WWW: Mouse emulators. (n.d.). [Online]. Available Web page: http://www.ataccess.org/emulators.html

Products which enhance access to the WWW: Understanding. (n.d.). [Online]. Available Web page: http://www.ataccess.org/understanding.html

Products which enhance access to the WWW: Vision. (n.d.). [Online]. Available Web page: http://www.ataccess.org/vision.html

Reinen, I .J. and T. Plomp. 1994. *Gender and computer use: Another area of inequity?* New Orleans: American Educational Research Association. (ERIC Document Reproduction Service No. ED 376 174)

Roblyer, M. D., O. Dozier-Henry, and A. P. Burnette. 1996. Technology and multicultural education: The 'Uneasy alliance.' *Educational Technology* May-June, 5–12.

Rosenberg, M. 1998. Girls and technology: Making it work. *Equity: For the Education of Women and Girls* 3(1):1–4, 6.

Sayers, D. 1995. Educational equity issues in an information age. *Teachers College Record* 96(4):767–773.

Schwartz, W. 1995. A Guide to computer learning in your child's school. *ERIC Clearinghouse on Urban Education* [Online]. Available: http://eric web.tc.columbia.edu/guides/pg3.html

Secretary's Conference on Educational Technology. 1995. *Issue 1: Access and equity.* [Online]. Available Web page: http://www.ed.gov/Technology/Plan/MakeHappen/Issue1.html

Sexism in education: Is there gender equity in your community school district? 1993. Los Angeles, CA: National Center for History in the Schools. (ERIC Document Reproduction Service No. ED 374 053.)

Schmid, R. E. 1996. Survey finds disparities in public schools' internet access. *New York Times*, February 17.

Secada, W. G. 1989. Educational equity versus equality of education: An alternative conception. *Equity in education.* New York: Falmer.

Silverman, S. and A. M. Pritchard. 1993. *Guidance, gender equity and technology education.* Hartford, CT: Vocational Equity Research, Training and Evaluation Center. (ERIC Document Reproduction Service No. ED 362 651.)

Stripling, B. K. 1992. *Libraries for the national education goals.* Syracuse, NY: ERIC Clearinghouse on Information Resources.

Sutton, R. E. 1991. Equity and computers in the schools: A decade of research. *Review of Education Research* 61(4):477.

Thompson, A., Simonson, M., and C. Hargrave. 1992. *Educational technology: A review of the research.* Washington, D.C.: Association for Educational Communications and Technology.

Title IX. 1972. [Online]. Available Web page: http://www.edc.org/WomensEquity/title9.html

Tucker, M., Seluke, S., and A. Tucker. 1997. Networking a community of learners. *Science Scope,* March, 68–72.

Urschel, J. 1996. How girls get scared away from computers. *USA Today,* June 26, D1–D3.

United States Department of Education. 1996. *Getting America's students ready for the 21st century: Meeting the technology literacy challenge: A report to the nation on technology and education.* [Online]. Available Web page: http://www.ed.gov/Technology/Plan/NatTechPlan/title.html

United States Department of Commerce. 1995. *Falling through the net: A survey of the "have nots" in rural and urban America.* [Online]. Available Web page: http://www.ntia.doc.gov/ntiahome/fallingthru.html

Valdes, G. 1998. The World outside and inside schools: Language and immigrant children. *Educational Researcher* 27(6):4–18.

Van Orden, P. J. 1995. *The Collection program in schools: Concepts, practices, and information sources,* 2ed. Englewood, CO: Libraries Unlimited.

Wakefield, D. (n.d.). *Cruising the information highway with text browsers.* [Online]. Available Web page: http://www.itpolicy.gsa.gov/coca/web_brow.htm

WGBH Online. 1997. *Access instructions for users with disabilities.* [Online]. Available Web page: http://www.wgbh.org/wgbh/access/accesswgbh.html#gen

Yeaman, R. J. 1991. Sociocultural aspects of computers in education. In *Proceedings of Selected Research Paper Presentations at the Convention of the Association for Educational Communications and Technology and Sponsored by the Research and Theory Division,* ed. M. R. Simonson and C. Hargrave, 1–7. Orlando, Florida.

Principles and Practices in Multicultural Science Education: Implications for Professional Development

Gerry M. Madrazo, Jr.
Mathematics and Science Education Network, UNC-Chapel Hill
Jack Rhoton
East Tennessee State University

Gerry Madrazo has been a science teacher, curriculum specialist, director of instruction, assistant superintendent, researcher, clinical professor, speaker, and author. He has taught biology, environmental science, physical science, oceanography, and marine biology. Currently, he is executive director of the University of North Carolina Mathematice and Science Education Network and clinical professor in ht eSchool of Education at UNC-Chapel Hill.

Jack Rhoton is professor of Science Education at East Tennessee State University. Dr. Rhoton's special research interest is in the area of professional development and its impact on science teaching and learning. He is widely published and has written and directed numerous science and technology grants. He has more than 30 years of science teaching experience at all levels. He has received many honors including the NSTA Distinguished Service to Science Education Awards.

T wenty-first century schools and classrooms are becoming more cultur-ally and ethnically diverse each day. Science teachers, science supervisors, and science education leaders face the challenge of designing and implementing strategies that will work in a multicultural society. As professional development providers, educators have an exciting opportunity to offer insight and leadership while bringing meaningful activities into the new multicultural setting (Madrazo, 1998). Science educators can contribute to the effort by actively promoting critical thinking and investigative skills.

Science teachers, in particular, can help students develop the decision making, problem solving, and social skills necessary for participation in a culturally diverse society. For example, teachers can use a reflective strategy, in which students are asked to repeat major concepts and explain how newly learned material relates to information previously learned about these concepts. Students will then understand the connections between the topics covered day to day. Reciprocal teaching, a method where the

Science leadership at the district level can influence professional development activities to bring about the kinds of changes necessary to achieve science literacy for all...

teachers and students take turns leading discussions of text material, allows students to take an active role in learning and encourages them to work together to construct meaning from the material. Finally, laboratory investigations can be incorporated in authentic activities that all students relate to their everyday lives and experiences.

The vision of the *National Science Education Standards* (National Research Council, 1996) is clear: science is for all students, regardless of age, gender, cultural or ethnic background, ability, aspirations, or interest and motivation in science. Both the National Science Teachers Association (NSTA) and National Science Education Leadership Association (NSELA) have issued similar position statements on multicultural science education. According to both professional associations, the welfare of the American classroom is ultimately dependent on the productivity of *all* students; *all* students can learn; and *all* those involved in the educational enterprise—the students themselves, science education leaders, parents, and community leaders—must be willing to dedicate resources and efforts toward this end.

The Role of Professional Development in Multicultural Education

Leadership is important. Attention to science curriculum and instructional issues through professional development activities should be an ongoing process in the school district to make them better reflect the vision of multicultural education and equity concerns. Science leadership at the district level can influence professional development activities to bring about the kinds of changes necessary to achieve science literacy for all, regardless of gender, ethnicity, social class, disabilities, or other attributes. Because teacher leaders, as well as district science coordinators, science department chairs, administrators, and other district personnel, can develop and refine models of teaching science that align with the *Standards,* they can be leaders in working with K–12 teachers in experimenting with a full range of content and pedagogical techniques that address multicultural education.

Multicultural and ethnic issues are important components in the reform agenda. Even though suggested multicultural curricular activities are plentiful for the K–12 educator, it is more difficult to achieve and sustain a viable professional development program that provides teachers with the necessary ongoing support and training to reflect the vision of a multicultural classroom. What can science leaders at the district level do to make the science classroom a better place for all students, especially those who are culturally diverse? They can:

◆ promote and contribute to the multicultural education agenda by securing additional resources, funds, and time commitments for classroom teachers

- bring together teachers, university personnel, and key individuals in the community to development models of multicultural education sequences that address the needs of all students
- introduce teachers to innovative techniques and material via locally-sponsored workshops
- develop policy aimed at encouraging more participation in science by minorities, girls, and culturally diverse students
- encourage parents of culturally diverse students to visit the classroom and observe how the science curriculum and science teaching strategies might impact on their students' success
- enlist the support and resources of professional organizations particularly concerned with multicultural education and equity issues, such as the National Science Teachers Association, in reform efforts
- disseminate as well as expand the research and knowledge base about diverse groups and how students learn science

Professional development leaders should encourage teachers to highlight role models and their diverse career opportunities, especially those individuals whose gender or ethnic background is typically under-represented in their field. These "living proof" individuals serve as concrete images of success for the students. Science educators can also help students learn about the influence of science and scientists on other fields, such as history, mathematics, literature, and art. This presents an excellent opportunity to promote the achievements of scientists from different backgrounds.

Multicultural Science Classrooms

The goal of multicultural education is to offer students an equal opportunity to learn and see the possibilities awaiting them in life. Science teachers and science education leaders have many opportunities to open a new world to students; science is the perfect field for exploring diversity. Integrating multiculturalism into the science curriculum begins with the *additive* process (Figure 1).

Adding "something multicultural" to science teaching and learning is a good beginning, but actually attaining of multiculturalism in the science classroom must be the goal. Habib (1992) articulated the following principles that should be reflected in the multicultural science classroom:

- The content and methodology of multicultural science curricula, including resource materials, should be significant to students in school and at home.
- The curriculum should help students see the connection between their local and global environments and think conscientiously and critically about their roles in these relationships.
- Teachers should encourage students to be active learners. Multicultural science emphasizes dynamic inquiry and exploration, not static, memorized, right-or-wrong answers.

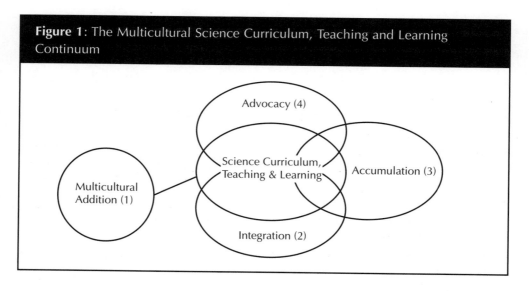

Figure 1: The Multicultural Science Curriculum, Teaching and Learning Continuum

◆ Science or mathematics instruction should represent a variety of traditional and historical viewpoints—integrating literature, history, and the arts! By presenting science as an ongoing, creative story with many parts, students will see their own cultural experiences reflected in the lesson (Figure 2).

The teaching and learning processes can then move from integration to accumulation and, finally, toward multiculturalism, also called "advocacy of multicultural science education (Figure 3)." Integration reflects the extent to which teachers and students relate information about various cultures to the concepts and theories of science. Teachers should help students understand how knowledge is constructed and how culture and customs play a role in its creation. Even scientists are influenced by cultural factors in the construction of their theories. The teaching and learning processes can only be enhanced by using one's own cultural knowledge and perspectives in the classroom. This mode of constructing knowledge is called accumulation.

Teachers can promote multiculturalism by presenting several examples of a newly learned concept to show students that the concept is applicable in many different settings. When teachers and students discuss the ways various viewpoints and cultural assumptions influence the accumulation of knowledge, they develop a multicultural perspective.

Implications for Multicultural Education

The demographics of our classrooms change so rapidly that one can no longer deny or ignore the magnitude of problems associated with the rapidly increasing cultural interactions in most schools. Professional development practitioners must provide leadership and mentoring by including the principles of multicultural education in all workshops and activities geared toward educators.

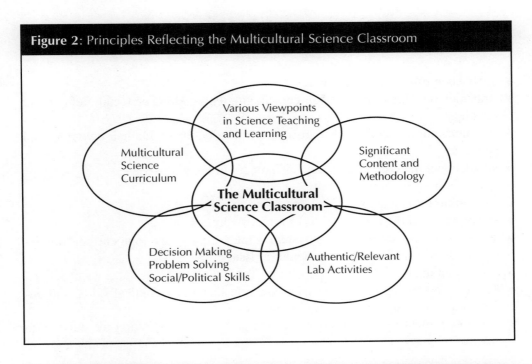

Figure 2: Principles Reflecting the Multicultural Science Classroom

Various Viewpoints in Science Teaching and Learning

Multicultural Science Curriculum

Significant Content and Methodology

The Multicultural Science Classroom

Decision Making Problem Solving Social/Political Skills

Authentic/Relevant Lab Activities

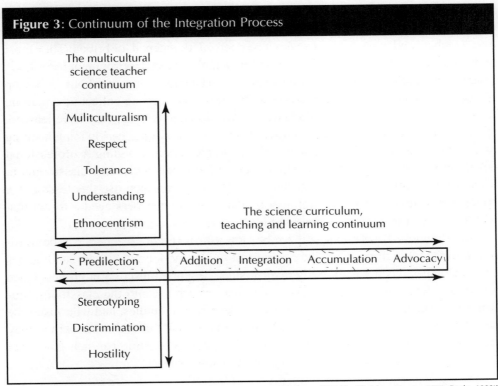

Figure 3: Continuum of the Integration Process

The multicultural science teacher continuum

Mulitculturalism

Respect

Tolerance

Understanding

Ethnocentrism

The science curriculum, teaching and learning continuum

Predilection   Addition   Integration   Accumulation   Advocacy

Stereotyping

Discrimination

Hostility

[Madrazo, 1997 (Modified from Hoopes, 1979; Banks, 1993)]

153

Teacher educators and others in leadership positions can start by incorporating the following into their own activities and schools:

- knowledge of represented cultures
- strategies for allowing and even encouraging expressions of racial and cultural identity
- communication in dialects that are a part of their culture, with their own rules and patterns
- instructional material that reflects differences in learning style
- appreciation of cultural diversity
- local minority resources
- an emphasis on the contributions of minority groups
- teacher participation in school system affairs, policy development, and implementation that may include multicultural issues
- ethnic pluralism
- teachers developing student decision making, social and political skills, and understanding of our ethnically diverse society
- a recommitment of all participants to the principle of expecting all students to achieve

Modeling, however, is not enough. Science educators can provide lesson plans geared toward the multicultural classroom as examples upon which teachers can build. However, teachers and administrators cannot be coerced, threatened, or bribed: They must understand and reflect on the issues. Building a multifaceted environment takes time. True understanding of multicultural issues cannot take place in a two-hour workshop or even a two-day intensive course. Teachers must have time to collect information; to be exposed to creative, useful ideas; and then to analyze what they have learned. Hands-on training following workshops or courses will assist teachers in implementing multiculturalism in their classrooms. For example, after providing a professional development workshop, the workshop leader might visit individual classrooms to teach a multicultural lesson to the students. Teachers can then use this lesson as a model for their own multicultural lesson plans. Finally, teachers need a forum that will allow them to exchange ideas and insights with their colleagues.

A multicultural classroom will not be attained overnight. Teachers can be introduced to the topic through guided readings of books and journal articles, audiotapes and videotapes, visits to culturally diverse sites, or guided discussion groups. Once aware, a teacher may foster understanding and transmit it into the classroom. Students who radiate self-esteem, who are confident in their studies, and who foster the understanding of differences will take these attitudes and "culture" with them as they enter the work force. They not only will find it easier to accomplish their goals, but also will likely make the workplace far more harmonious.

Our national motto—*E Pluribus Unum*—seems to be an appropriate multicultural goal, but *Unum* must reflect our nation's ethnic and cultural diversity. Sooner or later, our classrooms *will* reflect this diversity, and science educators have always been at the threshold of changes in our society. If all students are to achieve scientific literacy, changes that reflect diversity in today's society must occur in curricula, teaching, and learning. Science education leaders can be very instrumental in effecting these changes.

References

Barba, R. 1998. *Science in the multicultural classroom.* Boston: Allyn and Bacon.

Habib, D. 1992. A multicultural approach to science education. *Connect* 6(1):3–5.

National Research Council. 1996. *National science education standards.* Washington, DC: National Academy Press.

Madrazo, G. 1998. Embracing diversity. *The Science Teacher* 65(3):120–23.

Guided Index

Issues in Science Education: *Professional Development Leadership & the Diverse Learner*										
		Issue Matrix (see numbered descriptions below)								
Chapter	**First Author**	**1**	**2**	**3**	**4**	**5**	**6**	**7**	**8**	**9**
1	Pratt, H.		x	x						x
2	Vasquez, J.		x	x	x					x
3	Prather, J.	x	x	x						
4	Wallace, J.		x	x	x			x		x
5	Charles, K.		x	x			x	x	x	x
6	Moyer, P.		x	x		x	x			x
7	Walbert, D.	x	x					x		
8	Rowland, P.		x		x		x	x		
9	Tippins, D.		x		x		x	x		x
10	Davis, E.						x	x	x	
11	Sweeney, J.				x	x	x			
12	Butler, R.	x					x	x		
13	Madrazo, G.						x	x	x	

1. Online learning

A variety of new online delivery methods are available for professional development. They allow presentation to diverse audiences, provide resources beyond the range of any program planner, and are easily accessible. As in all delivery methods, there are good and bad ways to use online instruction. For discussion of the variety and use of online learning methods, see:

Butler, R. P., pp. 133–148.
Prather, J. P. & H. F. Field, pp. 23–36.
Walbert, D. J., pp. 77–86.

2.   **Teaching techniques in professional development**

As in teaching students, working with educators can benefit from proven techniques in accomplishing learning goals. Engaging teachers in inquiry and building instruction around assessment are a few methods described in this book. As you plan a professional development program, refer to the following chapters:

Charles, K. J. & F. D. Cummings, pp. 49–66.
Moyer, P. & E. D. Packenham, pp. 67–76.
Prather, J. P. & H. F. Field, pp. 23–36.
Pratt, H., pp. 1–10.
Rowland, P., D. Montgomery, G. Prater, & S. Minner, pp. 87–98.
Tippins, D. J. & S. E. Nichols, pp. 99–112.
Vasquez, J. & M. Cowan, pp. 11–22.
Walbert, D. J., pp. 77–86.
Wallace, J. D., C. R. Nesbit, & C. R. Newman, pp. 37–48.

3.   **Building a professional development program**

There may be a range of goals and outcomes you are planning in any level of professional development program. The following chapters offer insight into program design:

Charles, K. J. & F. D. Cummings, pp. 49–66.
Moyer, P. & E. D. Packenham, pp. 67–76.
Prather, J. P. & H. F. Field, pp. 23–36.
Pratt, H., pp. 1–10.
Vasquez, J. & M. Cowan, pp. 11–22.
Wallace, J. D., C. R. Nesbit, & C. R. Newman, pp. 37–48.

4.   **Motivation**

Students at every age learn better when they are in charge of their own learning. Motivational methods for professional development include such topics as constructivist processes and leadership development. See:

Rowland, P., D. Montgomery, G. Prater, & S. Minner, pp. 87–98.
Sweeney, J. K. & S. E. Lynds, pp. 125–132.
Tippins, D. J. & S. E. Nichols, pp. 99–112.
Vasquez, J. & M. Cowan, pp. 11–22.
Wallace, J. D., C. R. Nesbit, & C. R. Newman, pp. 37–48.

5.   **Community Collaboration**
     Successful school programs often benefit from community resources beyond the school, and professional development programs are no exception. Applying for grants, using informal science learning centers, tapping local cultural resources, and adopting systemic initiative strategies are a few methods described here. See chapters:

6.   **Equity/Diversity Issues**
     It is critical that we provide quality science education for all students in order to ensure a viable workforce and to meet the demands of society in the future. To do so, those who are currently underrepresented in those fields—women and minorities—must participate in greater numbers. For various ways professional development can help meet these needs, see chapters:

7.   **Promoting Change**
     Change is very difficult for most people, but it is essential if we are to have hope of meeting the recommendations found in reform documents. The change process can be facilitated in a number of ways through professional development. See the following chapters:

8. **Reform**

An in-depth understanding of the current reform efforts is essential if programs and curricula are to be aligned with them. Reform documents outline such topics as what students should know and understand at various grade levels, teaching, content, assessment, and professional development. See the following chapters for information on the nature of science and these documents in general:

Charles, K. J. & F. D. Cummings, pp. 49–66.
Davis, M. E., pp. 113–124.
Madrazo, G. & J. Rhoton, pp. 149–156.

9. **Leadership Development**

The development of effective leadership is critical for widespread implementation of reform efforts. For details of successful elements of leadership development, see:

Charles, K. J. & F. D. Cummings, pp. 49–66.
Moyer, P. & E. D. Packenham, pp. 67–76.
Pratt, H., pp. 1–10.
Tippins, D. J. & S. E. Nichols, pp. 99–112.
Vasquez, J. & M. Cowan, pp. 11–22.
Wallace, J. D., C. R. Nesbit, & C. R. Newman, pp. 37–48.